Building Web Applications with SVG

David Dailey
Jon Frost
Domenico Strazzullo

Published with the authorization of Microsoft Corporation by:
O'Reilly Media, Inc.
1005 Gravenstein Highway North
Sebastopol, California 95472

ISBN: 978-0-7356-6012-0

1 2 3 4 5 6 7 8 9 LSI 7 6 5 4 3 2

Printed and bound in the United States of America.

Microsoft Press books are available through booksellers and distributors worldwide. If you need support related to this book, email Microsoft Press Book Support at *mspinput@microsoft.com*. Please tell us what you think of this book at *http://www.microsoft.com/learning/booksurvey*.

Microsoft and the trademarks listed at *http://www.microsoft.com/about/legal/en/us/IntellectualProperty/Trademarks/EN-US.aspx* are trademarks of the Microsoft group of companies. All other marks are property of their respective owners.

The example companies, organizations, products, domain names, email addresses, logos, people, places, and events depicted herein are fictitious. No association with any real company, organization, product, domain name, email address, logo, person, place, or event is intended or should be inferred.

Acquisitions and Developmental Editor: Russell Jones

Production Editor: Holly Bauer

Editorial Production: Zyg Group, LLC

Technical Reviewer: Domenico Strazzullo

Copyeditor: Zyg Group, LLC

Proofreader: Zyg Group, LLC

Indexer: Zyg Group, LLC

Cover Design: Twist Creative • Seattle

Cover Composition: Karen Montgomery

Interior Composition: Zyg Group, LLC

Illustrator: Rebecca Demarest

I would like to dedicate this book to my wife, Caron: my friend and companion on so many adventures.

—DAVID DAILEY

I would like to dedicate this book to my mentors in the local community, who consistently demonstrate their authentic passion for improving our town by regularly organizing events that coordinate efforts to revitalize our world, and who manage it all with an inspiring degree of heartfelt warmth and charm: Eduardo Crespi of Centro Latino, Mark Haim and Ruth Schaefer of PeaceWorks and Sustainability, and Proffessor Miguel Ugarte.

—JON FROST

I dedicate this book to the community of SVG adepts and evangelists who have given so much time and effort.

—DOMENICO STRAZZULLO

Contents at a Glance

Contents

What do you think of this book? We want to hear from you!

Microsoft is interested in hearing your feedback so we can continually improve our books and learning resources for you. To participate in a brief online survey, please visit:

microsoft.com/learning/booksurvey

Chapter 7   Building a Web Application: Case Studies   215

Introduction

Scalable Vector Graphics, known as SVG, is the World Wide Web Consortium standard for graphical interactivity on the web and mobile platforms. SVG is a mature standard, first released more than a decade ago and has been under improvement by the W3C ever since. SVG is now available natively in all modern web browsers, as well as more than one billion mobile devices. SVG provides ways to create interactive graphics that can be rescaled without loss of clarity. Like HTML and HTML5, SVG coexists happily with technologies that are already familiar to web programmers, such as CSS, JavaScript, the Document Object Model, AJAX and, indeed, with HTML itself.

This book provides a comprehensive introduction to the language and how to use it for interaction and animation. The text also provides exposure to several important JavaScript packages and libraries, including D3, jQuery, and Pergola. While the book does not provide exhaustive coverage of every feature of the SVG language, it does offer essential guidance in using the key SVG components.

In addition to its coverage of basic SVG features, the book discusses a wide range of software tools for creating SVG and for embellishing it with scripted functionality. You'll also find solid introductions to complex topics such as SVG animation and filters. In many places, the book includes step by step examples and references numerous examples and downloadable sample projects that you can explore for yourself.

SVG Testimonials

Many people have been involved in the creation of SVG. As part of the Introduction to this book, we asked a handful of people who were closely involved in SVG's evolution to expound a little on what they think about SVG's past and future. Here are their statements.

Jon Ferraiolo

The W3C launched the Scalable Vector Graphics Working Group in 1998 to provide the vector graphics counterpart to HTML. The SVG WG chose to adopt all of the same general approaches as HTML (markup, DOM, scripting, styling) but replaced HTML's <div>, <p> and <span> elements with vector graphics element such as <rect>, <circle> and <path>. With various events in 2001 (SVG 1.0 Specification approval, Adobe SVG Viewer version 3 (ASV3) and bundling of ASV with Adobe Acrobat Reader 5), SVG was ubiquitous on desktop browsers, with the result that temporarily SVG took off like gangbusters, with tens of thousands of developers using SVG for various sorts of interactive graphics applications (flow charts, business graphics, and mapping). But SVG adoption dropped once Adobe abandoned ASV. Subsequently, the open source browser teams added SVG support (first Mozilla, then WebKit). With the open source project "SVGWeb" supporting older versions of SVG in IE6–8 and Microsoft's announcement of SVG support in IE9, SVG has once again regained ubiquity, and developers are now (re)discovering the power and coolness of DOM-based scriptable graphics.

The future for SVG looks quite exciting, particularly when using SVG as a component of HTML5. The W3C, in collaboration with the browser teams and the community, is generalizing many of SVG 1.0's best features (e.g., clipping, animation, filter effects) into CSS so these features will also be available to HTML, and cleaning up SVG to make it easier to use (e.g., removing SVG's XML requirement). There is active discussion about going to the next level with vector and raster graphics effects, particularly ones that are able to leverage CPUs. Given the automatic update features of the modern browser, developers will be able to take advantage of cool new features almost as soon as they are defined.

Background: Jon Ferraiolo was one of SVG's principal architects. He was the primary author of the PGML submission that served as the starting point for SVG and was the sole editor of the W3C's original SVG specification (SVG 1.0). While employed at Adobe Systems, Inc., he was the architect for several SVG-related projects at Adobe, including the Adobe SVG Viewer and Adobe Illustrator's SVG support. He is now a Distinguished Engineer at IBM.

Alex Danilo

In the early days of the web, browsers were rapidly changing and competition was fierce. When the W3C sent out a call for vector graphics proposals for the web, a collective cheer from thousands of graphics people could be heard. At last, to be free of those ancient bitmaps and bring the web into beautiful resolution and independent glory. This was the birth of SVG.

As we know, Rome wasn't built in a day, and over the years SVG was massaged and honed to perfection by an army of enthusiastic graphics aficionados. The result is a gem that's polished and can glisten with vibrant color when viewed in the right light.

SVG enables vivid interactive experiences that adapt to any display size, a way to bridge images with meaningful semantics, a powerful synergy with HTML and the DOM and just looks so good!

Background: Alex Danilo joined the W3C SVG Working Group at the start of 2002 and is now the representative of his company Abbra. Abbra's implementations both for mobile devices and web have always been at the cutting edge of the development of the SVG specification. Alex has very often produced the first proof of concept of new proposals for SVG. His current focus is development of a rich-media capable SVG engine for cross-platform application areas especially in resource constrained devices.

Cameron McCormack

It has been 10 years since the W3C Recommendation for SVG 1.0 was published, and having been involved in the SVG community for most of that time period, I can say with first-hand knowledge that SVG's fortunes have definitely been mixed. This is not an indictment on the technology itself, which is solid, but a historical problem of implementation availability.

In the early 2000s, there was a good deal of interest in SVG, as evidenced probably most clearly by the activity on the SVG Developers Yahoo Group mailing list, a forum that is still running today. Authors were creating visually rich, graphical, dynamic web applications with SVG before it became popular (or possible) to do so with other open web technologies. That this was possible at the time was, in my view, nearly entirely due to Adobe's investment in SVG and their development of the Adobe SVG Viewer plug-in. It did not matter that browsers' support for SVG was not up to scratch or did not exist at all—through the use of the Adobe plug-in, SVG was available to everyone. (Technically not everyone, of course, as the plug-in was limited to particular operating systems and architectures, but for most authors this was good enough.)

The last release of the Adobe plug-in, a preview of version 6, was made available in 2003. The preview release was somewhat unstable, but demonstrated attractive new features, including a componentization model for SVG content whose fundamental ideas even today garner interest despite a number of false starts in standardization groups. However, for a long time after this release not a word was heard out of Adobe on their plans for development. This caused growing consternation within the SVG developer community, as progress of native browser implementations had been slow to catch up to the features and performance of the plug-in. Interest in SVG began to wane, and Adobe's acquisition of Macromedia and the Flash platform only served further to fuel the notion that SVG was dead. The years following were the Dark Ages of SVG.

Although native browser implementations did improve during this time, there was still a perpetual sense by developers at large that SVG wasn't ready for prime time. What was probably the biggest impediment to authors publishing SVG content was the lack of implementation in Internet Explorer. With the arrival of one particular version of IE or Windows, I don't remember which, the unmaintained Adobe plug-in stopped working altogether. This was a blow to developers, as Microsoft had no plans to implement SVG at all, unlike the other major browser vendors who all were committed to supporting it.

In 2008, a major development occurred: the addition of SVG (and MathML) to the HTML5 specification, which allowed authors to write HTML documents with inline vector graphics without having to use mixed-namespace XML documents. This was a welcome simplification, but importantly it helped to sell SVG as being a first class part of the web platform.

By 2009—the same year that Adobe finally announced what everyone knew already, that their plug-in was no longer being maintained—sentiment had finally managed to shift away from the notion of SVG being a neat technology unsuitable for publishing on the web due to Microsoft's intransigence. This was helped by the release of SVG Web, a Flash-based SVG renderer developed by a team at Google. Once again, authors had a way to target SVG content to Internet Explorer, as most Windows computers already had Flash installed. Not only did SVG Web provide a way to render SVG in IE, it did so with reasonably complete coverage of the SVG specification and with great performance.

But perhaps the most welcome news to the SVG community came in 2010 when Microsoft announced a preview release of Internet Explorer 9, the first version of IE to support SVG. Finally it would be possible to publish SVG content using open web technologies and have all desktop browsers consume it without the need for any plug-ins or workarounds. Hooray!

Today, SVG is in its strongest position yet. Browser implementations continue to improve by leaps and bounds. Standards groups continue to draw SVG and CSS ever closer, allowing the use of SVG features such as filters, patterns, and gradients in HTML documents. The SVG Working Group itself is busy working on the next major revision of the SVG specification itself to address issues and add features that have been requested by the persevering SVG community over the years. JavaScript toolkit writers are choosing SVG as their graphical output technology.

And the developer community is reinvigorated. SVG is very much alive!

Background: Cameron McCormack has been involved in SVG since 2003 and has served as coeditor of the SVG specification and cochair of the SVG Working Group from 2007 to the present. As a graduate student at Monash University in Australia, Cameron also spearheaded the implementation of SVG in Batik—sometimes called the most extensive implementation of SVG yet. He has since gone on to work at Mozilla Corporation, where his work with SVG and other web standards continues.

Jeff Schiller

I became involved with Scalable Vector Graphics (SVG) around the time that Firefox was planning to ship its first partial implementation of SVG Full in Firefox 1.5. At that time, native support was mostly a curiosity given that there was a very mature browser plug-in (Adobe SVG Viewer) and sound alternatives to rich vector graphics in web applications (Macromedia's Flash). But what intrigued me about native SVG support was the integration with HTML: a DOM, an event model, scripting in JavaScript, styling with CSS. This would allow graphical web applications to take advantage of the AJAX bubble that was happening at the time: rich, dynamic applications that worked cross-browser without a plug-in.

More SVG Full implementations began showing up, first in Opera which set the standard for Full support, then in WebKit and finally in Internet Explorer, making it ubiquitous across the web and mobile. As native SVG support began showing up in the wild, HTML5 really started to take shape in the minds of browser vendors and I've been delighted to follow both SVG and HTML as their paths became aligned. I believe the arrival of graphics in the browsers (SVG and HTML Canvas) were essential in making the web platform compelling for application developers: a powerful markup vocabulary, a document model, a simple authoring syntax, and continuously improving support in all major browsers. Refinement of both the implementations and the specification have made SVG a really effective weapon in the web developer's arsenal and I'm constantly amazed at what people are doing with it.

Background: Jeff Schiller's name is a familiar one in the SVG community. In addition to being the originator of and contributor to the popular and useful tools SVG-Edit and Scour, he has also for many years maintained the web's most definitive site for cross-browser comparison of the completeness of the implementation of SVG. He also spearheaded and chaired the W3C's SVG Interest Group, and has made numerous contributions to the evolution of the standard itself. Jeff began his work with SVG while working at Motorola and is now a Google employee.

Doug Schepers

The fundamental idea of SVG is beautiful: take the best from popular vector programs like Illustrator, and the structure, dynamic adaptability, and hyperlinking of web formats like HTML and CSS, and then add in animation and raster effects like filters to make it fun, funky, and functional.

Now that it's supported in every modern browser, with tons of applications that output SVG, the W3C SVG Working Group is turning its eye toward SVG 2. What's in the cards? Certainly more seamless integration with HTML5 and the assorted APIs that go into making awesome web apps (though most of them already work with SVG), and a general tidying up of the language to make common tasks easier for developers and implementers, and a massive improvement to the DOM API to increase speed and usability. We're also working closely with the CSS Working Group on shared features, like filters for HTML, and we plan to adopt some new CSS features, including complex text wrapping into and around shapes, a long-standing SVG request.

And while it may sound a bit boring, we have a plan to work on smaller, more modular specs; what this means to developers and designers is more features more quickly. Look for things like parameters (highly adaptable images) and features for mapping (like non-scaling strokes and declarative level-of-detail) to come out as modules. And we are always looking for use cases and requirements that solve real-world problems for developers.

Background: Doug Schepers has been involved in SVG as a developer since the very early days, starting in 2001. He was deeply involved in raising the public's awareness of SVG. In 2007 he was hired by W3C itself to serve on the Working Group. Doug's footprints can be seen all over the SVG specification from its earlier days through the present.

Who Should Read This Book

This book is designed as both a basic introduction and a more advanced treatment that delves deeply into some of the advanced aspects of SVG. It should be equally accessible to a professional web programmer, an undergraduate student with a few semesters of computing coursework, a scientist who wants to make large datasets more interactive, or a graphical designer with a strong technical side. In short, if you are familiar with the basics of web development and computer graphics and have an interest in developing websites that are richly graphical and interactive, then this is the right book for you.

Assumptions

This book assumes some familiarity with HTML and web graphics. Prior experience with programming is not a requirement, though prior programming experience will clearly help you understand some of the chapters (such as Chapter 4 and Chapter 7) that involve programming. Familiarity with the basics of coordinate geometry and fluency with high school algebra will likely also aid in comprehension—though that would be true with any treatment of graphics involving the x-y plane—so the foray into mathematics you'll find here should prove to be a gentle one.

With a heavy focus on database concepts, this book assumes that you have a basic understanding of relational database systems such as Microsoft SQL Server, and have had brief exposure to one of the many flavors of the query language known as SQL. To go beyond this book and expand your knowledge of SQL and Microsoft's SQL Server database platform, other Microsoft Press books such as *Programming SQL Server 2012* offer both complete introductions and comprehensive information on T-SQL and SQL Server.

Who Should Not Read This Book

A graphical artist who finds notation distasteful will probably not find either SVG or this book to his or her liking. SVG is a declarative language based on XML; accordingly, it has a rigorous syntax that is not forgiving of grammar errors. If you're interested in a purely point-and-click environment, or simply want to create a graphical user interface containing drawings and illustrations, then a package such as Inkscape or Illustrator may prove to be a better direction for your creative expression.

Web authors who primarily develop web pages with a package such as Microsoft Expression Studio or Adobe Dreamweaver rather than coding HTML by hand may be interested in some of the new software tools being developed for integrating SVG and HTML. However, while this book discusses some of these tools briefly, the book is not intended as a tutorial in the use of design packages.

Organization of This Book

This book is organized in seven chapters. Chapter 1, "SVG Basics," orients the reader to SVG itself, showing how to get started, the contexts in which SVG can be created and viewed, and a diverse sampling of examples that may whet the reader's appetite. Chapter 2, "Creating and Editing SVG Graphics," and Chapter 3, "Adding Text, Style, and Transforms," get into the dynamics of the core of SVG: the basic shapes, patterns, gradients, clips, masks, and images. Chapter 4, "Motion and Interactivity," introduces the two fundamental aspects of SVG interactivity: animation and scripting. Chapter 5, "SVG Filters," discusses filters, one of the most complex and powerful parts of the graphical language. Chapter 6, "SVG Tools and Resources," and Chapter 7, "Building Web Applications: Case Studies" introduce and provide examples of the broad range of tools and libraries that support SVG development.

Conventions and Features in This Book

This book presents information using conventions designed to make the information readable and easy to follow.

- This book has numerous examples in which the reader may examine the illustration itself and the code used to create the example.

- On occasion, the code shown is an excerpt showing only the parts needed for understanding the narrative text. In such cases, a link is provided to a working example on the web, so that the reader may examine a complete working example.

- In cases of very lengthy source code, the example has been annotated in a table so that blocks of code and explanatory comments may be seen side by side.

About the Companion Content

Most of the chapters in this book include exercises that let you interactively try out new material learned in the main text. The working examples can be seen on the web at:

http://go.microsoft.com/FWLink/?Linkid=257519

or

http://cs.sru.edu/~svg

The examples are organized by chapter number as well as linked from the above addresses.

Installing the Code Samples

There's no need to "install" the code samples for this book—you simply need a browser that can display SVG.

System Requirements

You will need the following hardware and software to be able to follow along with the step-by-step examples in this book:

- A modern web browser: Microsoft Internet Explorer 9 or 10, Firefox 6 or higher, Opera 8 or higher, or Safari or Chrome (any version).

- For mobile users: either Opera Mobile, the Android Ice Cream Sandwich OS, or the iPhone will suffice, though in truth, there are dozens of SVG-enabled browsers too numerous (and quickly evolving) to mention.

- A simple text editor (such as NotePad) or a syntax-completion environment (such as *http://notepad-plus-plus.org/* or *http://www.htmlkit.com/*) for editing your own examples.

- If you wish to share your content on the web: a web server that serves the proper mime type for .svg files, namely as "image/*svg*+xml".

- Internet connection to view examples that accompany the book.

Acknowledgments

Jon Frost initially came up with the idea for this book; his motivation brought it about and saw it through to completion. David Dailey was instrumental in bringing the vision of the book to light through his insight and wisdom and brought a healthy down-to-earth style to the writing process. Jon and David were fortunate to be joined by Domenico Strazzullo, originally brought in as a technical reviewer. His contributions were so energetic and thorough that we just had to have him write a chapter—and who better to do that than the author of Pergola himself?

David: I'd also like to thank my family for their patience and understanding during the writing process and my academic department and university for their generous support with my SVG-related endeavors. Also to the creators of SVG and the SVG Open folks: thanks for the language and for the fun.

Jon: I am grateful for my supportive family, my super-supportive and playful wife, my super-playful and loving dog, and my good friends from cultures around the world who continue to teach me the vital necessity of sharing and caring.

Domenico: I'd like to thank Microsoft Press and the editors at O'Reilly for giving us this terrific opportunity to expose SVG to the greatest number of developers, and help it reach a long deserved status.

Errata & Book Support

We've made every effort to ensure the accuracy of this book and its companion content. Any errors that have been reported since this book was published are listed on our Microsoft Press site at oreilly.com:

http://go.microsoft.com/FWLink/?Linkid=257518

If you find an error that is not already listed, you can report it to us through the same page.

If you need additional support, email Microsoft Press Book Support at *mspinput@microsoft.com*.

Please note that product support for Microsoft software is not offered through the addresses above.

We Want to Hear from You

At Microsoft Press, your satisfaction is our top priority, and your feedback our most valuable asset. Please tell us what you think of this book at:

http://www.microsoft.com/learning/booksurvey

The survey is short, and we read every one of your comments and ideas. Thanks in advance for your input!

Stay in Touch

Let's keep the conversation going! We're on Twitter: *http://twitter.com/MicrosoftPress*

CHAPTER 1

SVG Basics

I decided that if I could paint that flower in a huge scale, you could not ignore its beauty.

Georgia O'Keefe

Scalable Vector Graphics (SVG) is a graphical standard maintained and endorsed by the World Wide Web Consortium (W3C), the same group that created and continues to maintain HTML, CSS, XML, and other technologies that constitute the World Wide Web.

The What, Why, and Where of SVG

SVG is much more than its name suggests. It is true that SVG is a language that allows for the creation of two-dimensional vector elements, which are simply mathematical representations of graphical objects, and that these vectors are infinitely scalable and can be transformed within the bounds of the 2D coordinate system. However, SVG is unique in that it is an open standard defined by the W3C (*http://w3c.org/svg/*), and like other W3C languages such as HTML and XML, it has its own Document Object Model (DOM) that brings with it many benefits, and it's interoperable with other open standard languages such as JavaScript, CSS, and HTML.

SVG has been in the works over the past decade and has matured a great deal during that time, with collaboration from interested parties around the world. The great appeal of SVG is that, like HTML, it's easy to read and edit, while allowing for complex interactivity and animations through scripting and Synchronized Multimedia Integration Language (SMIL), which is another W3C standard. Browsers have matured over the last few years, and all the major ones now natively support much of the SVG specification, so you no longer need to fuss with proprietary SVG plug-ins. All of these capabilities allow for a much greater degree of creativity, with complex interactivity mixing with animation and real-time data, all within the context of SVG-enhanced web applications. This is ideal for modern designers and developers, as demonstrated throughout this book.

The What

SVG is based on vectors rather than pixels. While a pixel-based approach (used by programs such as Adobe Photoshop) places pigment or color at xy-coordinates for each pixel in a bitmap, a vector-based approach (used by programs such as Adobe Illustrator) composes a picture out of shapes, each described by a relatively simple formula and filled with a *texture* (a term used broadly here to refer to a mixture of colors, gradients, and patterns).

SVG is scalable. As you may already know, if you zoom in on pixel-based art, you will eventually reach a maximum resolution. Even with the 10-megapixel cameras that are now commonplace (or the 100-megapixel cameras that can be had for a small fortune), increasing the zoom factor much beyond screen resolution will cause pixelation. Scalability is a tremendous advantage for the emergence of the mobile web, as well as for very-large-display devices (as for outdoor advertising).

The following image shows the difference between what happens when you zoom into a vector graphic (left) and a bitmap (right).

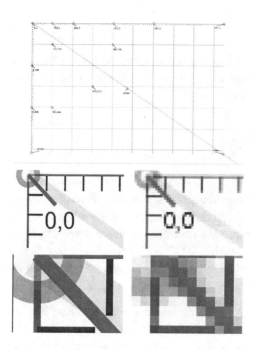

The Why

Some of the advantages of SVG are now discussed, with brief explanations:

- **Client-side graphics**   Because SVG uses client-side graphics, its impact on your web server is light. In addition to being scalable, SVG is dynamic and interactive. A user can interactively explore the data underlying a picture in novel ways.

- **Open source (XML)**   Anyone can view the source code that underlies the graphic. It's readable by humans and looks a lot like HTML.

- **Accessibility**   Because the SVG source code is written in XML, it is also readable by screen readers and search engines. While a picture might be worth a thousand words, a megapixel image is not worth much at all to someone who can't see it. The ability of SVG to bring geometry to those who cannot see it extends its reach into many domains that pixel-based imagery just cannot go.

- **Open standard**   Because it was created by the W3C (the same organization that brought us HTML and the web itself), SVG is nonproprietary and vendor neutral.

- **Familiar technologies**   SVG uses technologies already familiar to web programmers: DOM, JavaScript, CSS, and AJAX. Rather than having to learn entire realms of technology, programming languages, and terminology to deal with the complex and technical area of computer graphics, designers, programmers, and web professionals can leverage skills learned elsewhere.

- **Web applications**   SVG is suitable for incorporation with HTML5, web-based applications, and rich Internet applications (RIAs). The last 10 years have seen a great elevation of the status of the phrase *web-based application*. Not so many years ago, people in the web community used to respond with sarcasm or disbelief when someone talked about wanting to create a web-based application that lived primarily in the browser. A cursory inspection of the history of HTML5 reveals that the creation of web applications was one of the primary intentions behind the development of this emerging specification. The incorporation of inline SVG into the HTML5 specification is a great advantage for web developers.

- **SMIL**   SMIL is a W3C declarative language supporting multimedia and animation for nonprogrammers. SMIL is partially incorporated into the SVG specification. Those who have had more than a cursory exposure to programming animation in JavaScript may find themselves enamored of the ease with which certain complex animations can be authored using SVG animation (or SMIL), as well as the ability to update many objects on the screen almost concurrently. While SVG also supports scripted animation through JavaScript, SMIL brings convenience, parsimony, and elegance to the table.

- **The adoption of SVG**   As of 2010, SVG is supported natively by the most current versions of the five major web browsers. Additionally, it can be found in the chip sets aboard several hundred million mobile phones, with major support being offered from Nokia, Ikivo, Sony

Ericsson, Opera Mobile, Samsung, iPhone, and several others. This will be discussed further in the next section.

- **Other technologies** SVG has overlap with Flash, Vector Markup Language (VML), and Silverlight—but it has the advantages of being nonproprietary, standardized, cross platform, and interoperable with other XML languages and W3C standards.

The Where

Vector graphics are everywhere. The art world, for example, is replete with examples of the use of vector graphics. As Professor Jerrold Maddox wrote in "SVG and Art: Expanding the possibilities, different times and different places," "Image making based on vector-like forms is the way most of the art of the world is and has been made" (*http://www.personal.psu.edu/jxm22/svgopen/*). He continues, "The Song [dynasty] in China and Renaissance Europe are only times and places where tonal art ever took off—and photography made it seem like the only way to do it" (personal correspondence, 2011). Accordingly, from a global and historical perspective, we might see images that are not vector based as more the anomaly than the rule.

SVG, nowadays, is also pretty much everywhere. As of this writing, an estimated 1.5 billion devices in the world are SVG enabled (from *http://en.wikipedia.org/wiki/Usage_share_of_web_browsers* and *http://marketshare.hitslink.com/browser-market-share.aspx?spider=1&qprid=2*).

If we add to this the two mobile manufacturers whose devices are SVG enabled (Ikivo with 350 million users [*http://www.ikivo.com/04about.html*] and Apple, whose iPhone boasts another 100 million [*http://mashable.com/2011/03/02/100-million-iphones/*]) and Abbra's estimate that "Today over 700 million mobile phones have been shipped with in-built support for SVG version 1.1—more than twice as many as the nearest competing technology—FlashLite" (*http://abbra.com/products.html*), then our estimate rises to close to two billion devices that are SVG ready!

Adobe provided the first support for SVG in the browser (via a plug-in known as ASV 3) as early as 2000, though support in other applications (such as CORELDraw and Microsoft Visio) came earlier (*http://www.w3.org/G6raphics/SVG/History*). SVG has had considerable support in drawing programs, including Illustrator, CORELDraw, and Inkscape, for many years now, and it's also supported in a variety of Internet Protocol Television (IPTV) applications and in the popular KDE desktop environment for Linux.

In the browser market, Konqueror was the first browser to support SVG natively, in 2004 (*http://en.wikipedia.org/wiki/Scalable_Vector_Graphics#Native_support*). As of early 2005, the Opera browser had fairly extensive SVG support, and Firefox developed support for basic SVG shortly thereafter in version 2. By mid-2007, Safari had implemented basic support as well. Google debuted its Chrome browser in 2008, and in 2009 Microsoft announced that Internet Explorer would finally have native support, rounding out SVG support for all the major browsers.

Beyond browsers, there are several dozen software applications that read or export SVG content (see the list at *http://en.wikipedia.org/wiki/Scalable_Vector_Graphics*).

Getting Started: A Simple Overview

You'll see a more detailed step-by-step example at the end of this chapter, but it is important that you gain some idea of what's involved in viewing and creating SVG at the outset.

Viewing SVG

Start up any modern browser and point it at the website related to this book, *http://cs.sru.edu/~svg .com*. Internet Explorer, Firefox, Chrome, Safari, and Opera all support viewing SVG on the web, so you can use any of those. The most important exception is this: if you are using Internet Explorer, you will either need to upgrade to Internet Explorer 9 (which requires Microsoft Windows Vista or later), or you will need to download the free SVG plug-in (ASV version 3.03) from Adobe, at *http://www.adobe .com/svg/viewer/install/mainframed.html*. For all the other browsers listed, using the latest version will always prove helpful, because all of these browsers are making steady and frequent progress on their implementations of the SVG specification.

SVG is a big specification—one that's not trivial to implement. SVG 1.1 is generally the version against which browsers are compared. As of this writing, no browser implements all of SVG 1.1, despite the specification having reached recommendation status (meaning that it is officially a W3C standard) in 2003 (*http://www.w3.org/Graphics/SVG/History*). Improvements to browser support tend to appear on a monthly basis, so it is best to make sure that you're using the latest release of whatever browsers you use.

As another example of the importance of using current browser versions, Firefox 3.6 does not support SMIL animation, while Firefox 4.0 does. You'll see more about the idiosyncrasies of browser support in the discussions of the relevant topics, but note that the parts of SVG that pertain to animation, filters, and fonts are most likely to show browser differences.

Writing SVG

There are many different paths that one can follow to develop SVG. This book will show you several of those in more detail in Chapter 6, "SVG Tools and Resources." In the meantime, we recommend using any simple text editor—for example, Notepad for Windows or TextEdit (properly configured for Mac; see *http://support.apple.com/kb/HT2523*)—or any of the plethora of editing tools in Linux or UNIX (nano, pico, emacs, vi, ed, kate, vim, kwrite, gEdit, etc.).

First, enter this very simple SVG file into your text editor, and save the file with the name **myfirstfile.svg** (you can save the file to your local hard drive or a remote server, so long as you know how to get to it from your web browser):

```
<svg xmlns="http://www.w3.org/2000/svg">
<circle r="50"/>
</svg>
```

The file is also visible at *http://cs.sru.edu/~ddailey/svg/simplest.svg* should you have any problems seeing the file you've created.

You'll see information about more advanced editing environments at the end of this chapter, and you'll of course see many more examples of SVG code throughout the rest of the book.

Thirteen Examples That Show the Capabilities of SVG

To fully appreciate the power of SVG, complete with its interactivity and animation capabilities, I encourage you to take a look at the tutorial page on this book's website (*http://cs.sru.edu/~svg*), which contains links to interesting examples, and also to explore and read the examples illustrated and briefly discussed below.

> **Note** We haven't yet defined the terms for the effects described below, but we'll make them clear later on. At this point, we simply want to ensure that you have some idea of what SVG can accomplish before you begin working with it. How else to know the lay of the land?

Example 1: Dynamic Random Landscape Drawn with JavaScript and SVG

The scenery here, inspired by one author's frequent drives from his homeland in New Mexico to his graduate school in Colorado, shows the effect of motion parallax on the various mountain ranges leading from the foothills to the Continental Divide. As the vantage point moves continually north-ward toward the badlands of Wyoming, a slightly impressionistic hot-air balloon follows. Its vertical position, speed, and wind deformation change somewhat randomly as we move. The various layers of mountains recede behind us to the left, with the taller peaks remaining visible longer. Owing to the use of random elements, no two landscapes will ever be the same (ignoring the infinitesimal probability of extreme coincidence). The example can be seen at (*http://srufaculty.sru.edu/david .dailey/svg/balloon.svg*).

Here's how it's done:

- **The sky**   The sky consists of two rectangles. One, the background, is simply filled with a linear gradient consisting of colors that move from brighter shades of sky blue to gray, from bottom to top. The second rectangle provides a snow globe effect. The foreground and smog, due to the overpopulation of communities along the front range, are simulated through the color transitions in the foothills and the overlay of gray stemming from the background and foreground.

- **The snow globe effect**   This is produced using a radial gradient of varying transparency in the foreground. With SVG gradients, you vary not only the colors as they change gradually from one to another, but also their relative opacity.

- **The balloon**   The balloon is entirely handled through JavaScript. A series of almost parallel Bézier curves is created with start points and endpoints that coincide. The control points differ and change over time. The entire group (a *<g>* element in SVG) then has its horizontal and vertical positions varied through a timed loop that refreshes the screen every 10 milliseconds.

- **The drawing of the mountains**   There are four layers of mountains, each filled with a linear gradient that changes from yellow-brownish in the plains and foothills to the blue-white of the snowcapped peaks of the Continental Divide. The hint of green in the second range behind the foothills is meant to suggest the presence of the forests there. The heights of the peaks are randomly determined, with an array of random xy-coordinates being first generated and then sorted by their x-values. Then they are divided into triplets so that the peaks can be connected by a series of curves, each having the previous endpoint and the next separated by points in a cubic Bézier curve.

- **The movement of the mountains**   The foreground layers are simply shifted leftward more quickly than the layers in the back. Each array has its first element removed so that another random element can be added onto the end of the array without the array becoming arbitrarily large. Any memory of what has happened is systematically purged.

Example 2: Equidistant Positioning Points along a Bézier Curve

The mathematics of Bézier curves, while quite accessible to a mathematician, are not trivial. Bézier curves were, after all, not discovered until 1959 (see *http://en.wikipedia.org/wiki/B%C3%A9zier_curve*), 130 years after Évariste Galois resolved the theory of roots of polynomials and laid the foundation for much of the algebra of the 19th and 20th centuries. Fortunately, SVG (following the lead of Adobe Illustrator 88) gives direct and intuitive access to these wonderfully expressive curves in terms of the ability to draw, measure, subdivide, orient, and animate them. In this example (visible at *http://srufaculty.sru.edu/david.dailey/svg/curve.svg*), the curve is drawn with a simple set of markup commands, and each time the user clicks the curve or near it, JavaScript is used to measure the curve and divide it into an increasingly larger number of parts, with the option of animating the process ultimately being offered to the user.

Here's how it's done:

- **Drawing the curve**   The markup used is quite simple:

```
<path d="M 10 150 C 200 80 350 300 450 100" id="B"
      stroke="black" fill="none" stroke-width="4"/>
```

> **Note**   The drawing of SVG paths is one of the most powerful and expressive aspects of the language; it's covered in Chapter 2.

- **Measuring and subdividing the curve**   The JavaScript language binding of SVG allows you to interrogate properties of things that have been drawn either through markup or dynamically, and to manipulate them using methods. In this case, we are using two function calls: $L = B.getTotalLength();$ and $P = B.getPointAtLength(L * i / n);$. The first measures the path, B, and returns a numeric value; the second returns a point (an object with both x and y values) a given fraction of the distance along B. Script is then used to create new ellipses of different colors at those fractional mileposts.

Example 3: Simple Animation (Just 38 Lines of Markup and No Script)

This example, visible at *http://srufaculty.sru.edu/david.dailey/svg/ovaling.svg*, has been cited by others for the richness it achieves even with such simplicity. The example uses SMIL animation to simultaneously vary 4 different attributes of 26 different objects. At the SVG Open 2010 conference in Paris, one of Microsoft's demonstrations showed that this particular example could be animated using one of several SMIL emulators for SVG, although as of this writing, most browsers can run the animation without additional assistance. Creating such a rich animation with other technologies, such as the HTML5 *<canvas>* tag or Java Applets, would take much more code, thought, experimentation, and time to develop.

Here's how it's done:

- **Drawing one petal of the flower**   An ellipse is drawn with a given centroid and differing radii in the x and y directions. It is made slightly more transparent than opaque (the *opacity* is set to 0.4). It is then filled with a gradient (in this case, a linear gradient moving from red to blue and then through green to yellow).

- **Replicating the petal**   SVG allows considerable reuse of code. In this case, the initial petal is reused four times through a series of *<use>* elements, each of which applies a different rotation to the petal. This creates a petal cluster, which itself is then grouped and reused 5 more times, for a total of 25 petals being drawn with only 9 lines of markup.

- **Animating the illustration** The initial petal of the flower (which is later replicated) has three separate animations applied to it. The first gradually changes its orientation from 0 to 360 degrees over a period of 7 seconds. The next 2 animations vary the x value of the centroid and the radius in the y direction over, respectively, 8 seconds and 3 seconds. Because 3, 7, and 8 are relatively prime, the entire animation will repeat every 168 seconds (3 × 7 × 8 = 168). Because the animation is applied to a petal that is then reused 24 times, each of the 25 petals inherits the same animation, with the rotation and repositioning being applied relative to each differing initial position. One more circle at the center of the composition has its own color animated to add a pleasant bit of chromatic variety.

Example 4: Use of Gradients and Patterns

This example, visible at *http://srufaculty.sru.edu/david.dailey/svg/grid2.svg*, consists of just 19 lines of markup (not counting its animations) and no JavaScript. It demonstrates that some rather intriguing results can be concocted by juxtaposing some quite simple SVG elements.

After you have grown accustomed to SVG, animations of this sort will be remarkably easy to create and experiment with on your own.

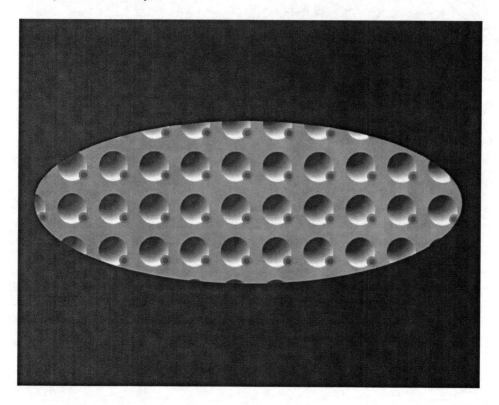

Here's how it's done:

- **Creating the repeating pattern**   In this case, the pattern consists of two circles (one filled with an off-center radial gradient and the other with a flat color and a different-colored stroke).

- **Restricting the pattern to a shape**   The pattern is then applied to an ellipse (which of course is animated).

Example 5: Intersecting Clip Paths

The example at *http://srufaculty.sru.edu/david.dailey/svg/newstuff/clipPath4.svg* demonstrates four things:

- SVG allows bitmapped images (.png, .jpg, and .gif) to be imported and used in conjunction with other graphical primitives. As you will see later, this is done through the *<image>* element.

- Images and other shapes can be clipped to the confines defined by a given shape (in this case, a five-pointed star) using the *<clipPath>* element.

- There is more than one way of making clip paths intersect. Here, the lavender rectangle intersects the five-pointed stars in two rather different ways.

- Like almost all things in SVG, clip paths can be animated. The example uses SMIL animation to rotate the stars, revealing different parts of the underlying faces.

  This particular example, first constructed in 2006, has served as a mini-benchmark test for browsers. Originally, it only worked properly in Internet Explorer with ASV. Over time, Opera came to handle the multiple clip paths and the animation, and each of the other browsers has been gradually phasing in correct handling of intersected clip paths as well.

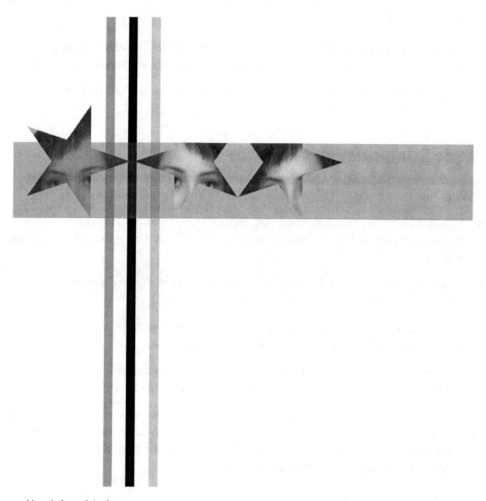

Here's how it's done:

- **Clipping an image by a shape** The leftmost image is defined by an *<image>* element. Its attribute *clip-path="url(#CPST)"* references the element *<clipPath id="CPST">*, which itself contains a star-shaped *<path>* element.

- **Clipping a clip path** This is done in either of two ways in this example: First, the *<image>* element to which a clip path has been applied is reused with a *<use>* element. The *<use>* element then has another clip path applied to it (which happens to consist of the lavender rectangle). The two clip paths intersect as would be expected. The other approach is to build a *<clipPath>* that has its own *clip-path* attribute defined. This works in Internet Explorer 9, Opera, and Internet Explorer with ASV, as you would expect, and is the same regardless of whether the secondary clip path is applied to the parent *<clipPath>* or the elements within it. The other browsers show a variety of idiosyncratic responses to this approach.

Example 6: Animated Text Crawling Along a Bézier Curve

To anyone who enjoyed the excitement of new applications being unveiled in the Macintosh environment of the mid-to-late 1980s, Adobe Illustrator's ability to allow the layout of text to follow an arbitrary curve, using a simple graphical user interface (GUI), fell in the category of "utterly cool." The example at *http://srufaculty.sru.edu/david.dailey/svg/newstuff/textpath1.svg* demonstrates that SVG can do this—and go one step further: it can animate the text moving along that curve!

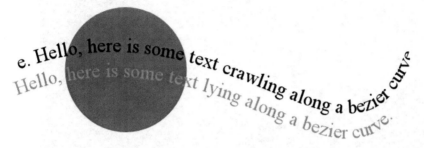

Here's how it's done:

- **Laying text along a path**   While this will be discussed with examples later in the book, it works rather like this: First, running text (a sequence of characters) is placed in an SVG *<text>* element. Also in the *<text>* goes a *<textPath>* element that has a simple URI reference to the ID of the *<path>* element.

- **Animation of text following a path**   One attribute of *<textPath>* is *startOffset*. Its value determines an offset for the initial position of the text. That is, a value of zero means that the text will begin at the start of the path; higher values mean that the text will begin closer to the endpoint. The effect is accomplished by simply animating that value with an SVG *<animate>* element.

Example 7: Animated Reflected Gradients with Transparency

Some of the effects offered by SVG seem to be more interesting than useful. This is often true of things like pure mathematics, until one's imagination discovers (or invents) their utility. The radial gradients available in SVG have the ability to repeat bands of color, using the values of *reflect* or *repeat*.

When seen in motion at *http://srufaculty.sru.edu/david.dailey/svg/newstuff/gradient11c.svg*, this example is quite impressive. It's best rendered by Chrome and ASV.

Here's how it's done:

- **The two swirly gradients**   SVG has two primary sorts of gradients: linear and radial. The radial gradient allows for a special type called a *reflected* gradient. In this case, two identical ellipses are located one atop the other. Both have alternating bands of opacity and transparency coinciding with their alternating colors, which allows us to see through to the background.

- **The animation**   The center and focal points of the reflected gradients are then independently animated using SMIL animation.

Example 8: Clock with Impressionist Tinge

There are lots of SVG clocks on the Web. Displaying time is a medium of expression ripe with opportunity, it seems. This particular one is probably not the most artful, elegant, appealing, fanciful, decorative, or marketable version available, but its ability to do what it does with only 79 lines of code (about half JavaScript and half SVG) may help to illustrate the ease and brevity with which you can achieve rich effects. You can find an animated version of this (for browsers that support SMIL animation) at *http://srufaculty.sru.edu/david.dailey/svg/ballclock.svg*.

Here's how it's done:

- **The animation** All animation is handled declaratively (using SMIL). That is, there are no JavaScript statements involving *setTimeout()* or *setInterval()* (used for conventional web animation). A generic animation that handles the rotation of the clock's hands is declared in markup and then cloned through JavaScript, with its properties being modified in a simple loop that handles the details of how fast each hand should move. Likewise, the gears are each cloned from one protogear, with the dash patterns around their edges and their rotations being assigned different speeds.

- **The markup** The markup is kept minimal by using script to replicate many copies of similar things. SVG does not yet have a *<replicate>* element that might allow some of this script to be handled declaratively. In the meantime, we can use markup and script for what each does best—SVG allows the pleasant intermingling of both. The JavaScript is also used to assign colors, sizes, and speeds to the various gears, and to determine the actual time of day so the clock's hands may be initialized.

- **The clock face** The hour marks are also done declaratively by setting the *dash-array* attribute of the stroke around the clock face. The appearance of a slight curvature to the clock face is provided through a radial gradient.

Example 9: Using a Filter to Create Pond Ripples over an Image

This example shows some of the more advanced aspects of scripted animated gradients used in conjunction with filters to distort an image. The animated version shows ripples (customizable by the user using HTML input elements) moving across an image—much as ripples would disrupt the reflection of an image in a pond.

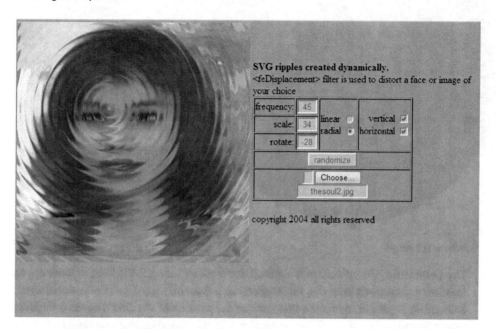

Here's how it's done:

- **Creating concentric circles**   The circles are created with script. A gradient can have different color bands, called *stops*, defined within it. In this case, a series of concentric stops (orange and green) is created through script and added to a gradient, which is then applied to an ellipse under the image of a face.

- **Animating concentric circles**   The radius (or offset) of each stop is then modified gradually through subtle changes in a *setTimeout* loop defined in JavaScript. Interestingly, the script for this example resides in the HTML rather than within the SVG, and the SVG DOM is accessed from there.

- **Distorting the image**   Once the above two things have been done, the rest is rather easy. A filter is created that brings in both the concentric circles and the face as layers, and then distortion is applied through a filter effect known as *<feDisplacementMap>*, using the red channel of the gradient to determine the degree of distortion associated with the image. Because green doesn't contain red but orange does, *<feDisplacementMap>* provides the differential distortion in concentric bands.

Example 10: Using <replicate> to Simulate Digital Elevation Maps

SVG is still evolving. Version 2 of the specification is presently under deliberation by the W3C's Working Group. While the language currently has only two types of gradients (linear and radial), several proposals exist for increasing that number. One, the proposal to allow declarative markup to create many objects that are tweened from one another—like animation, only spatial rather than temporal—is to use *<replicate>*. While *<replicate>* would handle a wide variety of issues (such as this rotatable 3D portrayal of a geographic landform), other proposals are considerably less broad in scope.

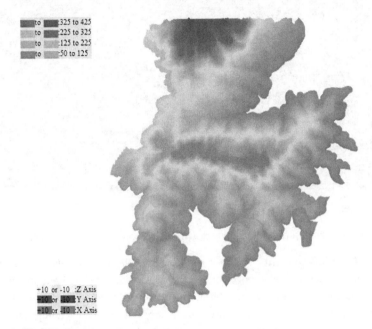

Here's how it's done:

- **Interpolating between paths**   In this example, which you can find at *http://srufaculty.sru .edu/david.dailey/svg/dem/DEM_1.svg*, many concentric polygons (with varying numbers of points in their definition) are defined through interpolation and then cloned.

- **Simulating 3D rotation**   Script then manipulates the data to enable rotation in three dimensions.

Example 11: Non-Affine Cobblestones

Here's another example showing the use of *<replicate>* (see *http://srufaculty.sru.edu/david.dailey/svg/ replicate/repRectsGrad2g.svg*). This example replicates interpolated polygons in two directions. While *<replicate>* is not (yet) supported by the SVG specification, it is supported through an open source JavaScript initiative that allows SVG-like declarative markup to be interspersed with actual SVG to create a wide range of effects.

Here's how it's done:

- **The basic shape**   First, a quadrilateral is drawn with SVG using a *<path>* element.

- **Replicating from left to right**   It is then replicated by placing a *<replicate>* element inside the *<path>*. The *<replicate>* element instructs the quadrilateral's shape and position to be gradually duplicated from left to right. Additionally, the gradient applied to the quadrilateral is retrieved, and one of its defining color bands (or *stops*) is gradually changed from red to green, and finally to purple (with the color values of that gradient being modified as well).

- **Replicating vertically**   The results of the first replication are viewed as part of a group that is then replicated upward, with its scale being modified as it is cloned.

Example 12: Triangular Tiling

While SVG has a *<pattern>* element, which allows the creation of repeated rectangular tiles, if you wish to use nonrectangular tilings or to individually modify the elements from one part of a pattern to another, then script may be the way to go. The juxtaposition of opacity, rotation, gradients, and triangles is something easily done in SVG. The rotation of the inner triangles creates a bivalent appearance of either clover leaves or honeycombs, depending on orientation. You can see this example at *http://srufaculty.sru.edu/david.dailey/svg/triBraids4.svg*.

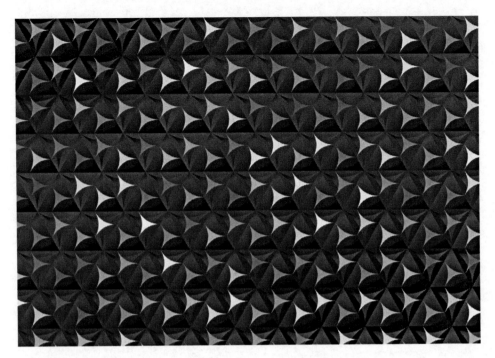

Here's how it's done:

- **The basic shapes**   We begin with two triangles, having different orientations and gradient fills. Some opacity in the gradients is used to allow the background to be seen.

- **Duplication using script**   In this case, script is used to build a triangular tiling through cloning of the initial triangles. The center of each triangle is then filled with another triangular shape filled with random colors (from a very select range of possibilities).

- **Finishing effects**   An underlying gradient is applied and slowly animated to give an almost subliminal sense of "atmosphere." For browsers that support SMIL animation, some of these effects, including rotation, are animated.

Example 13: A Web Application for Drawing Graphs (Networks)

This particular application has been built and rebuilt by its authors in many different languages (cT, HyperTalk, Java, VML, and now SVG with JavaScript) over the past 25 years. It has proven invaluable for the teaching of discrete mathematics to undergraduate students. Basically, using a few thousand lines of JavaScript, it builds a click-and-drag GUI interface to allow the creation, editing, replication, storage, and retrieval of finite graphs. Like many emerging web applications, the SVG here is sort of secondary, with JavaScript and event handling consuming the predominant effort. SVG can be used to play a crucial role in the increasingly important realm of web applications.

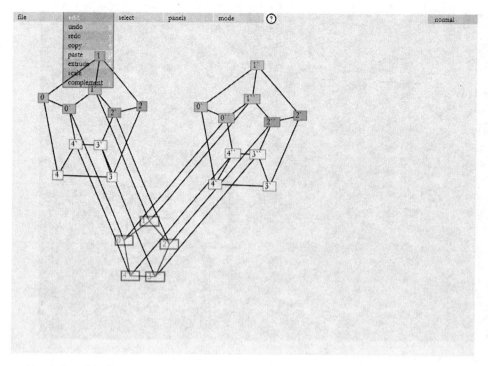

Here's how it's done:

- **Drawing**   One advantage of using SVG—instead of comparatively lightweight graphical technologies, such as *<canvas>* in HTML—for building web applications is that objects in SVG are in the DOM. This means that events can be easily attached to objects and SVG event handling, much like those in the nongraphical parts of HTML. Thus, mouse coordinates (as well as the targets of events) can easily be interrogated to allow the creation and repositioning of objects, in the classical sense of a GUI.

- **Connecting**   Again, because SVG objects are in the DOM, it is easy to build JavaScript referents to those objects so that arrays of objects and their properties may be maintained along with connections back to their visible instantiations. It is easy to connect and disconnect nodes of graphs, precisely because they are objects, both in JavaScript and SVG.

- **Interface**   The example shown here uses JavaScript to build a menuing system along with dialog boxes, and the ability to export and import the user's drawings. However, much of this functionality can also be provided through higher-level tools, such as D3, and Pergola (discussed in later chapters).

Diving In: A Step-by-Step Approach to Building a Simple SVG Document

The following exercises are presented at a deliberately slow pace. Once you get the hang of how SVG works (in some general way), the pace will quicken a good deal.

A first file

We already introduced a very simple example of an SVG file in this chapter, in the "Writing SVG" section. Let us recommence at that point:

1. Open a trusty text editor (something that allows you to see and save plain text—typically plain ASCII or UTF-8 in .txt format).

2. Create a file containing the following lines of code, and save it as *first.svg*:

```
<svg xmlns="http://www.w3.org/2000/svg">
  <circle r="50"/>
</svg>
```

3. Open the same file in a web browser. You can leave your text editor open because you may wish to later revise the file to add new things. For your browser, you may use a current version of Chrome, Firefox, Internet Explorer (see notes on this from the "Viewing SVG" section earlier in the chapter), Opera, or Safari.

   You should see something that looks like the image below, which shows screen shots of Firefox, Chrome, Opera, Internet Explorer, and Safari (from left to right, top to bottom).

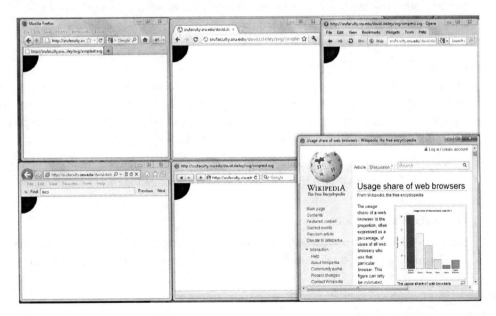

4. If you wish to serve this file from your own server, then make sure that the server is serving its mime type as *Content-Type: "image/svg+xml"*. You may have to contact your systems administrator to make sure the server is properly configured. If problems arise, please refer to the document SVG MIME Type, at *http://planetsvg.com/tools/mime.php*.

Intermission and Analysis

Next, we'll discuss the code from the preceding exercise so you can see what it does.

```
<svg xmlns="http://www.w3.org/2000/svg">
  <circle r="50"/>
</svg>
```

SVG As XML

The first and last lines show that SVG, as an XML dialect, is a markup language. Each element—in the simplest case, a single word between the angle brackets—must have a beginning (the *<svg>* in this case) and an end (the *</svg>* in this example). You can end the tag like this:

```
<svg></svg>
```

Or you can end it like this:

```
<circle ... />
```

This second example is called a self-terminating tag, because the slash (/) occurs at the end of the tag itself. Note that the second line in this example is indented as a convention for making the code more readable—the indentation isn't required.

Attributes

All SVG elements have a collection of attributes that are divided into two categories: regular attributes and presentation attributes (*http://www.w3.org/TR/SVG/attindex.html*). The first category includes, for example, geometrical attributes, such as *x*, *cx*, and *width*. The second category includes, for example, paint attributes, such as *fill*, *stroke-width*, *display*, and *opacity*.

The *<circle>* element, for example, has an attribute *r* (meaning *radius*). The fact that the *r* attribute has a value of 50 means (in the simplest and standard case) that the circle's radius will be 50 pixels.

The SVG Namespace

The *<svg>* element has the attribute/value pair *xmlns="http://www.w3.org/2000/svg"* (meaning that the XML namespace used to interpret the document will be one specified by the W3C).

The *xmlns* attribute (which appears not to have been a part of the language originally, because the Adobe and Opera viewers are unique in not requiring it) is necessary for most browsers to be able to display the code as SVG.

Essentially, the *xmlns* attribute merely tells the browser that it will be speaking a new dialect of XML. This is because most browsers of the 20th century assumed that the only language they would need to know was HTML. Writing *<svg>* isn't sufficient to let the browser know this, because the XML specification requires a namespace. It is rather unfortunate, from the perspective of teachers and learners, that the computer languages we learn are filled with mysteries that have no apparent purpose until one becomes a guru. However, you can think of the code *xmlns="http://www.w3.org/2000/svg"* within the *<svg>* element as just that: a mysterious incantation probably placed in the language to make sure that casual learners know to be on their guard. It turns out that it is not all that important to understand.

Screen Coordinates

Before beginning the second exercise, in which you'll begin experimenting with SVG, consider the drawing space itself—the browser window. Each point within the drawing space (also known as the Cartesian plane) is identified by a pair of coordinates (x and y). The upper-left corner of the screen is the point (0,0) and—depending on screen resolution and the current size of the window—the lower-right corner could have coordinates such as (800,640), (951,651), or (1440,900). The number of pixels determines the resolution of the screen. The resolution on mobile devices varies considerably; 240×320 pixels is a popular size for smaller and older devices.

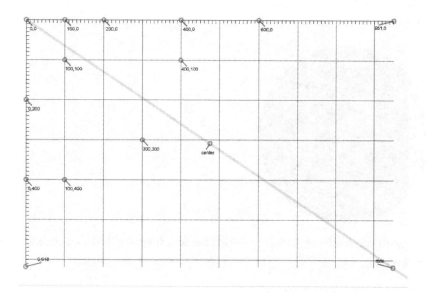

Modifying your code and experimenting

In this exercise, you'll experiment with the circle you drew in the previous exercise by changing its location, size, and color, rebuilding it so that only its outer boundary remains black.

1. Move the circle to the center of the screen. You do this by setting the x and y coordinates of the center of the circle (*cx* and *cy*, respectively) to 50 percent, which is measured relative to the width and height of the browser window.

```
<svg xmlns="http://www.w3.org/2000/svg">
  <circle r="50" cx="50%" cy="50%"/>
</svg>
```

2. Increase the radius and set it as a fixed proportion of the browser's width.

> **Note** A geometric attribute, such as *cx*, *cy*, or *r* in this case, can be set as either a proportional value (relative to window size) or an absolute value (pixels, by default).

```
<svg xmlns="http://www.w3.org/2000/svg">
  <circle r="25%" cx="50%" cy="50%"/>
</svg>
```

3. Change its color. You can do this by setting the *fill* attribute to a named color, or in a variety of other ways (e.g., using CSS or HTML hexadecimal values, RGB values, or HSB values).

```
<svg xmlns="http://www.w3.org/2000/svg">
  <circle r="25%" cx="50%" cy="50%" fill="darkorange"/>
</svg>
```

4. Change the code so that just the outside of the circle is colored. This actually involves three tasks: setting the fill of the circle to *none* so that its interior is transparent, setting its stroke to some color (e.g., *darkorange*), and defining a width for the stroke. The code below also adjusts the color from the named color *darkorange* to *#e60*, which is a bit lower on the red channel and a good bit lower on the green channel than the *darkorange* hexadecimal equivalent, #FF8C00.

```
<svg xmlns="http://www.w3.org/2000/svg">
  <circle r="25%" cx="50%" cy="50%" fill="none" stroke="#e60" stroke-width="25"/>
</svg>
```

5. Make the inside transparent. You can accomplish this by putting another opaque circle behind it and scooting it a bit to the left. Note that the first object defined appears behind objects that appear later in the document tree. In this case, we've also added another namespace identifier (which is not strictly needed here, but will become necessary for elements that use the SVG linking facilities to link to external documents or code fragments defined elsewhere within the same document). It's here so you can become accustomed to seeing it, because it's part of the standard declaration of a typical SVG document.

```
<svg xmlns="http://www.w3.org/2000/svg"
     xmlns:xlink="http://www.w3.org/1999/xlink" >
  <circle cx="30%" cy="50%" r="25%"
          fill="lightgreen" stroke="#e60" stroke-width="25"/>
  <circle cx="50%" cy="50%" r="25%"
          fill="none" stroke="#e60" stroke-width="25"/>
</svg>
```

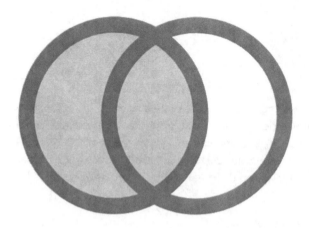

Accomplishing a given effect

In this exercise, we will present a picture and ask you to analyze and then try to draw it.

1. Observe the following SVG drawing, referred to as "the objective":

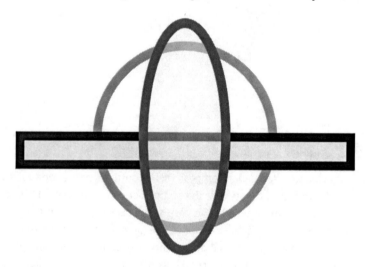

2. Identify the type of objects that seem to be used in the drawing.

Tip Until we introduce the full range of graphical primitives, we will restrict the drawing to circles, ellipses, and rectangles, all of which are somewhat self-explanatory once you see the syntax.

In this case, it appears that there are three objects: a circle (that very much resembles our earlier one), an oval (called an ellipse in SVG), and a rectangle.

3. Identify the order in which the objects are drawn. The front-most object appears to be the ellipse, and its yellowish fill pattern appears slightly transparent, because you can see through it to the objects behind it. From back to front (which coincides with the order in which the objects will be drawn), there appears to be a circle, then a rectangle, and finally an ellipse. It's important to note that the topmost object (the ellipse) is transparent in its interior but not its boundary.

4. Determine whether the objects seem to be drawn using relative values (percentages) or absolute values (pixels) for their geometric attributes.

   You may find it useful to view the drawing on the web, where you can see how the drawing is affected by resizing the browser. You can find the drawing here: *http://granite.sru.edu/~ddailey/svg/lesson3.svg*.

   In this case, it makes sense to begin with the assumption that the geometry has been drawn relative to the window size for three reasons: because the circle seems to be the same as in the second exercise (which used relative values for its geometry), because the rectangle's top line seems to coincide with the center of the circle, and because the ellipse appears to share the same center as the circle.

5. Start off with the same file you created at the end of the previous exercise, because it appears that the two files share the same circle, and the objective illustration would involve placing that circle beneath the other objects—which means earlier in the markup code.

```
<svg xmlns="http://www.w3.org/2000/svg"
  xmlns:xlink="http://www.w3.org/1999/xlink" >
  <title>Collage involving &lt;rect&gt; , &lt;circle&gt; and &lt;ellipse&gt; </title>
  <circle cx="50%" cy="50%" r="25%" fill="none" stroke="#e60" stroke-width="25"/>
</svg>
```

The preceding code contains one additional line: a *<title>* element. As an image format, SVG has great potential to address issues of accessibility for visually impaired people, so it is best to get in the habit of adding a title to all your documents. You'll see more about accessibility later in this book, because it is an important topic, particularly for SVG.

6. Add a light-blue rectangle on top of the circle and adjust its size, position, color, stroke, and stroke width:

```
<svg xmlns="http://www.w3.org/2000/svg"
xmlns:xlink="http://www.w3.org/1999/xlink" >
  <title>Collage involving &lt;rect&gt; , &lt;circle&gt; and &lt;ellipse&gt; </title>
  <circle cx="50%" cy="50%" r="25%" fill="none"
    stroke="#e60" stroke-width="25"/>
  <rect x="10%" width="80%" y="50%" height="10%"
    fill="#8ff" stroke="black" stroke-width="6" />
</svg>
```

The <rect> element, like the *circle*, can have *fill*, *stroke*, *stroke-width*, and other attributes. The *x* and *y* attributes specify the rectangle's upper-left corner, and *height* and *width* specify its size. Because you want the top of the rectangle to coincide with the center of the window, you can set *x* to "50%". You also want it centered on the screen horizontally, so the distance of its rightmost extent (specified by *x* + *width*) to the right edge of the window should equal *x*. By experimenting a bit with different values of *x* and the corresponding value of *width* (determined by the centering constraint), you can visually estimate the values above (or similar values). Note that 100% − (80% + 10%) = 10%, which means that the rectangle will be centered horizontally, even though it is not centered vertically. The values for *stroke-width* and *fill* can likewise be estimated through experimentation.

7. Put an oval atop everything and fill it with a transparent shade of yellow, while keeping its stroke opaque:

```
<svg xmlns="http://www.w3.org/2000/svg"
  xmlns:xlink="http://www.w3.org/1999/xlink" >
  <title>Collage involving &lt;rect&gt; , &lt;circle&gt; and &lt;ellipse&gt; </title>
  <circle cx="50%" cy="50%" r="25%" fill="none" stroke="#e60" stroke-width="25"/>
  <rect x="10%" width="80%" y="50%" height="10%" fill="#8ff"
    stroke="black" stroke-width="6" />
  <ellipse cx="50%" cy="50%" rx="10%" ry="40%" fill="yellow" fill-opacity=".45"
    stroke="purple" stroke-width="15" />
</svg>
```

An ellipse, like a circle, has a center defined by *cx* and *cy*. However, owing to the difference in its vertical and horizontal extents, it has two radii: *ry* and *rx*, respectively. Because this oval is taller than it is wide, you can approximate the values above fairly closely by testing a few values and seeing what happens. Alternatively, you could actually measure the drawing on the screen to duplicate the effect more precisely.

The preceding code introduces a new attribute: *opacity*. All the typical drawn objects (such as *rect*, *circle*, *polygon*, *ellipse*, and *path*) all have an *opacity* attribute. When *opacity* is set to "1.0", an object's stroke and fill are completely opaque. When *opacity* is set to "0.0", the object is completely invisible. If you don't specify *opacity*, the browser assumes that *opacity* is 1. If you wish to specify different levels of opacity for an object's stroke and fill, you can do so using the attributes *stroke-opacity* and *fill-opacity*.

The code you end up with for this exercise should closely match the code of the example at *http://granite.sru.edu/~ddailey/svg/lesson3.svg*.

Summary

With this chapter, we hope to have given you a sense of how useful, elegant, and important SVG is for building informative and appealing graphics. You can accomplish a broad range of effects with this technology, ranging from practical to artistic, while making your graphics both dynamic and interactive. SVG is a powerful technology, and yet it allows you to easily begin the process of experimenting and learning. We feel it is a valuable technology that is just beginning its ascent to widespread deployment.

CHAPTER 2

Creating and Editing SVG Graphics

Order becomes beauty
beyond infinite planes
and the undeciphered dense text
a mosaic flower, fiery,
chaos tamed in fullness,
spring.

Orides Fontela

In this chapter:

By the end of this chapter, you will have explored the core concepts and practiced the basic skills to begin tapping into your visual creativity. One great thing about programming graphics is that you can usually visualize your work almost immediately. To demonstrate this, you'll walk through a process that uses all of the basic shape elements of SVG. As a teaser, here's a look at one of the graphics that you will build in this chapter.

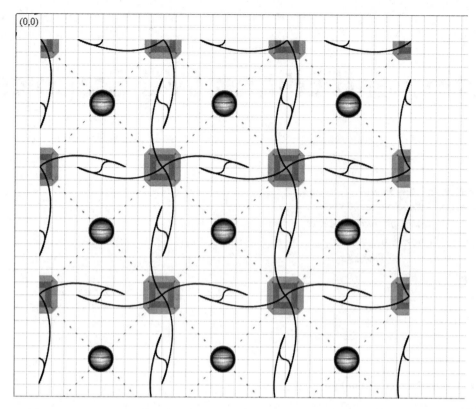
(0,0)

This graphic incorporates all of the basic shapes, the simple Bézier curve, more complex cubic Bézier curves, and bitmap images. It also demonstrates the logical grouping and reusing of related graphics, and finally, how to pull everything together into a reusable tiling pattern, which is also known as *tessellation of the plane*.

Note Although mathematical functions underlie the creation of SVG, and getting the most out of SVG requires a decent grasp of mathematical concepts, those of us who have limited mathematical talents can still harness the power and creative potential of SVG.

Creating Basic Vector Shapes

To get started, we'll go over the six basic shape elements: *<line>*, *<rect>*, *<circle>*, *<ellipse>*, *<polyline>*, and *<polygon>*.

Lines

To create a visible line in SVG, simply set the *x2* and *y2* values of the *<line>* element. You can set the line's color and other properties as well using the stroke-related attributes.

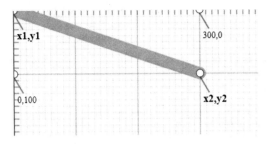

```
<line x2="300" y2="100" stroke="green" stroke-width="10" stroke-linecap="round" />
```

> **Note** By default, most SVG shape properties have initial or default values. For example, the initial value of most positioning properties is zero, which is why you do not have to specify the *x1* and *y1* values for the *<line>* element. Also, the default fill color for shapes is black, so the shape *<circle r="50" />* or *<polygon points="850,75 850,325 742,262 742,137" />* will appear black even though the fill has not been specified.

Brief Review of SVG Presentation Attributes

Besides the command attributes that define a shape's position, radius, width, and height, SVG also has many attributes that define a shape's style. You are probably already familiar with attributes such as *display, visibility, font,* and *letter-spacing.* SVG also has many SVG-specific styling properties (as in the example above, which shows how the *stroke* attribute allows you to define the color of the line).

SVG presentation attributes can help you quickly set the paint and geometrical values of SVG elements; apply gradients, filters, and clipping; and control the interactive behavior. Chapter 3, "Adding Text, Style, and Transforms" covers presentation attributes in more depth, but Table 2-1 provides a quick reference for common properties that you will be using in this chapter.

TABLE 2-1 Common SVG Presentation Attributes

Attribute	Values
stroke	This specifies the color of the stroke. The valid color values are the same as in CSS3 and HTML5: named color (e.g., "blue"), hexadecimal (e.g., "#f34a12"), RGB (e.g., "rgb(255,255,255)"), HSL (e.g., "rgb(100%,50%,90%)"),%), and so on. More detail about SVG colors can be found here: *http://www.w3.org/TR/SVG/color.html.*
stroke-width	This specifies the width of the stroke for a shape or text using either a percentage or a length value. When using a length value, we recommend specifying the type of unit (px, cm, etc.) to prevent cross-browser issues. It is worth pointing out that the units specified in the outermost *<svg>* tag are inherited by all descendants, and that the default value is *px.* You can find more details about possible length values here: *http://www.w3.org/TR/SVG/types.html#DataTypeLength.* Note that the stroke is centered on the edge of a shape, so if *stroke-width* is set to a large enough value, the shape's fill may not even display.
stroke-opacity	This is a number between 1.0 and 0.0. A value of 1 makes the stroke entirely opaque and 0 makes it invisible.
stroke-dasharray	This is a list of user coordinate values (px) that determines the length or pattern of the invisible spacing to be drawn between segments along the stroke of text or a shape.

Attribute	Values
stroke-linecap	This defines the shape at both ends of a line. The options are *butt* (the default), *round*, and *square*.
stroke-linejoin	This determines the shape to be used at the corners of paths or basic shapes. The options are *miter* (the default), *round*, and *bevel*.
fill	This specifies the color of the shape or text.
fill-opacity	This is similar to the stroke opacity. Note that if the opacity is between 0 and 1, and the stroke value is set to a different color or opacity than the fill color, then the inner portion of the stroke will be a different color than the outer portion of the stroke, which can create some nice effects.
fill-rule	This determines which portions of a shape will be filled. The options are *nonzero* (the default) and *evenodd*. Note that this is usually straightforward, but for more interesting or complex shapes, the result of *fill-rule* can be less obvious, as explained in the "Fill Properties: nonzero and evenodd" section.

Rectangles

The rectangle element (*<rect>*) requires *width* and *height* attributes, but you can also specify *x* and *y* attributes, which specify the position in relation to the top-left corner of the SVG canvas. If they are not specified, they default to (0,0). Optional *rx* and *ry* attributes are also available, which apply a uniform rounding to all the corners. If only *rx* is specified, *ry* is equal to *rx*.

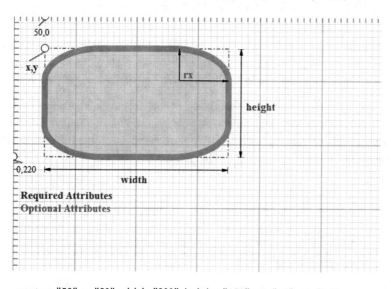

```
<rect x="50" y="50" width="300" height="170" rx="90" ry="50"
      stroke="darkseagreen" stroke-width="10"
      fill="lightgray" fill-opacity="0.6" />
```

Circles

As mentioned in Chapter 1, "Stepping into SVG," the SVG *<circle>* element only requires a value for the radius. In the following image, the *cx* and *cy* values are set to (100,50).

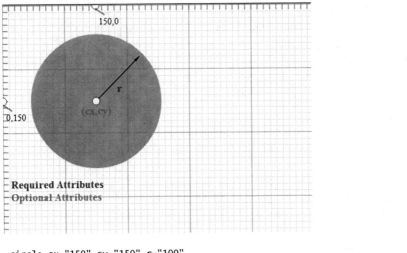

```
<circle cx="150" cy="150" r="100"
        stroke="darkseagreen" stroke-width="10" fill="grey" fill-opacity="0.6"/>
```

Ellipses

The *<ellipse>* element provides the additional attribute *ry* so that both the x and y radius values can be set as shown below:

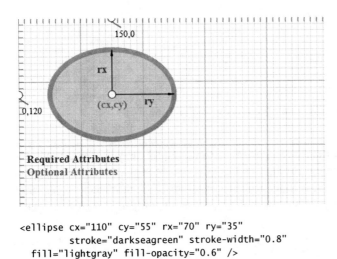

```
<ellipse cx="110" cy="55" rx="70" ry="35"
         stroke="darkseagreen" stroke-width="0.8"
  fill="lightgray" fill-opacity="0.6" />
```

Polylines and Polygons

There are just two additional basic shapes: the polyline and the polygon. They are very similar to each other in that they both simply require the *points* attribute, which contains a list of x,y value pairs. Both of these shapes allow for drawing a series of straight lines, as if a pen were set down and used to draw on paper.

The primary difference between the *<polyline>* and *<polygon>* shape elements in SVG is that the polyline path will not be closed by default—that is, the two endpoints will not be connected unless you specify that they should be. If you wish a polyline shape to be closed, you need to specifically draw an endpoint that meets back up with the starting point. The polygon, on the other hand, will automatically close the shape from the last specified point, as shown in this example:

```
// open
<polyline points="200,60 240,230 310,230 350,60"
          fill="lightcyan" fill-opacity="0.7"  stroke="darkviolet"
          stroke-width="25" stroke-linecap="round" stroke-opacity="0.2" />

// closed
<polygon points="100,50 115,120 150,150 115,180 100,250 85,180 50,150 85,120"
         fill="darkorange" fill-opacity="0.5" stroke="papayawhip"
         stroke-width="20" stroke-opacity="0.7" stroke-linejoin="miter"/>
```

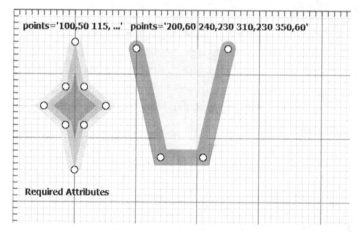

Note how the *stroke-linejoin* and *stroke-linecap* attributes affect the shape.

> **Note** All of these basic shapes have been purposely designed by the W3C community for ease of use, and each type of shape element carries an inherent semantic meaning as well. As discussed in the previous chapter, there are many benefits of semantic languages, and the well-defined shape elements of SVG have inherent benefits for projects such as mapping, CAD, and graphic design.

Creativity with Basic Shapes

The beauty of the SVG language is that with just this basic knowledge, you are already able to start building some complex vector graphics that will render in all the major browsers. As an example, this next image demonstrates some of the fancy things that you can already do with a little creativity and knowledge of SVG shape properties.

This next example shows how the *<line>* element can be styled, with surprising results. All of the shapes on the left of the figure were created with a single *<line>* element, and all of the shapes on the right were created with just two *<line>* elements.

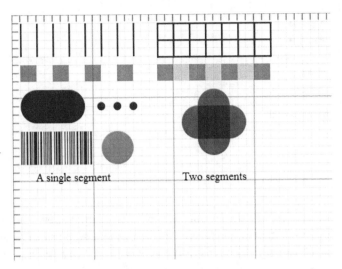

Even more interesting, the following minimalistic example demonstrates how to create fancy circular shapes using just one or two *<circle>* elements.

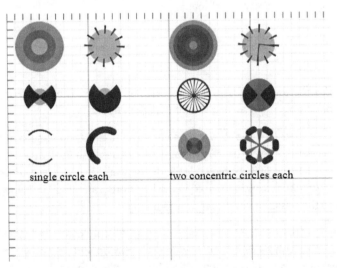

This third example uses only one or two *<polygon>* elements—again with interesting results:

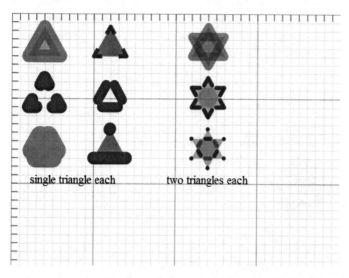

single triangle each   two triangles each

I encourage you to open the code samples (see the Introduction for instructions on downloading the code samples) that come with this book to better understand how these interesting shapes were created. This will provide you with valuable insights into the workings of presentation attributes such as *stroke*, *opacity*, *dash array*, and others.

In addition to the basic shape elements, SVG provides the much more expressive *<path>* element, which allows you to create any type of two-dimensional shape.

Paths in SVG

The *<path>* element is the most flexible drawing primitive in SVG. It contains subcommands that allow it to mimic all of the other basic shapes. As such, it is a bit trickier to learn.

Like other drawing primitives such as *<rect>* and *<ellipse>*, *<path>* can take attributes such as *fill*, *stroke*, and *dash array*. On the other hand, *<path>* uses a special syntax to describe the way it actually visits points on a plane. It borrows some of its origin (at least ideologically) from *turtle graphics* (*http://en.wikipedia.org/wiki/Turtle_graphics*), which are used in the Logo programming language to help introduce younger children to the basics of computer programming.

The SVG *<path>* element is very expressive due to the range of powerful path commands that it uses. As with the HTML5 *<canvas>* element, paths can be used to draw pen-up and pen-down movements, quadratic and cubic Bézier curves, and elliptical arcs, all within a single path. That is, you move the pen (or drawing point) from position to position, raise it and lower it, and make strokes of varying types. These instructions within the *<path>* syntax are called *subcommands* of the path object. In SVG, you'll find them in the data attribute (*d*) of the *<path>*.

Paths typically begin with the *M* subcommand, which instructs the drawing to begin at a specific (x,y) point, such as (100,100), like so:

```
d = "M 100,100 ..."
```

From there, you continue adding points—that is, (x,y) pairs—describing segments to be joined along the path. The following section shows how this works.

<path> Subcommands: M and L

Start by specifying where the drawing will begin. As the first command for the *d* attribute, you insert a notation such as *M x y*, where *x* and *y* are numbers. You can think of *M x y* as meaning "Move the pen to the coordinates (x,y)." From there, you have the option of drawing a line (*L*), a quadratic curve (*Q*), a cubic curve (*C*), or an arc (*A*). For example, *d="M 50 50 L 150 150"* would draw a diagonal line from the point (50,50) to the point (150,150).

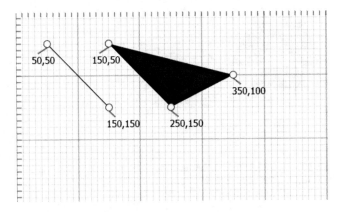

```
<path stroke="black"
      d="M 50 50 L 150 150"/>
<path d="M 150 50
      L 250 150 350 100"/>
```

You should note several things about this example:

- The second path does not specify a stroke; by default, the figure is filled with black. If you specify *fill="none"*, the figure will be invisible unless you specify a stroke.

- You can, for the sake of legibility, use commas between pairs of coordinates, in which case the space after the comma is optional.

- You can omit the command letter on subsequent commands if the same command is used multiple times in a row, as shown in the second path, where the *L* command is followed by two pairs of values. Note also that if a MoveTo command (*M* or *m*) is directly followed by multiple pairs of coordinates, the subsequent pairs are treated as implicit LineTo commands.

Fill Properties: nonzero and evenodd

Since a path is filled with black by default, it is natural to wonder what happens when a path crosses itself. As mentioned in Table 2-1, the default *fill-rule* value is *nonzero*, which means that by default, the union of the regions traversed by the path is filled unless you specify otherwise. You can find more information on this in the "Fill Properties" section of the SVG specification, at *http://www.w3.org/TR/SVG/painting.html#FillProperties*.

Here is an example to show the difference between the *fill-rule* values *nonzero* and *evenodd*.

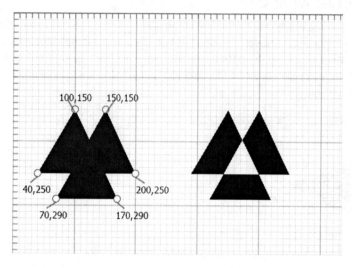

```
<path d="M 70,290 L 150,150 200,250 40,250 100,150 170,290"/>
<path d="M 70,290 L 150,150 200,250 40,250 100,150 170,290"
      fill-rule="evenodd" transform="translate(250,0)"/>
```

This example demonstrates the default fill technique, as well as the *evenodd* fill rule on a shape that intersects itself in more than one place.

> **Note** To demonstrate how the *fill-rule* attribute rule works in this example, we moved the second path shape, which has *fill-rule="evenodd"* applied to it, 250 units along the x-axis through the use of the *translate* method of the *transform* attribute. You will learn more about the *transform* capabilities in Chapter 3.

An Example of Building Complex Shapes

This section shows how you can use the pen-down command *M* to make more complex shapes with *<path>*.

The following code creates two paths, with one apparently drawn inside the other (in the sense that the coordinates of one are contained inside the polygon defined by the other):

```
<path d="M 100,350 300,100 500,350" fill="none" stroke="black" stroke-width="20"/>
<path d="M 250,320 250,220 350,220 350,320" fill="none" stroke="black" stroke-width="20"/>
```

The figure contains two paths: one with three points, the other with four. Note how the triangle encompasses the rectangle.

Next, we add the simple *z* subcommand (shown below in bold) at the end of each of the strings, which closes the path by drawing a final line back to the path's starting point. After we do that, the paths will be closed rather than left open between endpoints.

```
<path d="M 100,350 300,100 500,350 z" fill="none" stroke="black" stroke-width="20"/>
<path d="M 250,320 250,220 350,220 350,320 z" fill="none" stroke="black" stroke-width="20"/>
```

The new rendered SVG image looks like this:

Alternatively, you could create the preceding image using only a single *path* object (see *http://www.w3techcourses.com/svg_images/onepath.svg*), as follows:

```
<path d="M 100,350 300,100 500,350 z
         M 250,320 250,220 350,220 350,320 z"
       fill="none" stroke="black" stroke-width="20"/>
```

This method can save a bit on markup, but is a little harder. However, there are some additional benefits to this approach that are worth considering. By combining the two shapes above into one compound path, you can define the fill rule of that path as *evenodd*. The net effect of this is that the shape's fill color will not be applied to the interior region (although it would be applied to regions inside the interior region). Try this combined code:

```
<path d="M 100,350 300,100 500,350 z
M 250,320 250,220 350,220 350,320 z"
  fill="#ff8" stroke="black" stroke-width="15" fill-rule="evenodd"/>
```

You can see the advantage in the next graphic. The rectangles that underlie the triangle are visible through the rectangular hole in the shape. This effect would be difficult to produce if the two parts of this compound path were separate paths, because to be visible, the rectangle would have to be on top of the triangle—but in that case, nothing inside it other than the triangle itself would be visible.

We have just demonstrated how to create a complex vector graphic shape using a single SVG path element that contains a yellow triangle with a rectangular hole showing pink and green rectangles underneath. The next section discusses creating shapes using Bézier curves.

Quadratic Bézier Curves: The Q Subcommand

I became aware of Bézier curves in the mid-1980s when I discovered that Adobe Illustrator had the ability to draw amazing curves quickly. You can find good treatment of the subject on Wikipedia, at *http://en.wikipedia.org/wiki/B%C3%A9zier_curve#Quadratic_curves*.

Here's basically how a quadratic Bézier curve works in SVG. You define an initial point (e.g., 100,200) using a pen-down command. From there, you set a course heading toward the next point; however, instead of actually moving to the next point, you just aim in that direction. So, for example, while "*M 100 200 L 200 400*" will make you actually arrive at the point (200,400), "*M 100 200 Q 200 400...*" will merely point you in that direction. Ultimately, you also need a final destination, which is the final coordinate pair required for a quadratic Bézier curve. In the example that follows, the command "*M 100,200 L 200,400 300,200*" draws a red path between (and reaching each of) the three points indicated. But simply replacing the *L* with a *Q* (i.e., "*M 100,200 Q 200,400 300,200*") produces a curve that passes through both endpoints and is a tangent to the associated lines of the allied line path at the endpoints of the segments.

Bézier Curve Example

This example clearly shows how the quadratic Bézier curve is created.

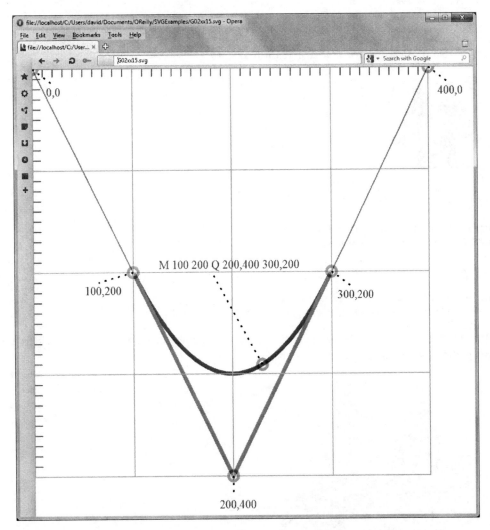

```
<path d="M 100 200 Q 200,400 300,200" fill="none" stroke="blue" />
<path d="M 100 200 L 200,400 300,200" fill="none" stroke="red"/>
```

While an infinite number of curves are tangent to both the line "*M 100 200 L 200 300*" at (100,200) and "*M 200 400 L 300 200*" at (300,200), only one quadratic shares these properties, even if you allow for rotations (in the sense of parametric equations) of the quadratic. That is, those three points in the plane uniquely define a specific curve. Likewise, any three noncollinear points in the plane determine one quadratic Bézier curve.

Revisiting the earlier example, which modified the fill rule to produce an empty space in the middle of the curve, you can draw the same curve with quadratic splines instead of lines to see the effect.

Here's an example of a graphic that uses a quadratic spline:

```
<path fill-rule="evenodd"
   d="M 70 140 L 150,0 200,100 L 40,100 100,0 L 170,140 70 140"/>

<path fill="red" fill-rule="evenodd"
   d="M 70 140 Q 150,0 200,100 Q 40,100 100,0 Q 170,140 70 140"/>
```

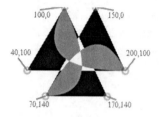

Note how the above example

```
<path id="H" fill="#bbb" fill-rule="evenodd"
   d="M 70 140 L 150,0 200,100 L 40,100 100,0 L 170,140 70 140"/>
```

can have its *L*s modified to *Q*s:

```
<path id="X" fill="#b42" fill-rule="evenodd"
   d="M 70 140 Q 150,0 200,100 Q 40,100 100,0 Q 170,140 70 140"/>
```

That produces a shape similar to the following (we've changed the colors and added in identifiers to the paths for easy reference in the text here):

The figure shows two paths produced from the preceding code. Both paths have the same points, but one is linear (*id="H"*) and the other is quadratic (*id="X"*).

Observe that the angles of the reddish shape (*X*) at which the curves actually meet are sharp rather than rounded. Let's look more closely. If you're familiar with trefoil knots (see *http://en.wikipedia.org/wiki/Trefoil_knot*), then that is the sort of shape we'll be aiming toward.

First, observe that if the desired shape were to pass through any of the six points of the linear path *H*, then in order for the parts of the curve that meet there to be smooth, and for any of them to be tangent to lines of *H*, the new curve would have to extend beyond the bounds of *X*. You could extend the lines of *X* into a larger equilateral triangle and then work on building your trefoil knot. You could do this with cubic Bézier curves by defining a curve that passes through the same three endpoints (*http://www.w3techcourses.com/svg_images/lineOutCub.svg*) that it already does, but that is guided by the control points consisting of the three points of the circumscribed triangle (shown in the next figure as the light green line).

```
<path fill="#c53" fill-rule="evenodd" opacity=".5"
   d="M 70 140 C 17.5 ,140 150,0 200,100 C 220, 140 40,100 100,0 C 127,-47 170,140 70 140"/>
```

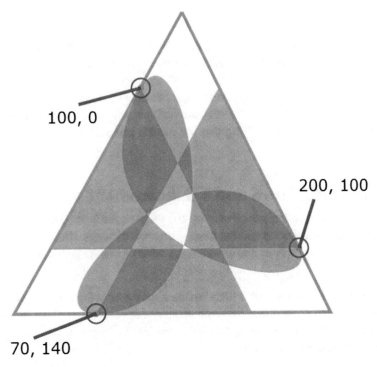

100, 0

200, 100

70, 140

As a final example, the following demonstrates how to stitch Bézier curves together smoothly. For this to happen, the slopes of the lines at either side of a segment's endpoint must be the same.

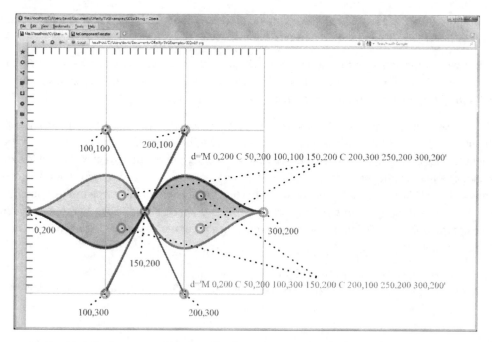

Notice that the brown and blue paths share the same beginning points and endpoints, initial and final control points, and midpoints (150,200). They differ only in terms of the control points surrounding the midpoint. The blue path aims toward (100,100) and then changes direction toward (200,300), passing through the midpoint on its way and tangent to the line, as shown. Because the three relevant points, (100,100), (150,200), and (200,300), are collinear, the slopes of both segments are the same at the point where they meet, implying that the curve is smooth (continuously differentiable) at that point.

Creating Smooth Curves: The S and T Subcommands

These shortcut commands help with creating smooth curves, and they require fewer data points than constructing cubic and quadratic Bézier curves without these shortcut commands. This is because one of the Bézier curve points is used simply as a reference point, which is then reflected to create a smooth curve.

You use the *S* command to draw a smooth cubic Bézier spline segment from the current point to a new point (x,y). The previous segment must also be a smooth cubic Bézier spline, and that second control point is then reused via reflection relative to the current point as the segment's first control point. The second control must be explicitly specified.

You use the *T* command to draw a smooth quadratic Bézier spline segment from the current point to a new point (x,y). The previous segment must also be a smooth quadratic Bézier spline, and that control point is then reused via reflection relative to the current point.

The following image demonstrates the automatic reflection process for both these commands:

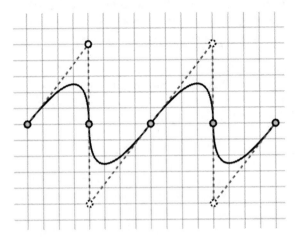

As you have seen, the *<path>* element can express both simple and complex shapes using the *L*, *H*, *V*, *Q*, and *C* commands. The geometric calculations involved are quite complex, which is why vector-drawing programs such as Inkscape, Illustrator, SVG-Edit, and Visio are very helpful in the SVG design process.

Elliptical Arc Example

One other often-used path command is the elliptical arc command (*A*), which allows you to quickly draw subsets of ellipses or intersecting ellipses. The arc subcommand of the *<path>* element has the following syntax: *A rx ry XAR large-arc-flag sweep-flag x y*.

The arc begins at the current point (which is determined by the last coordinate specified) and ends at (x,y), as demonstrated below:

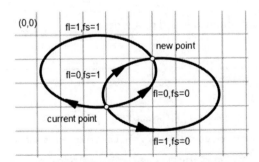

You now have the choice of four elliptical arc segments: two small ones and two large ones. These arc segments can have a positive angular orientation (clockwise) or a negative orientation. The *large-arc-flag (fl)* controls the angular orientation of the larger arc segment via *fl = 0 : small, fl = 1 : large*. The *sweep-flag (fs)* controls the angular orientation analogously, via *fs = 0 : positive*, and *fs = 1 : negative*.

Note For the special case where the endpoint coordinates (x,y) are equal to the *current point's* coordinates, the arc will not get rendered. Because this behavior is not intuitive when *large-arc-flag* is set to 1, this might be changed in the SVG 2.0 specification.

Using this elliptical arc information, here's the code to create a simple spiral:

```
<svg width="600" height="400" viewBox="0 0 400 300">
<path stroke="darkslategray" stroke-width="6" fill="none"
  stroke-linecap="round"
 d="M50,100
    A100,50 0 0 1 250,100
    A80,40 0 0 1 90,100
    A60,30 0 0 1 210,100
    A40,20 0 0 1 130,100
    A20,10 0 0 1 170,100" />
</svg>
```

That code produces the following spiral:

Table 2-2 provides a quick reference for the path commands and properties.

TABLE 2-2 Path Commands

Commands	Parameters	Instruction
M, m	x, y	Move to a new point (x,y).
L, l	x, y	Draw a line from the current point to a new point (x,y).
H, h	x	Draw a horizontal line from the current point to a new point (x,current-point-y).
V, v	y	Draw a vertical line from the current point to a new point (current-point-x,y).
A, a	rx, ry, x-axis-rotation, large-arc-flag, sweep-flag, x, y	Draw an elliptical arc from the current point to a new point (x,y). The arc belongs to an ellipse that has radii *rx* and *ry* and a rotation with respect to the positive x-axis of *x-axis-rotation* (in degrees). If *large-arc-flag* is 0 (zero), then the small arc (less than 180 degrees) is drawn. A value of 1 results in the large arc (greater than 180 degrees) being drawn. If *sweep-flag* is 0, then the arc is drawn in a negative angular direction (counterclockwise); if it is 1, then the arc is drawn in a positive angular direction (clockwise).

Commands	Parameters	Instruction
Q, q	x1, y1 x, y	Draw a quadratic Bézier curve from the current point to a new point (x,y) using (x1,y1) as the control point.
T, t	x, y	Draw a smooth quadratic Bézier curve segment from the current point to a new point (x,y). The control point is computed automatically as the reflection of the control point on the previous command relative to the current point. If there is no previous command or if the previous command was not a Q, q, T, or t, the control point is coincident with the current point.
C, c	x1, y1 x2, y2 x, y	Draw a cubic Bézier curve from the current point to a new point (x,y) using (x1,y1) and (x2,y2) as control points.
S, s	x2, y2 x, y	Draw a smooth cubic Bézier curve segment from the current point to a new point (x,y). The first control point is computed automatically as the reflection of the control point on the previous command relative to the current point. If there is no previous command or if the previous command was not a C, c, S, or s, the first control point is coincident with the current point. (x2,y2) is the second control point.

Relative vs. Absolute Path Coordinates

This next example uses a mixture of MoveTo (*M*), Vertical (*V*), LineTo (*L*), Bézier (*Q*), HorizontalTo (*H*), and ClosePath (*Z*) commands to generate a fairly elegant shape, as shown on the left of the following image. The example on the right requires less spatial brain power to generate the same shape because it uses *relative* versions of commands (i.e., lowercase commands). The coordinates of the new point are relative to the position of the previous point (40,80).

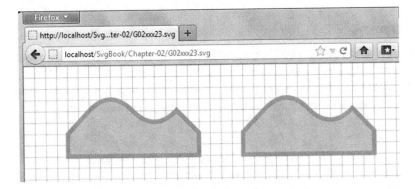

 Note The data of the path's *d* attribute actually follows a specific set of rules, called the Backus-Naur Form (BNF). You can find more detailed information on these rules at *http://www.w3.org/TR/SVG/paths.html#PathDataBNF*.

Accessing and Reusing Graphics

From buttons, icons, and window UIs, to building graphs and gaming graphics, there are many logical use cases for accessing and reusing raster and vector graphics in SVG.

Linking to both internal and external image data is worth a quick mention here because it is a common method for accessing and reusing SVG.

Referencing Vector and Bitmap Images

The SVG language provides the *<image>* element, which can reference other SVG images, as well as PNG and JPEG bitmap images. The syntax for the *<image>* element is similar to the *<rect>* element in that it has *x, y, width*, and *height* attributes.

The *<image>* element has the additional attribute *xlink:href*, which allows you to specify the location of the referenced image. Similar to HTML's *href* attribute, the *xlink:href* attribute allows the referenced image to be stored either locally or on the Internet. The code for referencing a bitmap image is as follows:

```
<image xlink:href="GrandMothersParty-121YO.png" x="340" y="0" width="140"
  height="160" opacity="0.5"/>
```

Referencing other SVG images is just as easy and becomes very useful in many application scenarios, such as reusing the same vector symbol on a page or dynamically loading vector images on demand.

The Group Element

The SVG group element, *<g>*, is great for logically grouping sets of related graphical objects. This group capability makes it easy to add styles, transformations, interactivity, and even animations to entire groups of objects. The following code groups a circle and a bitmap image together into a group named *iris*, which is then grouped together with an ellipse shape into another group named *eye*.

```
<!-- Group containing the eye. -->
<g id="eye">
  <!-- Draw the ellipse. -->
  <ellipse fill="#a1d9ad" fill-opacity="0.7" fill-rule="nonzero"
          stroke="#32287d" stroke-width="1" stroke-opacity="0.5" />

  <!-- Group containing the eye's iris. -->
  <g id="iris"
     cx="50" cy="50" rx="20" ry="14" />

    <!-- Draw the circle. -->
    <circle fill="black" fill-opacity="1" fill-rule="nonzero"
            stroke="#32287d" stroke-width="1" stroke-linecap="butt"
            stroke-linejoin="bevel" stroke-miterlimit="4"
            id="path3395" cx="50" cy="50" r="10" />
```

```
<!-- Reference the bitmap image (PNG) -->
<image id="bitmapCentralBall"
        width="5.5%" height="5.5%"
        x="39px" y="42px"
        xlink:href="iris-small.png"
        alt="NASA Photo of Jupiter" />
  </g>
</g>
```

With some creativity, you could then add some scripted interactivity such that the *iris* group could follow the mouse, while the *eye* group could blink randomly or at set intervals.

You'll see another great use for *<g>* during the discussion of transformations and interactivity in SVG in Chapter 4, "Motion and Interactivity." You can associate items together in a group and then define transformations to move, scale, or rotate all the items together so that their spatial relations to one another are maintained. Through the use of interactivity in SVG, you can assign, for example, an *onclick* event to an entire group so that all elements within the group respond to the event.

The <use> Element

The *<use>* element lets you reuse existing elements and thus write less code. Like the *<image>* element, *<use>* takes *x, y, height,* and *width* attributes, and it references other content using the *xlink:href* attribute.

As an example, you can reuse the following rectangle

```
<!-- Draw the upper-right rectangle. -->
<rect fill="#ada1d9" fill-opacity="1" fill-rule="nonzero"
    stroke="#32287d" stroke-width="10" stroke-linecap="butt"
    stroke-linejoin="bevel" stroke-miterlimit="4" stroke-opacity="0.4"
    id="rectangle" width="20" height="20" x="90" y="-10" />
```

by referencing it with the *<use>* element:

```
<!-- Reuse the first rectangle element and move it to a different position. -->
<use x="" y="" xlink:href="#rectangle" />
```

Creating Patterns

The SVG language helps you create and reuse patterns with ease. Patterns are extremely useful—in fact, the grid background found in many of this book's examples is just a simple pattern that consists of a single 10-by-10-pixel rectangle. The *<defs>* element can be used to store content that will not be directly displayed. This stored hidden content can then be referenced and displayed by other SVG elements, which makes it ideal for things such as patterns that contain reusable graphics.

To create a basic pattern in SVG, first place a rectangle within a *<pattern>* element, and then put everything inside of a *<defs>* element.

```
<defs>
  <pattern id="Pattern01" width="10" height="10" patternUnits="userSpaceOnUse">
    <rect width="10" height="10" fill="#FFFFFF" stroke="#000000" stroke-width="0.1"/>
  </pattern>
</defs>
```

Now, to use this pattern anywhere in your SVG graphic, simply set your element's *fill* attribute value to the *id* of the pattern, like this: *url(#Pattern01)*.

```
<rect id="Background" x="0" y="0" width="100%" height="100%"
  fill="url(#Pattern01)" stroke-width="0.5" stroke="#000000" />
```

Case Study: Designing a Reusable Pattern

The example in this section gives you a closer look at how to write SVG code that generates a pattern composed of both vector and bitmap graphics.

Adding Basic Shapes

Building upon your knowledge up to this point, you'll walk through each step of the design and creation process.

1. Create and save a file named *tile.svg* that contains the following lines of code:

    ```
    <svg xmlns="http://www.w3.org/2000/svg" xmlns:xlink="http://www.w3.org/1999/xlink"
      version="1.1"
      width="800" height="600"
      viewBox="0 0 400 300" preserveAspectRatio="none">
      <g id="layer1"></g>
    </svg>
    ```

2. With this framework in place, you can start adding some basic shapes. The next example shows a simple pattern design. Tile patterns are known mathematically as *tessellations of the plane*.

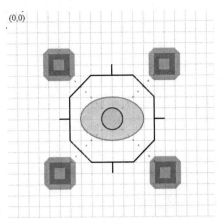

(0,0)

To create this pattern in SVG code, first create the following line:

```
<line stroke="#000000" stroke-width="1" stroke-linecap="round"
        stroke-linejoin="round" stroke-miterlimit="4" stroke-opacity="0.4"
        stroke-dasharray="1, 6" stroke-dashoffset="0"
        x1="90" y1="10" x2="10" y2="90"
        id="patternLine1" />
```

Now, as mentioned earlier, you can reuse the line. By changing the *x* and *y* values you can effectively rotate the line by 90 degrees. Also, to mix the pattern up a bit, you can override *stroke-opacity* and other style attributes that would otherwise be inherited from the referenced element:

```
<use stroke-opacity="1"
        transform="rotate(90, 50, 50)"
          xlink:href="#patternLine1"
          id="patternLine2" />
```

3. Next, draw the rest of the elements that you want to include in your pattern—for example:

```
<ellipse fill="#a1d9ad" fill-opacity="0.7" fill-rule="nonzero"
          stroke="#32287d" stroke-width="1" stroke-opacity="0.5"
          id="path3389" cx="50" cy="50" rx="30" ry="20" />

<!-- Draw the upper-right rectangle. -->
<rect fill="#ada1d9" fill-opacity="1" fill-rule="nonzero"
        stroke="#32287d" stroke-width="10" stroke-linecap="butt"
        stroke-linejoin="bevel" stroke-miterlimit="4" stroke-opacity="0.4"
        id="patternRect-upperRight"
        width="20" height="20" x="90" y="-10" />

<!-- Reuse the first rectangle element and rotate it 90 degrees each time. -->
```

```
                    <use transform="rotate(90, 50, 50)"
                            xlink:href="#patternRect-upperRight"
                            id="patternRect-lowerRight" />
                    <use transform="rotate(180, 50, 50)"
                            xlink:href="#patternRect-upperRight"
                            id="patternRect-lowerLeft" />
                    <use transform="rotate(270, 50, 50)"
                            xlink:href="#patternRect-upperRight"
                            id="patternRect-upperLeft" />

                    <!-- Draw the circle. -->
                    <circle fill="#d9d2a1" fill-opacity="1" fill-rule="nonzero"
                            stroke="#32287d" stroke-width="1" stroke-linecap="butt"
                            stroke-linejoin="bevel" stroke-miterlimit="4"
                            id="path3395" cx="50" cy="50" r="10" />

                    <!-- Draw the path using "relative"coordinates via lowercase path commands.
                        Note that we can easily switch to using the Polyline element by changing
                        the "d" attribute to "points". -->
                    <path fill="none" stroke="#000000" strGoke-width="1px" stroke-linecap="butt"
                            stroke-linejoin="miter" stroke-opacity="1"
                            d="m 0,50 10,0 0,20 20,20 0,0 0,0 20,0 0,10"
                            id="patternPath-lowerLeft" />

                    <!-- Reuse the first path, rotate it 90 more degrees for each of the four corners. -->
                    <use transform="rotate(90, 50, 50)"
                            xlink:href="#patternPath-lowerLeft"
                            id="patternPath-upperLeft" />
                    <use transform="rotate(180, 50, 50)"
                            xlink:href="#patternPath-lowerLeft"
                            id="patternPath-upperRight" />
                    <use transform="rotate(270, 50, 50)"
                            xlink:href="#patternPath-lowerLeft"
                            id="patternPath-lowerRight" />
```

These SVG elements form the basis for the pattern that you will create in the next step. You may have noticed the use of the *transform* attribute. You can see how the referenced rectangle and path shapes were moved into a different position via a rotate command. The next chapter will cover the usefulness of transformations in greater detail.

4. To create a more interesting pattern design, rather than using simple MoveTo (*M*) path commands, simply alter the *<path>* element's values to use a relatively positioned smooth quadratic Bézier curve using the *s* command, and an absolutely positioned cubic Bézier curve using *C*. So, the path's data becomes the following:

```
d="M 0,50 s 10,0 0,20 C 20,20 0,0 0,0"
```

5. Add a reference to a bitmap image of the planet Jupiter and position the image at the center. Also, move the graphics to the origin of the coordinate system, which equals the x,y value of (0,0), to complete your initial tile design. Now the tile looks like this:

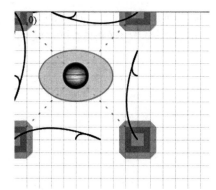

6. Finally, add the *<pattern>* element inside of a *<defs>* element and move the tile design graphics inside of the *<pattern>*.

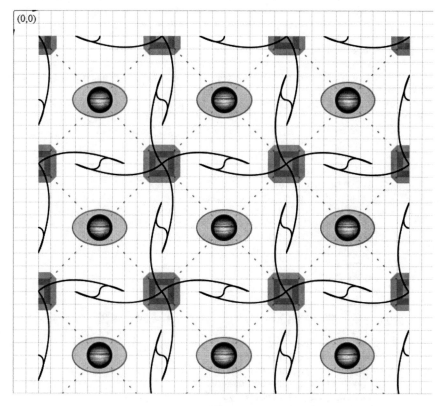

```
<defs>
  <pattern id="gridPatternWithTessellation"
           x="20" y="20" width="100" height="100
           patternUnits="userSpaceOnUse">
    <!--Insert the tile elements here.  -->
  </pattern>
</defs>
```

Below the *<defs>*, you then simply create a rectangle, path, or any other SVG shape and set its *fill* value to be the pattern, as shown at the end of the full code listing below.

```
<svg
    xmlns="http://www.w3.org/2000/svg"
    xmlns:xlink="http://www.w3.org/1999/xlink"
    id="chapter2-ShapesPatternsGroupsUse"
    version="1.1"
    width="800" height="600"
    viewBox="0 0 400 300" preserveAspectRatio="none"
>
  <defs>
    <!-- Begin Example -->
    <pattern id="gridPatternWithTessellation" x="20" y="20" width="100" height="100"
      patternUnits="userSpaceOnUse">
      <!-- Draw the lines. -->
      <line stroke="black" stroke-width="1" stroke-linecap="round" stroke-
linejoin="round"
          stroke-miterlimit="4" stroke-opacity="0.4" stroke-dasharray="1, 6"
          stroke-dashoffset="0"
          x1="90" y1="10" x2="10" y2="90"
          id="patternLine1" />
      <!-- Reuse the first line, rotate it 90 degrees, and update the style attributes.
-->
      <!-- For appendix or wiki - note that currently most browsers do not support
styling
      of Use elements using either CSS or SVG attributes -->
      <use stroke-opacity="1"
        transform="rotate(90, 50, 50)"
          xlink:href="#patternLine1"
          id="patternLine2" />
      <!-- Draw the upper-right rectangle. -->
      <rect fill="#ada1d9" fill-opacity="1" fill-rule="nonzero" stroke="#32287d"
          stroke-width="10" stroke-linecap="butt" stroke-linejoin="bevel"
          stroke-miterlimit="4" stroke-opacity="0.4"
          id="patternRect-upperRight"
          width="20"
          height="20"
          x="90"
          y="-10" />
      <!-- Reuse the first rectangle element and rotate it 90 degrees each time. -->
      <use transform="rotate(90, 50, 50)"
          xlink:href="#patternRect-upperRight"
          id="patternRect-lowerRight" />
      <use transform="rotate(180, 50, 50)"
          xlink:href="#patternRect-upperRight"
          id="patternRect-lowerLeft" />
      <use transform="rotate(270, 50, 50)"
          xlink:href="#patternRect-upperRight"
          id="patternRect-upperLeft" />
      <!-- Group containing the eye. -->
      <g id="eye">
        <!-- Draw the ellipse. -->
        <ellipse fill="#a1d9ad" fill-opacity="0.7" fill-rule="nonzero"
          stroke="#32287d" stroke-width="1" stroke-opacity="0.5"
```

```xml
          cx="50" cy="50" rx="22" ry="14" />
        <!-- Group containing the eye's iris. -->
        <g id="iris">
          id="path3389"
          cx="50" cy="50" rx="20" ry="14" />

          <!-- Draw the circle. -->
          <circle fill="black" fill-opacity="1" fill-rule="nonzero" stroke="#32287d"
            stroke-width="1" stroke-linecap="butt" stroke-linejoin="bevel"
            stroke-miterlimit="4"
            id="path3395"
            cx="50" cy="50" r="10" />
          <!-- Reference the bitmap image (PNG) -->
          <image id="bitmapCentralBall"
            width="5.5%" height="5.5%"
            x="39px" y="42px"
            xlink:href="iris-small.png"
            alt="NASA Photo of Jupiter" />
        </g>
      </g>
      <!-- Draw the path using "relative" coordinates via lowercase path commands.
      Note that we can easily switch to using the Polyline element by changing
      the "d"
      attribute to "points". -->
      <path fill="none" stroke="black" stroke-width="1px" stroke-linecap="butt"
        stroke-linejoin="miter" stroke-opacity="1"
        d="M 0,50 s 10,0 0,20 C 20,20 0,0 0,0"
        id="patternPath-lowerLeft" />
        <!-- Other interesting paths
            MoveTo Polyline-like d="m 0,50 10,0 0,20 20,20 0,0 0,0 20,0 0,10"
            Quadratic d="M 0,50 Q 10,0 0,20 S 20,20 0,0"
            Smooth Quadratic d="M 0,50 S 10,0 0,20 Q 20,20 0,0"
            Cubic d="M 0,50 C 10,0 0,20 20,20 S 0,0 0,0"
            Smooth Quadratic & Cubic d="M 0,50 s 10,0 0,20 C 20,20 0,0 0,0" -->


            -->
      <!-- Reuse the first path, rotate it 90 more degrees for each of the
      four corners. -->
      <use
        transform="rotate(90, 50, 50)"
        xlink:href="#patternPath-lowerLeft"
        id="patternPath-upperLeft" />
      <use
        transform="rotate(180, 50, 50)"
        xlink:href="#patternPath-lowerLeft"
        id="patternPath-upperRight" />
      <use
        transform="rotate(270, 50, 50)"
        xlink:href="#patternPath-lowerLeft"
        id="patternPath-lowerRight" />
    </pattern>
  </g>
  <pattern id="gridPattern" width="10" height="10" patternUnits="userSpaceOnUse">
    <path d="M10 0 L0 0 L0 10" fill='none' stroke='gray' stroke-width='0.25'/>
  </pattern>
</defs>
<g id="layer1">
```

```
<!-- background grid -->
<rect id="grid" width="100%" height="100%" x="0" y="0"
    stroke='gray' stroke-width='0.25' fill='url(#gridPattern)'/>
<!-- grid illustrations -->
<use xlink:href="#coords"/>
<text x="3" y="9" font-size='8'>(0,0)</text>
<!-- Begin Example -->
<rect id="gridWithTessellation" width="300" height="300" x="20" y="20"
    fill='url(#gridPatternWithTessellation)' />
</g>
<rect id="gridWithTessellation"
        x="20" y="20" width="300" height="300"
        fill='url(#gridPatternWithTessellation)' />
</svg>
```

With just these lines of code, you have created an interesting work of art and a useful tiling pattern that has all the benefits of SVG. To meet the needs of your company, group, or imagination, you only need to edit the base tile to create an entirely different design for your application.

Because there is a bitmap image within the pattern, if end users zoom in they will see a slightly pixelated graphic surrounded by the smoother, unpixelated vector graphics. You should consider bitmap pixelation when your project requires high-fidelity printouts.

Note There are several programs that assist with creating tiles for patterns. Inkscape, for example, has some excellent built-in pattern creation features, and there is a powerful pattern creation program on the LearnSVG.com website as well, which was originally developed by Michel Hirtzler (see *http://pilat.free.fr/tiling_loc/tile.svg*).

Summary

At this point, you should be off to a great start exploring the expressive language of SVG. This chapter showed you the basics of working with SVG in a very condensed form, including creating basic vector shapes and paths, building more complex shapes, and creating and working with patterns. In the next chapter, we will delve into animations and scripting, as well as gradient rotation, scaling, and other transformations.

CHAPTER 3

Adding Text, Style, and Transforms

I want to do with you what spring does with the cherry trees.

Pablo Neruda

You are now ready to move on to some of the slightly more advanced features of SVG. In this chapter, you will start adding more interesting effects and styles with SVG using text, colors, gradients, clipping, masking, CSS3, and coordinate system transformations. A thorough reading of this chapter will take your skills from novice to intermediate in your understanding of how SVG can be styled with and without the CSS language. By the end of this chapter, you will be able to create an SVG web page that makes use of CSS and SVG styling effects to create beautiful designs that automatically adjust to target a variety of end-user devices. Let's start with text.

Adding and Positioning Text

Adding text to SVG is quite simple after you understand the basic constructs. The main difference between text and the shape elements in SVG is that text is positioned at the lower-left corner of the first text character: the font's baseline (assuming the writing system flows from left to right, like English, Spanish, and Russian, but unlike Arabic or Hebrew).

Text in SVG can be styled, shaped, and spaced in a great number of ways, and if you wish to explore it in more detail, you can look to the SVG 1.1 specification for a plethora of rich details. For example, letter spacing and kerning, which control the space between text characters, are determined first by the default font rules, but can be overridden by the SVG *letter-spacing* and *font-kerning* consistent with *http://lists.w3.org/Archives/Public/www-svg/2012May/0101.html* attributes.

Due to the different text-rendering engines used by different implementers, text may not render exactly the same way. However, the homogeneity in the rendering is usually satisfactory, although it could be better.

Version 2 of the SVG specification will address what is considered a major limitation for text in the current version (1.1)—the inability to format the text flow (e.g., into a rectangle). To its benefit, however, SVG has the ability to define vector fonts and glyphs with remarkably flexible content.

Some of the examples at *http://srufaculty.sru.edu/david.dailey/svg/text/* will give you a good overview of what SVG can do with text. We also recommend you read the W3C's text specification, at *http://www.w3.org/TR/SVG/text.html*.

It is also worth watching the SVG 2.0 spec as it emerges, since some aspects of text-handling are being improved, amended and deprecated, to bring SVG's treatment into more compliance with CSS.

The \<text> Element

The classic Hello World example that follows shows how to make use of the *\<text>* element. Note that the *\<text>* element needs a closing tag after the text content, as shown here:

```
<svg xmlns="http://www.w3.org/2000/svg" xmlns:xlink="http://www.w3.org/1999/xlink">
    <text x="20px" y="55px" font-family="Verdana" font-size="43pt">Hello World!</text>
</svg>
```

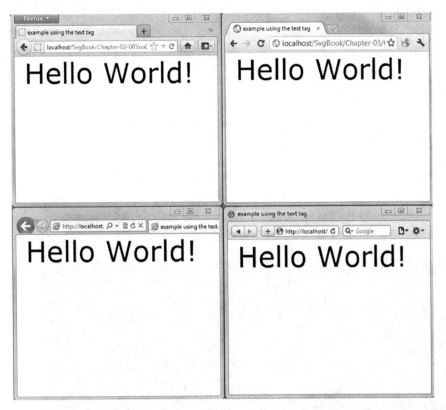

Some of the most useful attributes of the *<text>* element are *x* (for setting the horizontal position), *y* (for the vertical position of the baseline of the text), *fill* (for determining the text's color or pattern), *font-size*, and *font-family*, though there are literally dozens of other text attributes that you can experiment with. As a general rule, the use of attributes gives you precise control over layout and rendering. Size and positioning values can be expressed with unit identifiers, which are the same as in CSS: *em*, *ex*, *px*, *pt*, *pc*, *cm*, *mm*, and *in*. If you don't specify a font family in the outermost *<svg>* element (or through a style sheet) for the whole document, remember to always specify it for a particular *<text>* element or for its container element; otherwise, the browser will use the font family that has been set as the default in the browser's options.

Next is a more interesting example using a variety of features that allow effects commonly found in vector-editing software, such as gradients, rotation, and stretching textual content:

```
<linearGradient id="g">
  <stop offset="0" stop-color="#870"/>
  <stop offset=".2" stop-color="#520"/>
  <stop offset=".4" stop-color="#000"/>
  <stop offset=".6" stop-color="#840"/>
  <stop offset=".8" stop-color="#210"/>
  <stop offset="1" stop-color="#832"/>
</linearGradient>
<text id="T" fill="none" stroke-width="4" stroke="url(#g)" stroke-opacity="1"
  font-family="serif" font-stretch="ultra-expanded" stroke-dasharray="10 5"
  rotate="-25 -20 -15 -10 -5 0 5 10 15 20"
  textLength="90" lengthAdjust="spacingAndGlyphs" font-style="oblique"
  text-decoration="overline" font-size="50" x="5" y="65%" font-weight="bold">
Decorative</text>
```

The above example looks like this in the Opera browser, though if you try it in other browsers, you are likely to be surprised by how inconsistently it is rendered:

There is an imaginative little program called Textorizer (*http://lapin-bleu.net/software/textor-izer/*) that can create artistic effects in SVG using any bitmap image (e.g., PNG or JPEG) and overlay it with the text of your choice. As you will see in the code sample for the SVG image that follows, the program maps the colors of the background bitmap image with the color of each letter in the text that you specify. If you then remove the *<image>* element from the output file, you end up with an interesting work of art composed entirely of your text:

Some of you may recognize this beautifully uplifting three-story-high mural that I photographed in downtown Philadelphia. This graphic is composed entirely of SVG text.

The next sections will offer some guidance on how to deal with text in SVG.

The <tspan> Element

The *<tspan>* element allows you to group and associate characters, sentences, and even paragraphs, while allowing you to alter the placement of the contained glyphs.

For example, assuming we don't need to change the color and size of each character in the sentence, we could improve upon the previous example by using *<tspan>* like so:

```
<text x='116' y='7.6' font-size='6.1' fill='rgb(200,242,254)'>
  G
  <tspan x='5'>r</tspan>
  <tspan x='7'>o</tspan>
  <tspan x='9'>w</tspan>
  <tspan x='12'>w</tspan>
</text>
```

This repositions the individual characters along the x-axis relative to the parent *<text>* element's value for *x* using the *<tspan>* element's *x* attribute.

Note SVG 1.1 currently does not have built-in support for word wrapping. This is expected to be added to the next edition of the language, SVG 2.0. In the meantime, there are already several open source script-based approaches that add support for word wrapping.

Making Adjustments with dx and dy

Both the *<text>* and *<tspan>* elements provide the *dx* and *dy* attributes, which can be used to reposition one or more characters along the x-axis and y-axis. This allows for interesting effects, such as making words bend up or down, or even step up a staircase. The following image shows a sampling of commonly used text properties and their effects:

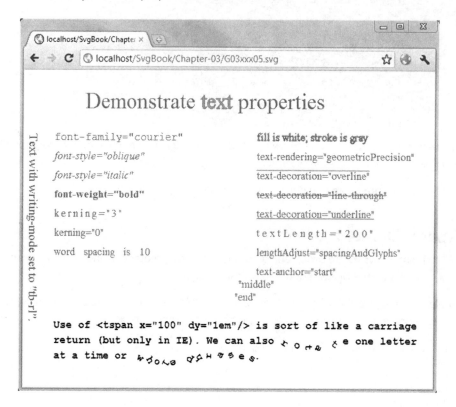

Text and Shapes on a Path: <textPath> and <mpath>

One of the most interesting and useful features of SVG is the capability of using paths for positioning shapes and text. As an example, all five of the primary browsers now support text effects such as the one shown in the following figure. This example demonstrates how to place text along a Bézier curve.

```
<defs>
  <path id="curve" d="M 10 100 C 200 30 300 250 350 50" />
</defs>
<text font-family="arial" font-size="16" fill="black">
  <textPath xlink:href="#curve">Hello, here is some text lying along a Bézier curve.</textPath>
</text>
```

The path above is defined inside a *<defs>* element, which serves to define the path, but without rendering it. You can use various flags, such as *startOffset*, to position the text along the path. The *startOffset* attribute of the *<textPath>* element lets you specify the distance in pixels from the beginning of the curve where the text will actually begin. When animated with SMIL (see Chapter 4), this attribute makes the text appear to crawl along the curve at a speed determined by the SMIL.

The <tref> Element

Another useful element is *<tref>*, which allows you to reuse letters and entire paragraphs of text. You can specify the referencing to the character data of another *<text>* element with a *<tref>* element like this:

```
<defs>
  <text id="ReferencedText">
    Reusable character data
  </text>
</defs>
<text font-family="arial" font-size="16" fill="black">
  <tref xlink:href="#ReferencedText"/>
</text>
```

Working with Colors in SVG

Thanks to the W3C's standardization efforts, there are many similarities in how we work with colors in HTML, CSS, and SVG, so some of the following information may already be familiar to you.

Named Color Values

SVG supports 147 colors, with names such as *white* and *blue*, and even *forestgreen*, *tomato*, and *cornsilk*. This makes it easy to remember specific colors.

HSL

Likely you have heard the acronym *HSL*, which stands for *hue, saturation, and lightness* (or *luminance*). If you have ever seen a circular color wheel in a drawing program, just picture that. With that picture in mind, most people can grasp HSL. This method of specifying colors is intuitive because our minds can fairly quickly comprehend the three concepts involved:

- **Lightness**   Lightness of colors ranges from solid (opaque) to invisible (transparent) (L = 0% to 100%).

- **Saturation**   Saturation of colors ranges from black to bright white (S = 0 to 360).

- **Hue**   Hue simply defines the degree along the circular color spectrum, with the circle running from red (0 degrees) to green (120 degrees) to blue (240 degrees) (H = 0 to 360).

RGB

RGB (red, green, blue) is probably the most common approach for specifying colors in SVG, mainly because HSL had not been an option until recently, and most drawing and IDE programs use RGB by default. The advantage of using RGB over named colors is the ability to quickly adjust color values incrementally, which would be difficult to do with named colors without an amazing memory or reference chart.

RGB values can be created as functional values between 0 and 255, or as percentages, such as *rgb(255, 0, 0)* or *rgb(100%, 0, 0)*. RGB can also be specified in three-digit or six-digit hexadecimal notation—for example, *#a2f* and *#aa22ff*, which are equal.

Creating Gradients in SVG

In the world of graphics, a gradient simply refers to the gradual transition, in some direction, of one color into another, or of combinations of such transitions involving multiple colors. The 19th century artist Georges Seurat did a lot to popularize the underlying scientific work showing how scenes can be simulated by collections of points of colored light. Seurat's points are numerous and their sizes nearly infinitesimal. Translated into the world of computer imagery, though, that implies big file sizes. But if we decompose regions not into monochromatic points (a process known as *posterization*), but into regions of smooth transition (namely gradients), we can transmit less data and yet still create high-quality, realistic images. Excitingly, the instructions for creating gradients can convey semantics as well as rendering instructions for the browser, and it's this that makes SVG amenable to indexing by search engines in a way that can't readily be applied to formats such as GIF, JPEG, or PNG. If you're in-terested in the broader topic of visual perception and information transmission, you might like to see some of the work of Marvin Minksy (see *http://courses.media.mit.edu/2004spring/mas966/Minsky%20 1974%20Framework%20for%20knowledge.pdf*), or the articles at *http://quantombone.blogspot .com/2010/08/beyond-pixel-wise-labeling-blocks-world.html* and *http://srufaculty.sru.edu/david.dailey/ engraver.htm* for a more modern take.

Applying Gradients to a Path

Let's get started with the basics here. This example shows the definition of a linear gradient and that of a radial gradient, which are then applied to the *fill* attribute of a path:

```
<path d="M 100 200 200 200 150 100 z" stroke="black" stroke-width="2" fill="url(#g)"/>
<linearGradient id="g">
 <stop offset="0" stop-color="white"/>
 <stop offset="1" stop-color="black"/>
</linearGradient>
<radialGradient id="g">
 <stop offset="0" stop-color="white"/>
 <stop offset="1" stop-color="black"/>
</radialGradient>
```

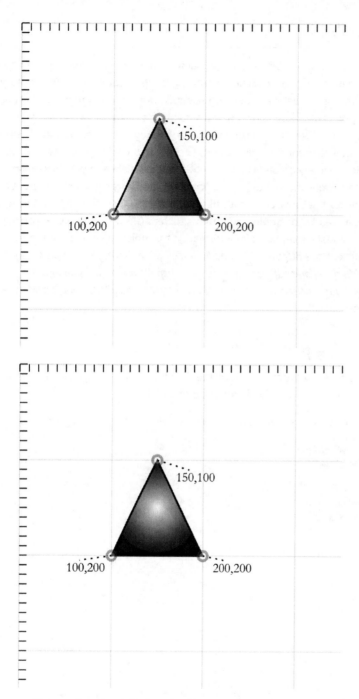

The gradient is applied to the *fill* attribute of an element using a local URL: *fill="url(#g)"*. This demonstrates that an object may have a color or a gradient as its fill, but not both.

Note that in the linear gradient above, two *<stop>* elements have been built. This means the gradient has two colors applied to it, one for each stop. Those colors are determined by the *stop-color* attribute. The *offset* attribute is either a number (between 0 and 1) or a percentage, and it determines where the gradient stop is placed in the direction established by the gradient vector, which is defined by attributes of the gradient element (*x1, x2, y1, y2* for a linear gradient, and *cx, cy* for a radial gradient). For the linear gradient in the example, white is applied at the leftmost part of the triangle, while black is applied to the rightmost part. Shades of gray gradually darken as we move to the right, with a grayscale value of 128/256, or 50%, occurring halfway across the image, or along the line where *x* equals 150. For the radial gradient, the midpoint of the bounding rectangle around the path is chosen as the center. From there, we apply our first stop color (zero percent of the way out toward the corners of the bounding box). Black will be applied to the four corners of the bounding rectangle, with shades of gray gradually lightening as we move toward the center.

The number of stops in a gradient need not be limited to two. In the example below, four stops are defined, with the offset values specified in percentages. The rectangles in the following figure are 200 pixels wide. That means the linear gradient is white at 0 pixels, black at 50 pixels, white at 150 pixels, and black at 200 pixels.

```
<stop offset="0" stop-color="white"/>
<stop offset=".25" stop-color="black"/>
<stop offset=".75" stop-color="white"/>
<stop offset="1" stop-color="black"/>
```

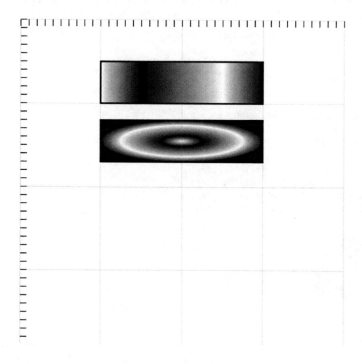

The stop-opacity Attribute

In addition to specifying the color of a *<stop>* within a gradient, you can also specify its opacity through an attribute known as *stop-opacity*. You can thus make gradients act like differential masks, allowing, for example, an image underneath to gradually fade into view. Here's an example of how *stop-opacity* works:

```
<stop offset=".8" stop-color="black" stop-opacity="0.5"/>
```

stop-opacity (like the regular opacity of drawn objects) takes values between 0 (transparent) and 1.0 (opaque). Here are some examples of using *stop-opacity* with gradients to allow differing amounts of what is underneath to be visible along a partly transparent gradient.

This example shows two different gradients defined and used in separate images. It creates a tricolor gradient by superimposing one on the other. Notice the use of the *transform* attribute to control the direction in which the gradient is applied. Here's the code:

```
<linearGradient id="r" >
  <stop offset="0" stop-color="red"/>
  <stop offset="1" stop-color="green"/>
</linearGradient>
<linearGradient id="t" gradientTransform="rotate(90,.5,.5)">
  <stop offset="0" stop-color="white" stop-opacity="0"/>
  <stop offset="1" stop-color="#208" />
</linearGradient>
<rect x="10" y="10" width="100" height="100" fill="url(#r)" />
<rect x="120" y="10" width="100" height="100" fill="url(#t)" />
<rect x="60" y="120" height="100" width="100" fill="url(#r)"/>
<rect x="60" y="120" height="100" width="100" fill="url(#t)"/>
```

This is similar to the previous example, but uses more than two colors in the gradient, as well as the *stop-opacity* attribute:

```
<linearGradient id="r" >
  <stop offset="0" stop-color="red"/>
  <stop offset=".5" stop-color="yellow"/>
  <stop offset="1" stop-color="green"/>
</linearGradient>
<linearGradient id="t" gradientTransform="rotate(90,.5,.5)">
  <stop offset="0" stop-color="#008" />
  <stop offset=".4" stop-color="cyan" stop-opacity="0"/>
  <stop offset=".6" stop-color="cyan" stop-opacity="0"/>
  <stop offset="1" stop-color="#22a" />
</linearGradient>
<linearGradient id="s" gradientTransform="rotate(45,.5,.5)">
  <stop offset="0" stop-color="#008" />
  <stop offset=".45" stop-color="red" stop-opacity="0"/>
  <stop offset=".55" stop-color="green" stop-opacity="0"/>
  <stop offset="1" stop-color="#22a" />
</linearGradient>
<rect x="10" y="10" height="100" width="100" fill="url(#r)"/>
<rect x="120" y="10" height="100" width="100" fill="url(#t)"/>
<rect x="230" y="10" height="100" width="100" fill="url(#s)"/>
<rect x="120" y="120" height="100" width="100" fill="url(#r)"/>
<rect x="120" y="120" height="100" width="100" fill="url(#t)"/>
<rect x="120" y="120" height="100" width="100" fill="url(#s)"/>
```

In this example, one simple gradient is used to impart a slightly asymmetric sheen that fades into darkness at the sides, to simulate the appearance of a rotating cylinder:

```
<linearGradient id="cylinder" x1="0" y1="1" x2=".2" y2="0">
  <stop offset=".1" stop-color="red"/>
  <stop offset=".1" stop-color="white"/>
  <stop offset=".2" stop-color="white"/>
  <stop offset=".2" stop-color="blue"/>
  <stop offset=".3" stop-color="blue"/>
  <stop offset=".3" stop-color="white"/>
  <stop offset=".4" stop-color="white"/>
  <stop offset=".4" stop-color="red"/>
  <stop offset=".5" stop-color="red"/>
  <stop offset=".5" stop-color="white"/>
  <stop offset=".6" stop-color="white"/>
  <stop offset=".6" stop-color="blue"/>
  <stop offset=".7" stop-color="blue"/>
  <stop offset=".7" stop-color="white"/>
  <stop offset=".8" stop-color="white"/>
  <stop offset=".8" stop-color="red"/>
  <stop offset=".9" stop-color="red"/>
  <stop offset=".9" stop-color="white"/>
  <stop offset="1" stop-color="white"/>
  <stop offset="1" stop-color="blue"/>
</linearGradient>
<linearGradient id="gradient1">
  <stop offset="0" stop-color="black"/>
  <stop offset="0.3" stop-color="white" stop-opacity="0"/>
  <stop offset="0.4" stop-color="white" stop-opacity=".8"/>
  <stop offset="0.6" stop-color="white" stop-opacity=".0"/>
  <stop offset="1" stop-color="black"/>
</linearGradient>
<rect x="10" y="10" height="250" width="55" fill="url(#cylinder)"/>
<rect x="10" y="10" height="250" width="55" fill="url(#gradient1)"/>
```

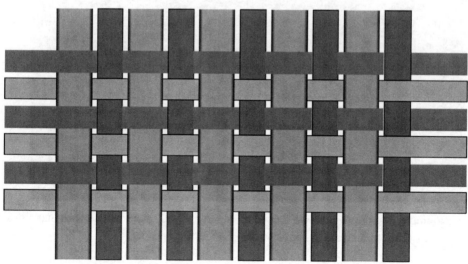

The following example shows how you can create the appearance of weaving by using a number of SVG elements linearly related to the number of threads. In the case of the dark green and the tan threads, a gradient is applied with discrete boundaries between opacity and transparency to give the illusion of the thread disappearing behind the other. Here's the code:

```
<stop offset=".20" stop-color="black"/>
<stop offset=".21" stop-color="#b83"/>
<stop offset=".29" stop-color="#b83"/>
<stop offset=".30" stop-color="black"/>
<stop offset=".30" stop-color="#b83" stop-opacity="0"/>
<stop offset=".40" stop-color="#b83" stop-opacity="0"/>
<stop offset=".40" stop-color="black"/>
```

Clipping and Masking with SVG

Like the slightly more complex <mask> (which we'll discuss later), the <clipPath> element gives you a way to define a collection of shapes that you can use to carve a given figure into more interesting shapes. You can apply a clip path to any drawn objects in SVG, including groups of objects, and the clip path itself can consist of many shapes. Masks are a lot like clip paths, but more flexible.

Some of the experiments with gradients might suggest that you can use the *stop-opacity* of a gradient to simulate certain kinds of cropping or clipping. In particular, let's use a radial gradient to restrict the appearance of a rectangular bitmap to an elliptical region.

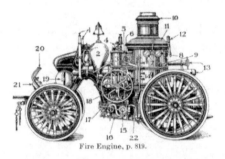

Fire Engine, p. 819.

```
<image x="15%" width="30%" y="15%" height="30%"
  xlink:href="fireenginefromWebsters1911.gif" />
```

```
<radialGradient id="r" fy=".55" >
  <stop offset=".3" stop-opacity="0"/>
  <stop offset=".8" stop-color="black" />
  <stop offset=".9" stop-color="white" />
  <stop offset="1" stop-color="brown"/>
</radialGradient>
<rect x="15%" y="15%" height="30%" width="30%" fill="url(#r)"/>
```

```
<radialGradient id="r" fy=".55" >
  <stop offset=".3" stop-opacity="0"/>
  <stop offset=".8" stop-color="black" />
  <stop offset=".9" stop-color="white" />
  <stop offset="1" stop-color="brown"/>
</radialGradient>
<image x="15%" width="30%" y="15%" height="30%"
  xlink:href="fireenginefromWebsters1911.gif" />
<rect x="15%" y="15%" height="30%" width="30%" fill="url(#r)"/>
```

This serves to illustrate some of the power of gradients, but it should be fairly straightforward to conclude that using linear and radial gradients (the only kinds available in SVG at present) to clip an image down to an arbitrary shape isn't easy.

You can use the following code to produce a similar effect just as easily, as the image that follows demonstrates:

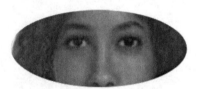

```
<clipPath id="CP">
  <ellipse cx="29%" cy="26%" rx="10%" ry="8%"/>
</clipPath>
<image y="0" x="10%" width="40%" height="55%" xlink:href='p17.jpg' clip-path="url(#CP)"/>
```

As this example shows, you can put elements, like gradients, inside a *<clipPath>*, and then apply the clip path (through its *id*) to the object or group of objects to be clipped.

Next, we'll illustrate an example that clearly differentiates between what you might accomplish with clip paths as opposed to gradients. In the following example, we insert numerous ellipses into the clip path, showing that the clipped regions can be complex.

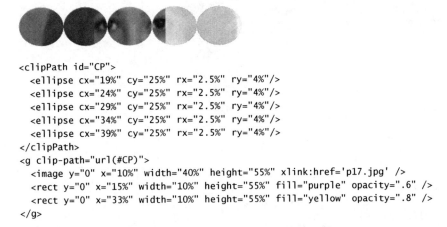

```
<clipPath id="CP">
  <ellipse cx="19%" cy="25%" rx="2.5%" ry="4%"/>
  <ellipse cx="24%" cy="25%" rx="2.5%" ry="4%"/>
  <ellipse cx="29%" cy="25%" rx="2.5%" ry="4%"/>
  <ellipse cx="34%" cy="25%" rx="2.5%" ry="4%"/>
  <ellipse cx="39%" cy="25%" rx="2.5%" ry="4%"/>
</clipPath>
<g clip-path="url(#CP)">
  <image y="0" x="10%" width="40%" height="55%" xlink:href='p17.jpg' />
  <rect y="0" x="15%" width="10%" height="55%" fill="purple" opacity=".6" />
  <rect y="0" x="33%" width="10%" height="55%" fill="yellow" opacity=".8" />
</g>
```

Note that the content of a *<clipPath>* cannot involve either groups (*<g>*) or complex uses (*<use>*). A clip path is limited to simple drawn objects and reuses of simple drawn objects. If we wanted to reuse content, we could do so through a *<mask>*, as follows:

```
<mask id="CP">
  <g id="U">
    <ellipse cx="19%" cy="25%" rx="2.5%" ry="4%" fill="white"/>
    <ellipse cx="24%" cy="25%" rx="2.5%" ry="4%" fill="white"/>
    <ellipse cx="29%" cy="25%" rx="2.5%" ry="4%" fill="white"/>
    <ellipse cx="34%" cy="25%" rx="2.5%" ry="4%" fill="white"/>
    <ellipse cx="39%" cy="25%" rx="2.5%" ry="4%" fill="white"/>
  </g>
  <use xlink:href="#U" transform="translate(0,40)" />
  <use xlink:href="#U" transform="translate(0,80)" />
</mask>
<g mask="url(#CP)">
  <image y="0" x="10%" width="40%" height="55%" xlink:href='p17.jpg' />
  <rect y="0" x="15%" width="10%" height="55%" fill="purple" opacity=".6" />
  <rect y="0" x="33%" width="10%" height="55%" fill="yellow" opacity=".8" />
</g>
```

While a clip path declares that content is either inside it (and hence visible) or outside it (and hence invisible), a mask allows degrees of visibility, depending on the brightness of the objects inside the mask.

The following example demonstrates both clipping and masking:

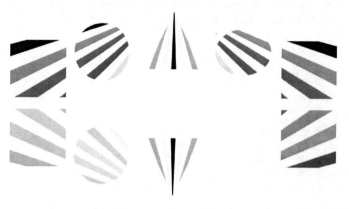

```
<defs>
  <clipPath id="clipRays">
    <rect x="5" y="80" width="100" height="100"/>
    <circle cx="170" cy="100" r="50"/>
    <polygon points="300 30 350 130 250 130" />
    <ellipse cx="425" cy="100" rx="50" ry="40"/>
    <rect x="494" y="80" width="100" height="100"/>
  </clipPath>
  <mask id="maskRays">
    <rect x="5" y="80" width="100" height="100" fill="red" />
    <circle cx="170" cy="100" r="50" fill="purple" />
    <polygon points="300 30 350 130 250 130" fill="white" />
    <ellipse cx="425" cy="100" rx="50" ry="40" fill="black" />
    <rect x="494" y="80" width="100" height="100" fill="orange" />  </mask>
  <g id="rays">
    <g id="RaysRight">
      <path d="M300,13.51c548.1,268.4,548.1,268.4,548.1,268.4
        s23.52-35.35,23.52-35.35-571.7-233-571.7-233" fill="red"/>
      <path d="M300,13.31c452.8,307.3,452.8,307.3,452.8,307.3
        s26.29-29.41,26.29-29.41-479.1-277.8-479.1-277.8" fill="green"/>
      <path d="M300,13.14c365.4,342.9,365.4,342.9,365.4,342.9
        s28.82-23.98,28.82-23.98-394.2-318.9-394.2-318.9" fill="blue"/>
      <path d="M300,12.97c282.9,376.5,282.9,376.5,282.9,376.5
        s31.22-18.84,31.22-18.84-314-357.7-314-357.7" fill="lime"/>
      <path d="M300,12.81c203.7,408.8,203.7,408.8,203.7,408.8
        s33.51-13.91,33.51-13.91-237.2-394.9-237.2-394.9" fill="purple"/>
      <path d="M300,12.66c127.1,440,127.1,440,127.1,440
        s35.73-9.153,35.73-9.153-162.9-430.9-162.9-430.9" fill="orange"/>
      <path d="M300,12.51c52.68,470.4,52.68,470.4,52.68,470.4
        s37.89-4.522,37.89-4.522-90.57-465.8-90.57-465.8" fill="yellow"/>
    </g>
    <use id="RaysLeft" xlink:href="#RaysRight" transform="translate(600) scale(-1, 1)" />
  </g>
</defs>
<!-- Light Ray 1 -->
<use xlink:href="#rays" x="0" y="0" clip-path="url(#clipRays)"/>
<!-- Light Ray 2 -->
<use xlink:href="#rays" x="0" y="0" transform="scale(1 -1) translate(0 -380)"
  mask="url(#maskRays)"/>
```

As you can see, both clip paths and masks can have a variety of shapes. The example above shows how clip paths simply behave like cookie cutters, while masks behave more like light filters.

Note that the ray-filled shapes at the bottom of the preceding image, which have a mask applied to them, filter out more color than the upper rectangles. The color that they filter out is defined by the fill color of the shapes that are used inside of the mask. When the color white is used in the mask, as in the triangle at the bottom of the image, then no colors are filtered out. When the color black is used in the mask, as in the invisible ellipse at the bottom, then all of the colors are filtered out, and none of the underlying masked graphic is displayed on the screen.

Note You can clip outside a clip path only by setting the fill rule to *evenodd* on the clipping object or with masks.

Here's another illustration of the difference between clip paths and masks:

```
<linearGradient id="gradient1" >
  <stop offset="0.0" stop-color="black"/>
  <stop offset="1" stop-color="white"/>
</linearGradient>
<mask id="Ma">
  <rect x="300" y="300" width="400" height="100" fill="url(#gradient1)"/>
</mask>
<text x="220" y="365" font-family="impact" font-size="52" mask="url(#Ma)"
  fill="black">The Masked Text:  it o</text>
```

Details of Transforms

The SVG language provides some useful methods for repositioning individual objects or entire groups of objects through these simple *transform* commands: *translate, scale, rotate, skewX, and skewY.*

The translate Command

One of the most useful transformation commands is *translate*, which allows you to reposition content by simply specifying the new xy-coordinates in this format: *transform="translate(50,10)"*. This simple command will shift graphical objects 50 units along the x-axis and 10 units along the y-axis. This effectively establishes a new coordinate system for the object or group to which the transform is applied, and often this makes it straightforward to apply other transformations, such as skewing, rotating, and scaling.

The scale Command

The syntax for the scale command looks like this: *transform="scale(2)"*. The *scale* command scales the graphical elements that it is applied to with respect to the origin of the coordinate system (0,0). This means that when the size of a shape that has positive x and y values is doubled, its top-left corner as well as the rest of the graphic is expanded horizontally along the x-axis and vertically along the y-axis. There are ways to center the graphic prior to applying the *scale* command, as you will see in later examples.

The next example shows the effects of the *scale* and *translate* commands:

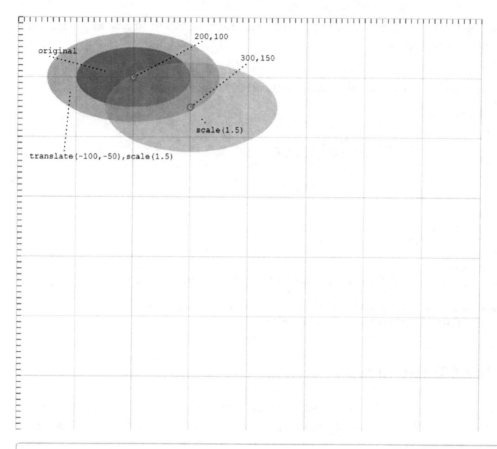

Note The order in which the transformation commands are applied affects the final result. For example, if you use the *translate* command before applying the scaling, the result will usually be quite different from applying them in the opposite order, because the origin of the coordinate system is often not centered on the graphic being transformed. In many cases, it is easier to first apply the *translate* command to center the graphic on the origin, and then apply other transformations.

Skewing: The skewX and skewY Commands

Using the *skewX* and *skewY* commands, you can skew shapes horizontally or vertically. For example, the command *<transform="skewX(25)">* will pull the graphic 25 units along the horizontal axis relative to the origin or top-left corner of the graphic, which produces a skewed effect.

The rotate Command

You can rotate vector and bitmap graphics using the *rotate* command. The following *rotate* command will rotate an object 50 degrees in the standard clockwise direction: *transform="rotate(50)"*. It is important to note that the *rotate* command actually takes up to three parameters—*degrees, cx,* and *cy*—where *cx* and *cy* (which are by default the point [0,0]) are the center about which the rotation will occur.

SVG transformations by example: Step by step

All of the transform commands can be used in combination with opacity and other style effects to create 2.5D (see *http://en.wikipedia.org/wiki/2.5D*) mirror-image effects. For example, you can reuse a shape or image via the *<use>* element, flip it using the *scale* command, and then reposition it to display below the original image. Adding the *skewX* command and making the graphic slightly opaque results in a reflection. The following exercise shows you how to do this:

1. Hand-code (or draw) the SVG shapes that you want to work with:

```
<line id="water" x1="-50" y1="110" x2="100%" y2="110"
                stroke="blue" stroke-width="1" stroke-opacity="0.7" />
        <g id="scene">
                <circle id="sun" r="50" cx="30" cy="30"
                        fill="orange" stroke="grey" stroke-width="1" />
                <circle id="venusInTransit" r="5" cx="15" cy="20"
                        fill="black" stroke="grey" stroke-width="1" />
        </g>
```

2. Add another grouping (a <use> element) within the current group, and add skewX, skewY, scale and transform commands to the new grouping

```
<use xlink:href="#scene" mask="url(#hazeIca)"
                transform="scale(1 -1) translate(30 -210) skewX(-20) skewY(5)"/>
```

The following image shows the result:

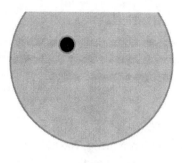

As you can see, this flips the graphic along the x-axis and then also along the y-axis. The *translate* command then repositions the object back at the correct location in the coordinate system so that the image displays below the original image.

The matrix Command

The *matrix* command is more complex and requires more mental power to make use of, but it allows for a more concise and efficient means of specifying precise transformations on an object. The format of this command will likely remind you of mathematics classes. The command has the format *matrix(a, b, c, d, e, f)*, which specifies a mathematical transformation matrix that looks like this: *[a b c d e f]*. This command is primarily used by SVG-editing programs that use mathematical functions to track and apply the transformations.

The best way to understand how this works is to observe the effects of the commands in an editor such as Inkscape. You can find more details on this command in the SVG specification, at *http://www .w3.org/TR/SVG/coords.html#TransformMatrixDefined*.

Adding Style Using CSS

In previous chapters, you saw how to add style using the SVG presentation attributes to modify many of the shape, text, and bitmap properties.

Just like in HTML, both the *class* and *style* attributes can also be used to add style in SVG. However, there are many advantages to using the *class* rather than *style* attribute, because the *class* attribute can take values from a style sheet that in practice requires fewer changes to the DOM.

Most of the SVG presentation attributes are available for us in CSS style sheets. For example, a rectangle's *fill* color and *stroke-opacity* attributes can be defined in CSS.

Using a style sheet in SVG is very similar to the usage in HTML5. You can define CSS rules inline using the *<style>* element. In this next example, several types of CSS selectors are used to target specific bars of a bar chart.

```
<svg xmlns="http://www.w3.org/2000/svg" xmlns:xlink=http://www.w3.org/1999/xlink
  height="170" width="450">
  <style type="text/css">
    svg {
      font: 12px sans-serif;
      shape-rendering: crispEdges;
    }
    text {
      fill:white;
      text-anchor:end;
      font-weight:bold;
    }
    g.bar rect {
      fill: green;
    }
    g > #LookAtMe {
      fill: steelblue;
    }
    rect#LookAtMe {
      fill: steelblue;
    }
    rect.custom {
      fill: orange;
    }
  </style>
  <g transform="translate(0, 4.5)" class="bar">
    <rect height="18" width="145.8" fill="papayawhip"></rect>
    <text text-anchor="end" fill="white" dy=".35em" dx="-6" y="9" x="145.8">39</text>
    <text text-anchor="end" dy=".35em" dx="-6" y="9" x="0">A</text>
  </g>
  <g transform="translate(0, 27)" class="bar">
    <rect height="18" width="31.5" style="fill:blue"/>
    <text text-anchor="end" fill="white" dy=".35em" dx="-6" y="9" x="31.5">12</text>
    <text text-anchor="end" dy=".35em" dx="-6" y="9" x="0">B</text>
  </g>
```

```
<g transform="translate(0, 49.6)" class="bar">
  <rect id="LookAtMe" height="18" width="91.3" fill="steelblue"/>
  <text text-anchor="end" fill="white" dy=".35em" dx="-6" y="9" x="91.3">26</text>
  <text text-anchor="end" dy=".35em" dx="-6" y="9" x="0">C</text>
</g>
<g transform="translate(0, 72)" class="bar">
  <rect class="custom" height="18" width="211.4" fill="steelblue"/>
  <text text-anchor="end" fill="white" dy=".35em" dx="-6" y="9" x="211.4">54</text>
  <text text-anchor="end" dy=".35em" dx="-6" y="9" x="0">D</text>
</g>
```

One thing worth noting here is how the CSS style sheet styles override the *fill* attribute of the first rectangle. Also notice how the *style* attribute in the second rectangle overrides the fill rule in the CSS style sheet.

Alternatively, style sheets can be pulled in from an external CSS file just as they are in HTML5. The main difference from HTML is the stricter XML syntax that is required for SVG documents:

```
<?xml-stylesheet href="bookStyles.css" type="text/css"?>
```

Using Media Queries to Enhance Usability

There are many examples of using CSS3 *media queries* (see *http://www.w3.org/TR/css3-mediaqueries/*) to improve the usability of HTML5 content. SVG can harness this same capability. One of the most common scenarios is automatically adjusting the layout based on the type of device the end user is using, or, more generally, the screen resolution. In this example, the web page layout changes to try to always fit the most important elements on the page.

For example, using the following media query CSS code, a number of changes to the document will take place automatically, depending on the end user's screen resolution:

```
@media screen and (max-width: 351px) {
    #pageContent {
        opacity: 0.3;
    }
    #backgroundGradient, #backgroundGridWithPattern {
        display: none;
    }
    #svgLogo01 {
        display: none;
    }
}
```

That is, when the end user's device's screen width is less than 351 pixels, the following takes place:

- The large logo graphic is hidden.

- The background gradient and grid are hidden.

- The opacity of the background is set to 0.3.

Additional Capabilities of CSS3

The newer CSS3 language offers several new features that can be used with SVG, including 2D transforms and transition effects. You can find more information about this on the Learn SVG website, at *http://learnsvg.com/CSS3/*. The CSS and SVG Working Groups have been working on consolidating the two approaches.

Among the anticipated features of CSS3 are the abilities to handle SVG filters, animation, gradients, and transforms through CSS.

Vector Graphics, Symbol, and Button Libraries

Perhaps because the SVG format is an open format as opposed to a proprietary one (such as Flash), many public-spirited projects such as Wikipedia and Inkscape have taken a liking to it. Likewise, many of the users of Wikipedia and Inkscape have taken to redistributing their artistic work in ways that are openly licensed for reuse. More and more graphics libraries and developer websites are using the Creative Commons Public Domain license, which gives end users complete rights to reuse "the work, even for commercial purposes, all without asking permission." The details of this license can be found at *http://creativecommons.org/publicdomain/zero/1.0/*.

The Inkscape users group, along with others, has contributed many fine examples to the Open Clipart Library, at *http://openclipart.org/Wikimedia Commons*. Under the auspices of the Wikimedia Foundation (which oversees Wikipedia), Wikimedia Commons is a collection of material, frequently used by authors on Wikipedia, that is believed to be reusable, either because of being in the public domain (no remaining copyright) or because of open licensing agreements (such as Creative Commons). The main Wikimedia Commons page can be visited at *http://commons.wikimedia.org/wiki/Main_Page*. However, to look for just SVG images at Wikimedia, you can either go to *http://commons.wikimedia.org/wiki/Category:SVG* (which categorizes much of the SVG content there), or to the IAN Symbol Library (*http://ian.umces.edu/symbols/*) or the Noun Project (*http://thenounproject.com/*).

Accessibility

Unlike many other image formats, and most conspicuously, the bitmapped formats used on the web, such as JPEG, GIF, and PNG, SVG is intrinsically accessible to screen readers because it is XML and composed of ASCII and Unicode. However, its ability to go further than this is vast. An author who is concerned about accessibility (as we all should be) can annotate each drawn element with its own descriptors, meaning that, in theory, both screen readers and search engines could separate the various pieces of a visual composition and translate those elements as well as their geometric relations into meaningful data that could be used as part of a query, rendered into tactile information, or excerpted in a variety of useful ways.

While semantic analysis of a bitmapped image requires artificial intelligence of the rendering device, for SVG, it only requires agreement among authors and browser manufacturers that this accessibility matters. Thus far, the SVG Working Group and the SVG Interest Group have given much attention to the topic, and it is generally believed that the SVG promise for accessibility is very strong.

Semantic Elements and Features

Most readers will be aware of HTML5 elements, so this is probably a good place to start. In HTML5, several new important semantic elements have been added, including *<nav>*, *<section>*, *<article>*, *<aside>*, *<header>*, *<footer>*, and even *<address>*. The way semantics plays out in HTML5 is that these new elements have defined meanings. For example, the *<section>* element is designed to hold sectioning elements so that modern browsers are able to know right where to look for hierarchical section and subsection information within web pages.

This improved semantic design makes the jobs of developers and even web development IDE programs that much easier, because all of this semantic logic is built into the language and the browsers. As a web-based example, the Semantic Notepad demo on the Internet Explorer Test Drive website (*http://ie.microsoft.com/testdrive/html5/semanticnotepad/default.html*) shows how useful the new HTML5 tags are with regard to semantics, or code that is designed to be aware of its own structure.

In SVG, semantics works much the same way, but the SVG elements have a different set of built-in meanings. For example, besides the shape elements, you can use metadata and microdata elements such as *title*, *desc* (description), *RDF*, *microdata*, and *data* attributes.

Note You can find more details about metadata in the SVG 1.1 specification here: *http://www.w3.org/TR/SVG/metadata.html*.

One important distinction between accessibility in SVG and HTML is that the fundamental semantic domain of HTML is text, while that of SVG is graphics. However, both have generally thus far provided the bulk of their accessibility in the textual domain. What it means, for example, for a red rectangle to be readable in sensory modalities other than the visual is intriguing, though shape and geometry, which are a major focus of SVG, clearly have tactile dimensions as well, and can relatively easily (in theory) be transfigured into that modality, as with Braille, in ways that extend the entire concept of accessibility. Text (the *T* in HTML) is historically based on an auditory medium (speech), so people's thinking about what accessibility means in the graphical environment is still rather fledgling.

The following resources have more information on the topics of SVG and accessibility:

- Accessibility Features of SVG: W3C Note 7 August 2000 (*http://www.w3.org/TR/SVG-access/*)

- SVG Content Accessibility Guidelines (2010) (*http://www.w3.org/TR/SVG/access.html#SVG AccessibilityGuidelines*)

- W3C Recommendation: "The <title> and <desc> elements" (2008) (*http://www.w3.org/TR/SVGTiny12/struct.html#TitleAndDescriptionElements*)

- SVG Interest Group (*http://www.w3.org/Graphics/SVG/IG/wiki/Accessibility_Activity*)

Case Study: A Simple SVG Web Interface

In this final example, you will pull everything you've learned so far together into a simple yet powerful SVG web interface that can be used by tiny devices, by mobile devices, and on desktop web browsers.

1. Create a rectangle with rounded corners, which will serve as a background area to contain all of the other graphics. Also set the rectangle's height and width to percentage values so that the background resizes as the user's screen expands and contracts.

2. Next, add a reference to the official SVG logo using the *<image>* element. You can find the SVG logo here: *http://www.w3.org/2009/08/svg-logos.html*. Also add a reference to a bitmap image and set its x and y position so that it is centered both horizontally and vertically in the middle of the screen, even when the browser is resized.

3. Next, add text that is centered horizontally but below the two images. Your SVG should now look similar to the following image:

```
<!-- Layer for content -->
  <g id="layer3">
<!-- Add background for primary content -->
    <rect id="pageContent" width="90%" height="85%" x="5%" y="5%" opacity="0.9" rx="50"
      ry="50" stroke="gray" stroke-width='0.25' fill='#333' fill-opacity="0.5"/>
<!-- Reference the official SVG logo as SVG -->
    <image id="svgLogo01" width="150px" height="150px"
      x="70px" y="50px" xlink:href="svg-logo-v.svg" alt="SVG Logo" />
<!-- Reference the bitmap image (PNG) -->
    <image id="bitmapCentralBall" width="25%" height="25%"  x="38%"
      y="37.5%"xlink:href="iris-small.png" alt="NASA Photo of Jupiter" />
    <g id="textForTargettedDevices">
      <text id="textTiny" x="50%" y="80%" fill="black" font-family="tahoma, serif"
        text-anchor="middle">Text for tiny devices.</text>
    </g>
  </g>
```

4. To spice up the user interface, add the background pattern created in the previous chapter. On top of that, add a linear gradient aligned from top to bottom, as shown here:

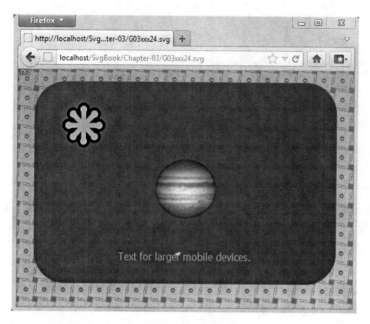

5. Next, add another reference to the SVG logo and position it toward the upper-right of the page. Also add two more *<text>* elements and give each of the *<text>* elements a unique ID so that the code looks like the following.

```
<text id="textBasic" display="none" x="50%" y="80%" fill="orange"
  font-family="Tahoma, serif" text-anchor="middle">
  Text for larger mobile devices.</text>
<text id="TextDesktop" display="none" x="50%" y="80%" fill="orange"
  font-family="Tahoma, serif" text-anchor="middle">
  Text for desktops and wide display devices.</text>
```

6. Finally, add logic to the media queries in the style sheet so that the layout and display of the page elements change depending on the end user's screen size.

```
<style type="text/css">
  @media screen and (min-width: 551px) {
    #svgLogo02 {
       display: inline;
    }
    #textDesktop {
       display: inline;
    }
  }
  @media screen and (max-width: 550px) and (min-width: 351px) {
    #textBasic {
       display: inline;
    }
  }
  @media screen and (max-width: 351px) {
    #pageContent {
       opacity: 0.3;
    }
    #backgroundGradient, #backgroundGridWithPattern {
       display: none;
    }
  }
@media screen and (max-width: 350px) and (min-width: 211px) {
    #textTiny {
       display: inline;
    }
    /* Not Yet Supported  #textTiny:before {content: "dynamic text inserted here...";}
*/
  }
  @media screen and (max-width: 211px) {
    #svgLogo01 {
       display: none;
    }
  }
</style>
```

You just created a solid start to a web application interface using the power of SVG and CSS to support a variety of end-user devices and screen sizes. This example demonstrates how CSS can be used to control the content of the SVG graphic based on various parameters, such as the width and height of the viewing area. CSS can be just as helpful for controlling the style and content of printouts as well. If you've made it this far, nice work!

Summary

So far, you have worked with static SVG, but as we will discuss in the next chapter, you can animate and script SVG as well.

We encourage you to read on. That said, there is already so much that you can do with SVG, so now might be an excellent time for you to tinker around with the examples you have learned so far.

CHAPTER 4

Motion and Interactivity

Neither love nor fire can subsist without perpetual motion; both cease to live so soon as they cease to hope, or to fear.

François VI, Duc de La Rochefoucauld

Although SVG can be a static image format suitable for illustrations, it was designed from its inception to be interactive and dynamic. There are two very important and radically different approaches to this dynamism: *declarative animation* and *scripting*. This chapter first introduces the powerful model of declarative animation that's used by SVG, and then introduces scripting. Scripting will come easiest to those readers who already have some programming experience; therefore, the treatment here proceeds gently. However, to take full advantage of scripting SVG, you will need some knowledge of basic web programming.

Declarative Animation with SVG

SVG animation, as it is often called, refers to the declarative constructs borrowed from another W3C standard: Synchronized Multimedia Integration Language (SMIL). Basically, the principle behind declarative animation (as with the allied concepts of declarative programming) is that the author tells the display device (computer screen, printer, mobile phone, etc.) what the end result is supposed to be and leaves the details of implementation up to the client software. For example, a programmer or developer can describe something like a circle and then let the device implement it to the best of its ability.

Before getting into the practical aspects of this topic, we need to explain several important notions:

- By *declarative animation*, we mean animation performed using markup rather than script.

- The term *SMIL* evokes different meanings for different audiences. Some use it to refer to the subset of SMIL incorporated into and then expanded within SVG. Others use it to refer to the much broader context of SMIL within the SMIL working group of the W3C. The latter is more correct, though the ambiguity has sometimes led to disputes in discussions about using SMIL within other W3C standards. The term *SVG animation* is more frequently used nowadays to refer to declarative animation in SVG; however, *SVG/SMIL* might be a better term to refer to this, because SVG also allows manipulation via CSS, and there is interest from several directions in bringing at least a subset of the power of SVG/SMIL into CSS so it can also be leveraged by HTML.

- All the major browsers except Internet Explorer have implemented declarative animation in SVG. A number of cell phone implementations also offer support for SVG animation—and some of these do not support JavaScript, leaving SVG animation as the only way for developers to perform animations in those platforms.

- To work with the following material, you'll need a browser that handles it well. Opera and the ASV plug-in for Internet Explorer are the best implementations for SVG animation, followed by Firefox 4 (or above). Chrome is slightly ahead of Safari at the time of this writing. You can easily discover whether your browser supports SVG. Check to see if the following example works in your browser. This example adds an ellipse containing two *<animate>* elements children to the standard SVG template:

```
<svg xmlns="http://www.w3.org/2000/svg"
  xmlns:xlink=http://www.w3.org/1999/xlink
  width="100%" height="100%">

  <ellipse id="E" cx="90" cy="90" rx="30" ry="40" fill="#448">
    <animate attributeName="rx" dur="5s" values="20;90;20" repeatCount="indefinite"/>

    <animate attributeName="ry" dur="5s" values="30;60;30" repeatCount="indefinite"/>
  </ellipse>
</svg>
```

Alternatively, you can point your browser to the same example here: *http://srufaculty.sru .edu/david.dailey/svg/animoval0.svg*. The browser should display an oscillating ellipse, the size of which changes periodically (with an aspect ratio that changes as well) over a five-second interval.

Note If the preceding example doesn't work for you, change browsers and continue experimenting with this section until you find one that works.

- The idiosyncrasies of browser support are somewhat to be expected, because Safari, Chrome, and Firefox all began their support for SMIL quite recently. The improvements within the past year have been dramatic.

- Almost all attributes of SVG objects can be animated declaratively. This implies that animation extends very broadly through the technology in ways that you might not always think of. Check *http://srufaculty.sru.edu/david.dailey/svg/#SMIL* and *http://srufaculty.sru.edu/david .dailey/svg/newstuff/Newlist.htm* for a variety of illustrations.

- Not all animations can be done declaratively (at least not yet) in SVG. Script is still far more powerful for creating complex effects. Later in the chapter, you'll see some examples that cannot be created using the declarative animation methods alone.

- Declarative animation is easy to use and appears (based on several years of anecdotal evidence) to cut development time down considerably.

Getting Started

Let's begin once more with the example described briefly above (and visible at *http://granite.sru .edu/~ddailey/svg/animoval2.svg*):

```
<ellipse id="E" cx="90" cy="90" rx="30" ry="40" fill="#448">
  <animate attributeName="rx" dur="5s" values="20;90;20" repeatCount="indefinite"/>
  <animate attributeName="ry" dur="5s" values="30;60;30" repeatCount="indefinite"/>
</ellipse>
```

Inside the ellipse are two *<animate>* elements. One controls the width, and the other controls the height of the ellipse during the animation. The attributes in this example control the following:

- ***attributeName***   This selects which attribute of the object will be animated.

- ***dur***   This is a measure (by default specified in seconds) that determines how long the animation will last.

- ***values***   This is a semicolon-delimited list of attribute values. These are often numeric, but need not be. In this case, there are three values, and the start and end values are the same. This means that the animation will start and stop with the same value.

- ***repeatCount***   A value of *indefinite* is the correct choice for animations that are to loop continually. Alternatively, you could put a positive integer here, specifying the number of times that the animation has to repeat.

The graphic that follows shows the animation at various times: when *t* is near 0, when *t* equals 1.25, and when *t* equals 2.5.

Just to give you a bit more exposure to the basic concepts, here's another example which duplicates the ellipse from above and shifts its position a little. Then it varies the *values* attribute of the second ellipse so that as one ellipse expands the other contracts. It also adds a rectangle (with rounded corners) and applies some transparency for fun. You can see this example at *http://granite .sru.edu/~ddailey/svg/animoval1.svg*:

```
<rect x="100" y="85" rx="12" height="30" width="150" fill="purple" stroke="black"
  stroke-width="3" />
<ellipse cx="100" cy="100" rx="30" ry="40" fill="#448" opacity=".75"
  stroke="black" stroke-width="3">
  <animate attributeName="rx" type="rotate" dur="5s" values="10;70;10"
    repeatCount="indefinite"/>
  <animate attributeName="ry" type="rotate" dur="5s" values="30;60;30"
    repeatCount="indefinite"/>
</ellipse>
<ellipse cx="250" cy="100" rx="30" ry="40" fill="#448" opacity=".75" stroke="black"
  stroke-width="3">
  <animate attributeName="rx" type="rotate" dur="5s" values="70;10;70"
    repeatCount="indefinite"/>
  <animate attributeName="ry" type="rotate" dur="5s" values="60;30;60"
    repeatCount="indefinite"/>
</ellipse>
```

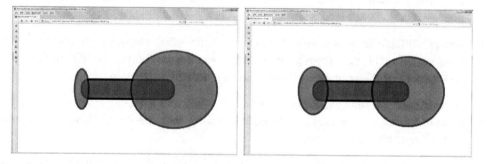

In the two previous examples, the timing associated with the attributes was set to five seconds. In the next example (visible at *http://granite.sru.edu/~ddailey/svg/animoval2.svg*), you'll explore what happens when you vary that interval for different attributes. Here is the code:

```
<rect x="100" y="85" rx="12" height="30" width="150" fill="purple" stroke="black"
   stroke-width="3" >
   <animate attributeName="width" dur="3s" values="150;100;150" repeatCount="indefinite"/>
</rect>
<ellipse id="E" cx="100" cy="100" rx="30" ry="40" fill="#448" opacity=".75" stroke="black"
   stroke-width="6"  stroke-dasharray="8,4">
   <animate attributeName="rx"  dur="3s" values="10;70;10" repeatCount="indefinite"/>
   <animate attributeName="ry"  dur="5s" values="30;60;30" repeatCount="indefinite"/>
</ellipse>
<ellipse  cx="250" cy="100" rx="30" ry="40" fill="#448" opacity=".75" stroke="black"
   stroke-width="6" stroke-dasharray="8,4">
   <animate attributeName="rx" dur="5s" values="70;10;70" repeatCount="indefinite"/>
   <animate attributeName="ry"  dur="3s" values="60;30;60" repeatCount="indefinite"/>
   <animate attributeName="cx" dur="3s" values="250;200;250" repeatCount="indefinite"/>
</ellipse>
```

This example adds a *stroke-dasharray* attribute to the ellipses and lets the position of the center of the second ellipse and the width of the rectangle vary (in synchrony with one another). This demonstrates that desynchronizing and synchronizing can yield rather fascinating effects. While this example appears to make the object rotate, this is simply because the circumference of the ellipse is changing (as *rx* and *ry* change). Also, because dash arrays are allocated in terms of absolute units (pixel widths), the number of dash segments needed to cover the ellipse also varies.

You might also experiment with the illusion of rotation by animating the *dash-offset* attribute. The example at *http://granite.sru.edu/~ddailey/svg/animoval3.svg* presents two apparently interlocking gears rotating in opposite directions.

It turns out that there is a better way of rotating objects than by animating the stroke. You can use the *<animateTransform>* element to change the scale, position, or rotation of an object. Observe this nifty extension of the preceding example, which uses *<animateTransform>*. You can see it at *http://granite.sru.edu/~ddailey/svg/animoval4.svg*, but here you'll examine a simpler case (*http://granite.sru.edu/~ddailey/svg/animoval5BW.svg*) in more detail:

```
<ellipse id="One" cx="200" cy="100" rx="30" ry="40" fill="#555">
   <animate attributeName="rx" type="rotate" dur="5s" values="50;20;50"
      repeatCount="indefinite"/>
   <animate attributeName="ry" type="rotate" dur="5s" values="10;60;10"
      repeatCount="indefinite"/>
</ellipse>
<use id="Two" xlink:href="#One" fill-opacity=".35" stroke="#d06" stroke-width="3">
<animateTransform attributeName="transform" type="rotate" dur="5s" from="0 200 100"
   to="360 200 100" repeatCount="indefinite"/>
</use>
<use xlink:href="#One" transform="translate(100,0)" />
<use xlink:href="#Two" transform="translate(-100,0)" />
```

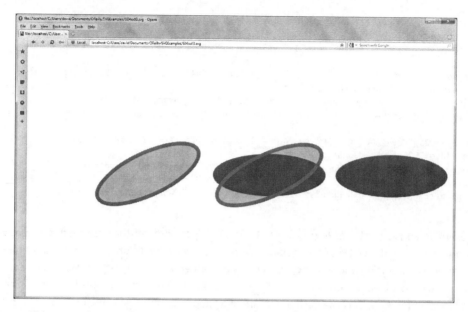

This example starts with a basic ellipse ("*One*") colored dark gray (#555) and animates both its *x* and *y* radii. It then reuses the ellipse three times: once in the same location ("*Two*"), once to the left, and once to the right. This example lets you see that the two gray ellipses oscillate only vertically and horizontally. However, both the reddish ellipses have an animation applied through an *<animateTransform>*, a child of the *<use>* element, so that they may be rotated as well. This should serve to demonstrate that rotation adds a new property to the ellipses. Note that because of the frequencies of oscillation, the reddish oval coincides precisely with the gray one four times in every five-second cycle—which you can see by pausing the animation, as shown at *http://granite.sru .edu/~ddailey/svg/animoval5BWpause.svg*.

Here's a more adventurous example using similar ellipses that both oscillate and rotate as a part of a clip path applied to an image that is then tiled through a pattern. This currently works best in Firefox 4, Opera, and Internet Explorer with ASV. You can view it at *http://granite.sru.edu/~ddailey/ svg/animoval4a.svg*.

SVG also has an *<animateColor>* element, intended for gradually changing colors over time; however, it has been deprecated. Instead, SVG provides the ability to animate nonnumeric values using a simple *<animate>* element with color names. So, you can use code such as the following to vary the fill of the gray ellipse above concurrently with some of its other attributes (you can see an example at *http://granite.sru.edu/~ddailey/svg/animoval5.svg*):

```
<ellipse id="One" cx="200" cy="100" rx="30" ry="40" fill="#555">
  <animate attributeName="rx" type="rotate" dur="5s" values="50;20;50"
    repeatCount="indefinite"/>
  <animate attributeName="ry" type="rotate" dur="5s" values="10;60;10"
    repeatCount="indefinite"/>
  <animate attributeName="fill" type="rotate" dur="5s" repeatCount="indefinite"
    values="red;plum;yellowgreen;red" />
</ellipse>
```

Motion Along a Path

Now let's play a bit more with the positioning of these ellipses by using *<animateMotion>* to make them follow a curve. You can see this example at *http://granite.sru.edu/~ddailey/svg/animoval7.svg*.

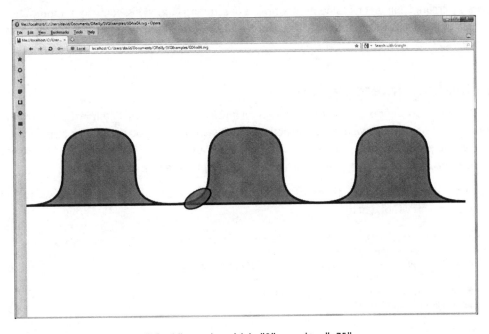

```
<path id="curve" stroke="black" stroke-width="3" opacity=".75"
    d="M 0,200
    C 100,200    0, 100, 100,100 C 200,100 100,200 200,200
    C 300,200 200, 100, 300,100 C 400,100 300,200 400,200
    C 500,200 400, 100, 500,100 C 600,100 500,200 600,200 z" >

</path>

<ellipse id="One" cx="0" cy="0" rx="20" ry="10" fill="inherit" opacity=".75" stroke="black"
    stroke-width="2">
    <animateMotion dur="10s" rotate="auto" repeatCount="indefinite">
      <mpath xlink:href="#curve"/>
    </animateMotion>
</ellipse>
```

This example draws three identical mounds (each 200 pixels to the right of the previous one). The path is closed by the *z* subcommand.

First, it is important to point out that the locus of the ellipse is specified to be on the curve by setting its center, *(cx,cy)*, to (0,0). Also notice that the ellipse takes its orientation from the curve itself, due to the *rotate="auto"* attribute. Also, because the distance traversed by the moving ellipse is greater along the mounds than it is along the straight line, and because its apparent speed remains constant, it takes less time to traverse the line than it does to traverse the mounds. That the shortest distance between two points is a straight line is perhaps illustrated by this example, *http://granite.sru .edu/~ddailey/svg/animoval7c.svg*, which takes the preceding code and passes a linear path through the same extremities of the smooth curve above. You can see another example that illustrates what happens when (*cx,cy*) equals (0,0) here: *http://granite.sru.edu/~ddailey/svg/animoval7b.svg.*

The *<animateMotion>* element allows you to move SVG content along a given path. If you have previously created animations using programming or scripting languages, you might appreciate the elegance of the declarative solution that *<animateMotion>* provides. The amount of code it saves is commendable.

Multivalued Interpolation

The last type of animation demonstrated here is *multivalued interpolation.* In this instance, attribute values are not single scalar values, but collections of values. To use it, you set up an interpolation between two paths. The only restriction is that the paths must have the same number of coordinates and the same types of subcommands (such as *L, Q, C,* or *A*) for the animation to work.

Consider the following example (visible at *http://granite.sru.edu/~ddailey/svg/animoval8.svg*), which animates two vertices of a path:

```
<path id="curve" stroke="black" fill="yellowgreen" stroke-width="3" fill-opacity=".5" >
  <animate attributeName="d"   dur="3s"
    values=" M 100,0  0,100   70,50  130,150  200,100  z;
        M 100,0  0,100    70,150  130, 50  200,100  z;
        M 100,0  0,100    70,50   130,150  200,100  z"
    repeatCount="indefinite"
  />
</path>
```

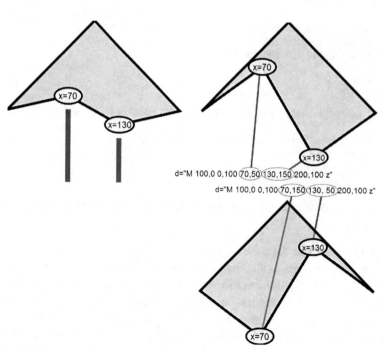

The key to understanding this example is to observe that the path's shape, *d*, is governed by three values (separated from one another by semicolons and typeset on separate lines for ease of reading). The first and last of those strings of coordinates are the same, and each string has exactly five points. The pentagon is animated by repeatedly morphing between the two shapes shown at the right of the illustration. Furthermore, by examining the first, second, and last points of the pentagon, you can see that we keep three of the vertices unchanged. Only the points where x equals 70 and 130 will be changed. As one of these vertices moves down the page from (70,50) to (70,150), the other will move up the same distance. The starting and middle values of the path are shown at the right of the animation.

Other examples that involve transition between paths are shown in the following images—and of course, we provide URLs so that you can view the live versions.

This graphic shows an example in which three curves are animated (see *http://granite.sru.edu/~ddailey/svg/animoval8b.svg*):

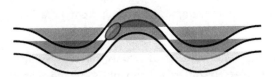

The following shows an example of transitioning between random polygons (*http://srufaculty.sru.edu/david.dailey/svg/SVGOpen2010/Polygons/polygons10.svg*):

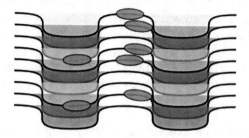

Interacting with Animation

SVG animations can be started or stopped based on user-generated events, such as mouse clicks and rollovers. You can trigger SVG animation from script, and conversely, trigger scripts to run upon completion of an SVG animation. Let's start with a simple example and work up from there, holding off on scripting until the next section.

In this example (visible at *http://granite.sru.edu/~ddailey/svg/animstart0.svg*), an ellipse is instructed to move along a curved path, as in previous examples. The difference, though, is that the animation does not begin until an object (G) is clicked.

```
<path id="curve" stroke="black" fill="none" stroke-width="3" fill-opacity=".5"
  d="M 0,100 C  100,150 100,50 200,50 C 300,50 300,150 400,100" />
<ellipse cx="0" cy="0" rx="16" ry="8" fill="orange" opacity=".85" stroke="black"
  stroke-width="2">
  <animateMotion dur="3s" rotate="auto" repeatCount="2" begin="G.click">
    <mpath xlink:href="#curve"/>
  </animateMotion>
</ellipse>
<g id="G">
  <ellipse  cx="200" cy="90" rx="33" ry="15" fill="yellow" stroke="black" stroke-width="2" />
  <text x="175" y="101" font-size="31" fill="black" font-family="arial">GO</text>
</g>
```

Here is how it works. First, the *<animate>* element contains the attribute *begin="G.click"*. This means that the action specified by the animation will begin exactly when an object having the *id* of *G* is clicked. Second, the object *G* is actually a group containing both an ellipse and some text. The reason for grouping them together is that ultimately, the developer cannot be sure whether the user will actually click the oval or the text object. By grouping them, the developer ensures that whichever one is clicked results in the animation activation. Third, the animation is instructed to run exactly twice, using the attribute *repeatCount="2"*.

A minor annoyance (which is actually two different minor annoyances that happen to look like one) is that when the animation is not running, part of the ellipse is visible at the corner of the page. This is because the ellipse has its centroid set to the coordinate (0,0), which is necessary to have the ellipse centered on the curve throughout the animation. Fortunately, there are ways to work around this, as you will see in the next example (visible at *http://granite.sru.edu/~ddailey/svg/animstart0a.svg*).

To modify the preceding code so that the ellipse doesn't blink at the end of the cycle, simply replace the first ellipse and its children by the following code:

```
<ellipse id="One" cx="0" cy="0" rx="16" ry="8" fill="orange" opacity="0" stroke="black"
   stroke-width="2">
<set attributeName="opacity" to=".75" begin="G.click" />
  <animateMotion id="A" dur="3s" rotate="auto" repeatCount="2" begin="G.click" fill="freeze">
    <mpath xlink:href="#curve"/>
  </animateMotion>
</ellipse>
```

This example employs two new aspects of SVG animation: the *<set>* element and the *"freeze"* value of the *fill* attribute. These accomplish two rather different effects.

The *<set>* element allows you to simply change the value of an attribute based on an event (either generated by the user or by the passage of time). Initially, the ellipse is invisible (*opacity="0"*); however, when *G* is clicked, in addition to the *<animateMotion>* starting as before, the *<set>* element makes the ellipse visible by changing the *opacity* value.

At the end of this animation, the *fill="freeze"* attribute specifies that the ellipse will remain at the last values specified—namely, at the end of the curve.

You could instead make the ellipse disappear at the end of the animation (as in the example at *http://granite.sru.edu/~ddailey/svg/animstart0b.svg*) by simply putting two *<set>* elements inside the *<ellipse>* element, thusly:

```
<ellipse id="One" cx="0" cy="0" rx="16" ry="8" fill="orange" opacity="0"
   stroke="black" stroke-width="2">
  <set attributeName="opacity" to=".75" begin="G.click" />
  <set attributeName="opacity" to="0" begin="A.end" />
  <animateMotion id="A" dur="3s" rotate="auto" repeatCount="2" begin="G.click">
    <mpath xlink:href="#curve"/>
  </animateMotion>
</ellipse>
```

We'll give one last example—an extension of the above—that employs a few more concepts to illustrate some of the additional power of declarative animation. You can see it at *http://granite.sru.edu/ ~ddailey/svg/animstart1.svg*.

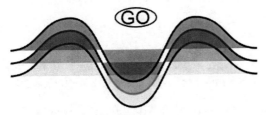

The code will be annotated in parts because there are several parts that illustrate different features.

Initially, for aesthetic purposes only, we lay down three curves, with two reusing the first with different values for the *fill* attribute. Then we lay down the yellow button:

```
<g id="G">
  <set attributeName="opacity" to="0" begin="G.click" />
  <set attributeName="opacity" to="1" begin="AM.end" />
  <ellipse cx="205" cy="30" rx="33" ry="15" fill="yellow" stroke="black" stroke-width="2">
    <set attributeName="fill" to="green" begin="G.mouseover" />
    <set attributeName="fill" to="yellow" begin="G.mouseout" />
  </ellipse>
  <text x="180" y="41" font-size="31" fill="black" font-family="arial"
    pointer-events="none">GO</text>
</g>
```

As in the earlier examples, this one identifies a group that contains an ellipse and some text. However, there are a few differences:

- The group is made to disappear when it is clicked and reappear when the *<animateMotion>* (#AM) terminates.

- The ellipse is made to change colors from green to yellow and back as the mouse moves over it or leaves. This is to signal to the user that the button is live and active. This direct affiliation of behavior with the object being animated results in code that is more understandable, easier to write, and easier to maintain than code that lives elsewhere, either in script or in a style sheet. It also results in a DOM that is fairly easily scripted.

- The text object within the group is given the attribute *pointer-events="none"*. This is because the browser will otherwise detect that the mouse has entered the text object, which will trigger a *mouseout* event on the ellipse.

Next, much as in the earlier example, the ellipse is created and instructed to follow one of the curves twice, taking three seconds for each traversal:

```
<ellipse id="One" cx="0" cy="0" rx="16" ry="8" fill="orange" opacity="0"

  stroke="black" stroke-width="2">
  <set attributeName="opacity" to=".75" begin="G.click+3" />
  <set attributeName="opacity" to="0" begin="AM.end" />
  <animateMotion id="AM" dur="3s" rotate="auto" repeatCount="2" begin="G.click+3">
    <mpath xlink:href="#curve"/>
  </animateMotion>
</ellipse>
```

The difference here is that instead of having the ellipse appear exactly when the button is clicked, the ellipse is told to become visible three seconds after the button is clicked (*begin="G.click+3"*).

```
<text x="180" y="40" font-size="35" fill="black" font-family="arial"  display="none">
  <set attributeName="display" to="block" begin="G.click" />
  <set attributeName="display" to="none" begin="G.click+1" />
// 3
</text>
<text x="180" y="40" font-size="35" fill="black" font-family="arial" display="none">
  <set attributeName="display" to="block" begin="G.click+1" />
```

```
    <set attributeName="display" to="none" begin="G.click+2" />
    // 2
  </text>
  <text x="180" y="40" font-size="35" fill="black" font-family="arial" display="none">
    <set attributeName="display" to="block" begin="G.click+2" />
    <set attributeName="display" to="none" begin="G.click+3" />
    // 1
  </text>
```

This cluster of text objects simulates a countdown from –3 seconds to –1 second. The countdown begins when *G* is clicked, but then, after each second, reveals a new number and hides the old number. The example could have just as easily used the *visibility* attribute, toggling its value from "hidden" to "visible" and back again; however, doing that causes the invisible object to take up screen real estate. When that's not desirable, using the *display* attribute (toggling between "block" and "none") removes that particular concern.

Scripting SVG

While SVG animation, following a declarative model, is pleasantly easy, scripting is still more powerful—but also typically requires more work and expertise. It is our hope that this section will be understandable to programmers and nonprogrammers alike; however, nonprogrammers should be aware that programming skill typically takes months or years to cultivate.

Excerpting a bit from the W3C document, "An SVG Primer for Today's Browsers" (*http://www.w3.org/Graphics/SVG/IG/resources/svgprimer.html#why_script*), let us cut to the chase:

Without programming in SVG we cannot

- *Create a new object wherever the user clicks the mouse;*

- *Build objects with random values for their attributes;*

- *Allow objects to have their attributes modified (nontrivially) by users;*

- *Allow moving objects to have their directions or velocities adjusted (nontrivially) by the user;*

- *Detect the distance between moving objects on the screen;*

- *Build a 3D rendering of a cylinder tumbling about in space;*

- *Build something which acts like a <select> object in HTML;*

- *Simulate the movement of armies of grasshoppers over an infinite meringue pie.*

Now, while not all SVG developers share all the above interests with equal enthusiasm, this may give you some idea of the range of possibilities that script enables. It is also worth mentioning that among the proposals for additions to SVG 2 (*http://www.w3.org/Graphics/SVG/WG/wiki/SVG2_Requirements_Mailing_List_Feedback*) are suggestions that might allow declarative access to random values, collision detection, and enhanced 3D capabilities.

Getting Started with JavaScript and SVG

To begin our discussion, the first example (*http://granite.sru.edu/~ddailey/svg/B/scriptstart1.svg*) is a sort of simplest case: a Hello World program in which the click of a button results in a simple scripted response.

```
<svg xmlns="http://www.w3.org/2000/svg" xmlns:xlink="http://www.w3.org/1999/xlink">
<script><![CDATA[
  function Here(){
    alert("hello")
  }
]]></script>
<text id="Text" x="87" y="100" font-size="26" fill="black">Click</text>
<rect id="Rect" onclick="Here()" x="75" y="76" height="30" width="80" stroke="black"
stroke-width="2" fill="green" opacity=".5" rx="10"/>
</svg>
```

Clicking the button results in an alert box being opened, containing the message "hello".

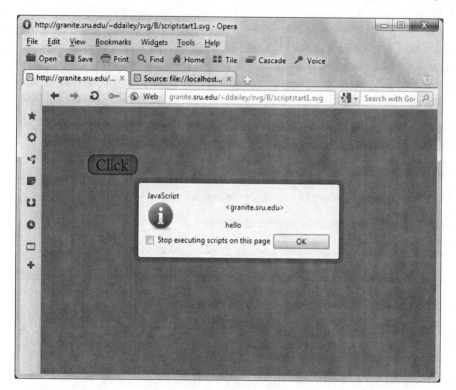

We want to point out several things about this code.

- JavaScript embedded in SVG typically resides within a *<script>* tag. Because SVG is actually XML, you must use:

    ```
    <script><![CDATA[
    ```

to begin a *script* tag and write:

```
]]></script>
```

to end the script tag. You define JavaScript functions and variables inside that script tag.

- Although the text is partly visible thanks to the *opacity* attribute set on the rectangle, a user cannot click it. To place the text in front instead, and make it sensitive to events, you can group the two objects by placing them inside a *<g>* element, first the rectangle, then the text (as in the earlier examples in the section "Interacting with Animation"), and then register the click event on the group rather than on the rectangle.

- When the user clicks on the rectangle, the event calls the JavaScript function *Here()*. Functions are used to define blocks of statements which can be reused by calling the function again.

- The commands—in this case, just one: *alert('hello')*—inside the curly braces (*{* and *}*) are the JavaScript program statements that will run when the function activates.

- The net result of the above example is that when the green button is clicked, the word "hello" will appear in an alert box.

- Alert boxes are not considered good user interface design; they are used primarily for debugging by programmers.

The examples that follow will all begin with this basic prototype and add things as needed. When beginning scripting, you may want to start with a simple scripting template (such as the one provided at *http://srufaculty.sru.edu/david.dailey/svg/simpleTemplate.svg*) because not all the syntax is easily memorable.

While the above example accomplishes very little, it serves the purpose of showing how to activate a JavaScript function from a mouse click within an SVG document, and it's intended to function only as a gentle introduction—the sort of Hello World program typically found in introductory programming texts. Programming is a big topic (as big as mathematics, indeed, as it holds the theory of computing within it), so this book can at best provide just a glimpse of what you can do with SVG and script working together.

Using Script to Find an Object and Change Its Attributes

Script presents the SVG author with several opportunities to manipulate objects in the SVG DOM. First, though, one must know how to find an object in the DOM. There are at least two different but effective ways to find an object so you can manipulate it.

Example 1

Here, you'll begin with the simple example above (*http://granite.sru.edu/~ddailey/svg/B/scriptstart1.svg*) and change the statement *alert('Hello')* so that, instead, the code retrieves the object named *rect* and then modifies it:

```
<svg xmlns="http://www.w3.org/2000/svg" xmlns:xlink="http://www.w3.org/1999/xlink">
  <script><![CDATA[
    function Here () {
      var R = document.getElementById("Rect");
      R.setAttributeNS(null, "fill", "red");
    }
  ]]></script>
  <text id="Text" x="87" y="100" font-size="26" fill="black">Click</text>
  <rect id="Rect" onclick="Here()" x="75" y="76" height="30"
    width="80" stroke="black" stroke-width="2" fill="green" opacity=".5" rx="10"/>
</svg>
```

When an element defined in an SVG document is built and inserted into the DOM, it is called a *node*. The DOM has a tree structure—computer scientists like to call the nodes "leaves." The *<rect>* element is a node that has been given an identifier using the *id* attribute: *id="Rect"*.

You use the method *getElementById()* to retrieve a particular node in the document, and the method returns a reference that you can store in a variable for future use. In the above code we have declared the variable *R* and we have assigned to it the node reference returned by the method. Think of *R* as an alias for *Rect*. However, remember that the variable *R* is a reference to the *Rect* node only within the body of the function (scope), because we have declared *R* as a *local* variable. If we wanted to be able to reuse it outside of the function, or within other functions, we would need to declare it as a *global* variable, right at the beginning of the script, and we would use it in the function body without the *var* keyword:

```
<script><![CDATA[

var R;
function Here () {
  R = document.getElementById("Rect");
  ...
}
```

We have declared the global variable R, and we have assigned a value to it in the function body. So long as we do not reassign that variable by giving it a new value, it will refer to the *Rect* node throughout the program.

When the function *Here()* is activated by the click event, the node *R* will have the value of its *fill* attribute changed to *red*. Note the use of the method *setAttributeNS()* instead of the more generic *setAttribute()*; although the latter would work equally well in this particular case, this is not true for methods that have an XML declination when used in documents using multiple namespaces, for example HTML and SVG. Therefore it is essential to get into the right habit of using the appropriate grammar.

Example 2

Here's a more general approach that would work for any item in the document for which you wish to change the fill color. You can see this example at *http://granite.sru.edu/~ddailey/svg/B/changeAttr2.svg*. The example begins the same as before, so the first lines are omitted here:

```
function Here (evt) {
  var R = evt.target;
  R.setAttributeNS(null, "fill", "red");
}
]]></script>
<text id="Text" x="67" y="100" font-size="26" fill="black">Click</text>
<rect onclick="Here(evt)" x="55" y="76" height="30" width="80" stroke="black"
  stroke-width="2" fill="blue" opacity=".5" rx="10"/>
<g transform="translate(100,0)">
  <text id="Text" x="87" y="100" font-size="26" fill="black">Click</text>
  <rect onclick="Here(evt)" x="75" y="76" height="30" width="80" stroke="black"
    stroke-width="2" fill="green" opacity=".5" rx="10"/>
</g>
```

Note the following about this example:

- Each of the two buttons, when clicked, sends a small gift (known as a *parameter*) to the function *Here()*. This parameter is the *event* (*evt*), which is an object that contains information about what just happened.

- The code *evt.target* is a way of referring to the thing that received the event. In this case, *evt.target* refers to whichever rectangle the user clicked.

- After you know what was clicked, you let *R* refer to that, and then change the attributes of *R* the same way as in the previous example.

Example 3

Notice that an object does not need to have a particular attribute specifically defined beforehand for you to add and then change that attribute in code (see the example at *http://granite.sru.edu/~ddailey/svg/B/changeAttr3.svg*, in which the *dash array* is adjusted by script even though the original element contained no such attribute to begin with). This is possible because in reality the majority of attributes are assigned to the element with an initial value (default) which, in the case of *dash array* for example, is set to "none".

```
function Here (evt) {
  var R = evt.target;
  if (evt.type == "mouseover") {
    R.setAttributeNS(null, "stroke-dasharray", "4,8");
    R.setAttributeNS(null, "stroke-width", "10");
    R.setAttributeNS(null, "fill", "green");
  }
  else if (evt.type == "mouseout") {
    R.setAttributeNS(null, "stroke-dasharray", null);
    R.setAttributeNS(null, "stroke-width", "2");
    R.setAttributeNS(null, "fill", "blue");
  }
}
]]>
</script>
<text id="Text" x="67" y="100" font-size="26" fill="black">Click</text>
<rect onmouseover="Here(evt)" onmouseout="Here(evt)" x="55" y="76" height="30" width="80"
  stroke="black" stroke-width="2" fill="blue" opacity=".5" rx="10"/>
```

Note the following about this example:

- The rectangle has both an *onmouseover* and an *onmouseout* event defined. Both fire the same function: *Here()*.

- The code uses the type of the event (*mouseover* or *mouseout*) to determine which block of code (inside the curly braces) to perform.

- The code adjusts several attributes during the call: *fill*, *stroke-width*, and *stroke-dasharray*.

- When the user moves the mouse out of the rectangle, the event fires and the function is called again restoring the attributes to their original values.

- You could easily add another block of code, using another *else if* statement to trigger a function or change attribute values when the user clicks the mouse.

Example 4

As you might expect, you can accomplish this just as well using the *<set>* element available in SMIL animation, as illustrated here (also see the example at *http://granite.sru.edu/~ddailey/svg/B/change Attr4.svg*):

```
<text id="Text" x="67" y="100" font-size="26" fill="black">Click</text>
<rect x="55" y="76" height="30" width="80" stroke="black" stroke-width="2"
  fill="blue" opacity=".5" rx="10">
  <set attributeName="fill" begin="mouseover" to="green"/>
  <set attributeName="stroke-width" begin="mouseover" to="10"/>
  <set attributeName="stroke-dasharray" begin="mouseover" to="4,8"/>
  <set attributeName="fill" begin="mouseout" to="blue"/>
  <set attributeName="stroke-width" begin="mouseout" to="2"/>
  <set attributeName="stroke-dasharray" begin="mouseout" to="none"/>
</rect>
```

Note the following about this example:

- As of this writing Chrome and Safari do not properly handle the rollover; they sometimes appear to be confused about whether the mouse has left or entered.

- Opera and Firefox disagree on the number of attributes left in the DOM after the process runs, as this example shows.

- This technique runs afoul of the popular approach of attempting to separate content, presentation, and behavior (into markup, styles, and script, respectively). Still, there is something nice about having all aspects of an object right there with it. It is also not clear, in a graphical language like SVG, what the distinction between the three necessarily is.

- The cross-browser issues associated with the SMIL approach, regardless of its elegance, might recommend the scripted approach instead.

Example 5

While on the topic of animation, here's an example of animating things using JavaScript (see *http://granite.sru.edu/~ddailey/svg/B/changeAttr5.svg*). Here are the key parts of the script:

```
if (evt.type == "mouseover") {
  R.setAttributeNS(null, "stroke", "green");
  R.setAttributeNS(null, "fill", "green");
  running = true;
  animate();
}
var w = 2;
var dir = 1;
function animate () {
  if (!running) return;
  w = w + dir;
  R.setAttributeNS(null, "stroke-width", w);
  if ( w > 5 || w < 1) dir =- dir;
  setTimeout("animate()", 50);
}
```

Note the following about this example:

- If the scripting looks complicated, realize that it is just a way of programming nondeclaratively. On mouseover, the code calls the function *animate()*, which repeatedly changes the stroke width.

- The *animate()* function uses the JavaScript command, *setTimeout()*, to repeatedly restart itself and redraw the screen every 50 milliseconds.

- The value of the variable *w* increases every 50 milliseconds until it reaches 5, and then it shrinks.

- You could obtain a similar effect rather easily using the declarative *<animate>* (which would probably be more understandable to prospective web authors).

Example 6

Next is an example that changes the text inside a text node. This is something that people often want to do at about this stage of their learning, but it turns out that the conceptual approach is somewhat different than what we've discussed so far. The words inside a text node are, in fact, not attributes of the text node, but rather the contents of its *child* node. You'll learn more about the distinction between parent nodes and child nodes later in this chapter, in the section "The SVG DOM." You can see the example running at *http://granite.sru.edu/~ddailey/svg/B/changeAttr6.svg*.

```
<script><![CDATA[
    function Here (evt) {

      var R = evt.target;
      var T = document.getElementById("Text");
      if (evt.type == "mouseover") {
```

```
      R.setAttributeNS(null, "fill", "green");
      T.textContent = "please";
      T.setAttributeNS(null, "font-size","20");
      }
     else if (evt.type == "mouseout") {
       R.setAttributeNS(null, "fill", "blue");
       T.textContent = "Click";
       T.setAttributeNS(null, "font-size", "26");
      }
   }
]]></script>
<text id="Text" x="67" y="100" font-size="26" fill="black">Click</text>
<rect onmouseover="Here(evt)" onmouseout="Here(evt)" x="55" y="76" height="30" width="80"
  stroke="black" stroke-width="2" fill="blue" fill-opacity=".5" rx="10"/>
```

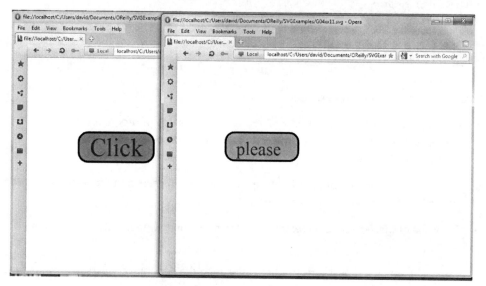

Note the following about this example:

- As before, the code changes the color of the <rect> element. But this time it also adjusts the font size of the <text> element named *Text*, so that it fits into its button a bit better. The code to do these two things uses the same techniques as in the earlier examples.

- The content of the text node is inside a node considered to be a child of the text node. As such, the value of that node is not an attribute, so you can set its *textContent*. Because the node inside is the first child of the text node, you could instead change the content of *firstChild* using the code *T.firstChild.nodeValue="please."*

- The code *T.textContent* does not work in the Adobe plug-in (meaning that it won't work with Internet Explorer 8 or below). If support for those browsers matters to you, then you can use the code *T.firstChild.nodeValue="please"*, which works in all browsers.

Adding New Content to an SVG Document

There are two functions for adding new content to an SVG document: *createElementNS()* and *cloneNode()*. Their purposes are similar, but their use cases are a bit different. Before getting into the details of each, in general you use the following steps for both methods:

1. Create the element, using either *createElementNS()* or *cloneNode()*.

2. Establish its properties (typically using *setAttribute*).

3. Insert the object into the SVG document.

So, let's use a script to create a new element. (This example is shown at *http://granite.sru.edu/ ~ddailey/svg/B/addNodes1.svg*.)

```
<svg xmlns="http://www.w3.org/2000/svg" width="100%"
  xmlns:xlink="http://www.w3.org/1999/xlink" >
  <script><![CDATA[
    xmlns="http://www.w3.org/2000/svg"
    xlink="http://www.w3.org/1999/xlink"

    function add (evt) {
        var C = document.createElementNS(xmlns, "circle");
        C.setAttributeNS(null, "r", 30);
        C.setAttributeNS(null, "cx", evt.clientX);
        C.setAttributeNS(null, "cy", evt.clientY);
        C.setAttributeNS(null, "opacity", .5);
        C.setAttributeNS(null, "fill", "red");
        document.documentElement.appendChild(C);
    }
]]></script>
<rect width="100%" height="100%" fill="white" onclick="add(evt)"/>
<text id="Text" x="67" y="90" font-size="17" font-family="arial" fill="black">
  Click anywhere to add something</text>
<rect x="55" y="70" height="30" width="285" onclick="add(evt)" stroke="black"
  stroke-width="2" fill="blue" opacity=".5" rx="10" />
</svg>
```

In this example, note the following:

- *onclick="add(evt)"* has been added to both the background rectangle and the button itself.

- *evt* is the click event. *evt.clientX* and *evt.clientY* refer to the x and y position of the click itself.

- Clicking a circle that has been added does not result in a new circle being added.

- *document.documentElement* refers to the drawing canvas within SVG—it corresponds roughly to the *<body>* tag in HTML. This is the container to which you're adding each new circle, and it's the same container in which the text and rectangle exist.

Instead of the *onclick="add(evt)"* statement, above, add a statement such as the following to *<script>* at the very beginning of the script (outside the function):

```
document.documentElement.addEventListener("click", function (evt) {add(evt);}, false);
```

After doing that, clicks will be allowed everywhere, including atop the newly added circles.

> **Note** The DOM Level 0 statement *document.documentElement.setAttribute("onclick","add (evt)")* accomplishes much the same thing, but is unlikely to meet the demands of modern applications.

The next example shows that you can use both declarative and scripted methods together in the same document (in fact, you can use both scripted and declarative animation together—and even combine them in ways that interact with one another). Consider the following (see the example at *http://granite.sru.edu/~ddailey/svg/B/addNodes2.svg*):

```
<svg xmlns="http://www.w3.org/2000/svg" width="100%"
  xmlns:xlink="http://www.w3.org/1999/xlink" >
<script><![CDATA[
var xmlns = "http://www.w3.org/2000/svg";
var xlink = "http://www.w3.org/1999/xlink";
function add () {
    var C = document.createElementNS(xmlns, "circle");
    C.setAttributeNS(null, "r", 50);
    var x = 20 + Math.random() * 300;
    var y = 20 + Math.random() * 150;
    C.setAttributeNS(null, "cx", x);
    C.setAttributeNS(null, "cy", y);
    C.setAttributeNS(null, "opacity", .5);
    C.setAttributeNS(null, "fill", Color());
    document.getElementById("underlayer").appendChild(C);
}
function Color () {
    var R = parseInt(Math.random() * 255);
    var G = parseInt(Math.random() * 255);
    var B = parseInt(Math.random() * 255);
    return "rgb(" + R + "," + G + "," + B + ")";
}
]]></script>
<rect width="100%" height="100%" fill="white"/>
<g id="underlayer" />
<text id="Text" x="67" y="90" font-size="17" font-family="arial" fill="black">
Click here to add something</text>
<rect x="55" y="70" height="30" width="250" onclick="add()" stroke="black"
  stroke-width="2" fill="blue" opacity=".5" rx="10">
  <set attributeName="fill" begin="mouseover" to="green"/>
  <set attributeName="stroke-width" begin="mouseover" to="5"/>
  <set attributeName="fill" begin="mouseout" to="blue"/>
  <set attributeName="stroke-width" begin="mouseout" to="2"/>
</rect>
</svg>
```

From this code, you can observe the following:

- Only the button (consisting of text under a *<rect>*) activates the function *add()*.

- To prevent the button from being covered with circles (and hence becoming unavailable for mouse clicks), a group named *underlayer* is created; it starts out without any content, but content will be added to it later. This layer appears before the button in the markup, so it lies under the button and thus can't interfere with mouse events on it. (If it were atop the button, then it would receive the mouse clicks.)

- Some declarative techniques are employed (namely, *<set>*, as discussed earlier in this chapter) to give the button a rollover effect. If you wanted to avoid declarative techniques, you could easily do this with script instead, using *setAttribute()*, as triggered by *mouseover* and *mouseout* events.

- For fun, each new circle appears at a random location in the rectangle, ranging from x and y values of (20,20) to values of (320,170).

- We added a random color to each circle by independently constructing random values for each of its R, G, and B values.

Cloning Nodes

Cloning an existing object instead of building a new one can save a lot of code. We'll show you two examples of this. Here's the first:

```
<script><![CDATA[
  function add (evt) {
    var C = evt.target;
    var N = C.cloneNode(false);
    N.setAttributeNS(null, "x", Math.random() * 300);
    N.setAttributeNS(null, "y", Math.random() * 200);
    document.documentElement.appendChild(N);
  }
]]></script>
<text font-size="17" font-family="arial" y="40" x="20" fill="black">
Click any blue shape</text>
<rect x="55" y="50" height="50" width="85" stroke="#503" onmousedown="add(evt)"
stroke-width="3" fill="blue" fill-opacity=".5" rx="20" stroke-dasharray="9,5,2,5"/>
```

In this relatively simple example (visible at *http://granite.sru.edu/~ddailey/svg/B/addNodes30.svg*), the *<rect>* is armed to call the function *add()* whenever it is clicked. The function first finds the node itself (namely the *<rect>*) and clones it. The parameter value *false* means that it does not copy any child nodes it may find inside the rectangle. This leaves most of the object's 11 attribute values intact, but the 2 of them responsible for its positioning—x and y—have been altered.

In the next example (visible at *http://granite.sru.edu/~ddailey/svg/B/addNodes3.svg*), the advantages of cloning are even clearer. Unfortunately, this doesn't work in Internet Explorer 9 or Safari yet, because of the dynamic SMIL nodes. But it does work with current releases of Chrome, Firefox, Opera, and Internet Explorer with ASV.

```
<svg xmlns="http://www.w3.org/2000/svg" width="100%"
  xmlns:xlink="http://www.w3.org/1999/xlink">
<script><![CDATA[
  xmlns="http://www.w3.org/2000/svg"
  xlink="http://www.w3.org/1999/xlink"
  function add (evt) {
      var C = evt.currentTarget;
      var N = C.cloneNode(true);
      N.setAttributeNS(null, "fill", Color());
      var s = (4 * Math.random() + 1);
      N.firstChild.setAttributeNS(null, "dur", s);
      document.documentElement.appendChild(N);
  }
  function Color () {
    var R = parseInt(Math.random() * 255);
    var G = parseInt(Math.random() * 255);
    var B = parseInt(Math.random() * 255);
    return "rgb(" + R + "," + G + "," + B + ")";
}]]></script>
  <g onmousedown="add(evt)" fill="blue"><animateTransform attributeName="transform"
    type="rotate" dur="5s" values="0,100,100;360,100,100" repeatCount="indefinite"/>
    <text x="67" y="70" font-size="17" font-family="arial" fill="black">Click me</text>
    <rect x="55" y="50" height="30" width="90" stroke="black" stroke-width="2"
    fill="inherit" opacity=".5" rx="10" />
  </g>
</svg>
```

Note the following about this code:

- The text and the rectangle are placed inside a group that is being rotated by an *<animateTransform>*.

- It is the group element that actually sends the event to the function. (We use a *mousedown* event because the object is moving, and it is easier for the user to aim at and click down on a moving object than to click both down and up on it.)

- It turns out that the target of the event in this case is actually the rectangle or the text, not the group. To identify and clone the group, we need to use *evt.currentTarget,* the object on which the event was registered, instead of *evt.target,* which is the object that triggers the event.

- The parameter passed to the *cloneNode()* method is set to *"true"*. This means that its children— namely, the *<animateTransform>*, the *<text>*, and the *<rect>*—are all cloned along with the group.

- We then modify the fill of the group to a random color, and this is inherited by the *<rect>*.

- Finally, to separate the various buttons from one another, we find the first child of the group—namely, the *<animateTransform>*—and modify its duration (*dur*) to be a random amount of time.

- Note that the *<animateTransform>* is not separated by any whitespace from the *<g>* element—and they are both in fact typed on the same line of text. This is important, because the *firstChild* of the group would otherwise actually be a text node consisting of the white space.

Evaluating Nodes (getAttribute)

Just as *setAttributeNS()* lets you change attribute values, the method *getAttributeNS()* provides a way to retrieve the current value of some attribute of a given node. As an example, to get the x-coordinate of the center of a circle with *id="C"*, you might use syntax like this:

```
var myCircle = document.getElementById("C");
var value = myCircle.getAttributeNS(null, "cx") ;
```

The following example (at *http://granite.sru.edu/~ddailey/svg/B/DOMplay0.svg*) uses *getAttributeNS()* to find the size values for a particular object, and then uses those to construct slightly smaller objects.

```
<svg xmlns="http://www.w3.org/2000/svg" width="100%"
  xmlns:xlink="http://www.w3.org/1999/xlink" >

<script><![CDATA[
  xmlns = "http://www.w3.org/2000/svg";
  xlink = "http://www.w3.org/1999/xlink";
function add (evt) {
  var C = evt.target;
  var N = C.cloneNode(true);
  var rx = C.getAttributeNS(null, "rx");
  var ry = C.getAttributeNS(null, "ry");
  var cy = C.getAttributeNS(null, "cy");
//  N.setAttributeNS(null, "cy", cy - 5);
// above line doesn't work because this value
// is overridden by animation
  N.setAttributeNS(null, "rx", rx - 10);
  N.setAttributeNS(null, "ry", ry - 5);
  N.setAttributeNS(null, "transform", "translate(0," + (62 - ry) + ")");
  document.documentElement.appendChild(N);
}]]>
</script>
  <radialGradient id="r1" cx="50%" cy="90%" r="34%" fy="80%" spreadMethod="reflect"
    gradientUnits="objectBoundingBox">  <stop offset=".1" stop-color="black" stop-opacity="0"/>
    <stop offset=".8" stop-color="orange"/>
    <stop offset=".9" stop-color="white" stop-opacity="0"/>
    <stop offset="1" stop-color="grey"/>
  </radialGradient>
  <text font-size="23" font-family="serif" x="20" y="40" fill="black">Click the oval</text>
  <ellipse ry="60" rx="110" fill="url(#r1)" stroke="black" onmousedown="add(evt)"
    stroke-width="2" >
    <animate attributeName="cx" type="translate" dur="9s" values="5%;90%;5%"
      repeatCount="indefinite"/>  <animate attributeName="cy" type="translate" dur="13s"
    values="5%;90%;5%" repeatCount="indefinite"/>
  </ellipse>
</svg>
```

In this example, you should note the following:

- The position of the ellipse has been animated with different periodicities for its horizontal (*cx*) and vertical (*cy*) movements. Because 9 × 13 = 117, the animation will repeat every 117 seconds.

- The ellipse has been filled with a reflected radial gradient, just for fun.

- The *onmousedown* attribute is used on the ellipse because it is easier to mouse down than to click a moving object.

- The *mousedown* event calls the function *add()*, which recognizes the event that activated it, and likewise the target of that event: the ellipse that was clicked (there may be more than one target).

- The value *true* passed to the *cloneNode()* method means that the cloning of the target (the ellipse) will include its children.

- The method *getAttributeNS()* is called to find the size of the clicked ellipse, to gather the values so the code can create a smaller one. As with setAttribute and setAttributeNS, if we are working only in the SVG namespace, we could use the simpler *getAttribute0* and save ourselves the need to specify the null attribute value.

- The new ellipse is placed down just a bit from where its predecessor was. But because the value *cy* is controlled by the animation, assigning a value through script has no effect.

- The code uses a transform instead to move each new ellipse's center a bit lower (because of the reasons mentioned in the previous point).

- As the number of ellipses increases, you'll see the animation slow down considerably.

- If you were to use a centralized *<animateTransform>* for the group of ellipses, it would be more difficult to vary the horizontal and vertical cycle frequencies independently.

The last three points are addressed somewhat in this very similar example (visible at *http://granite .sru.edu/~ddailey/svg/B/DOMplay0b.svg*). The differences in the code are briefly considered here.

```
function add (evt) {
  var C = evt.target;
  var N = C.cloneNode(false);
  var rx = C.getAttributeNS(null, "rx");
  var ry = C.getAttributeNS(null, "ry");
  var cy = parseInt(C.getAttributeNS(null, "cy"));
  N.setAttributeNS(null, "cy", cy + 5);
  N.setAttributeNS(null, "rx", rx - 10);
  N.setAttributeNS(null, "ry", ry - 5);
  C.parentNode.appendChild(N);
}
```

- The new node is added to the *parentNode*—the group that contains whatever object has been clicked. This provides a first glimpse of the topic of the next section, "SVG DOM."

- In the earlier example, *cy* could not be used because it was being animated. Now it can be.

- The function *parseInt()* converts the string value stored in *cy* to an integer. The subtraction operation in the earlier case didn't need to do this, because subtraction automatically casts the result into integer arithmetic. Here, if you don't use *parseInt*, you'll get a "not a number" error, at least in some browsers.

This example introduced only one new concept, the *parentNode* property, but it provided a chance to explore some of the earlier ideas in a bit more detail.

SVG DOM

To those who have not already programmed with the DOM in HTML or XML, this topic can be fairly complex. As you read this chapter, we encourage you to spend a week or two playing with some of these examples and others at the authors' websites (for example, see *http://srufaculty.sru.edu/david .dailey/svg/createElementBrowser.html*). If you are not already a programmer, you may want to skip this section.

To recap, the following two lists show topics that have already been covered in this chapter and those that have not, respectively. Once you become familiar with all of these concepts, you will be able to do most anything you will ever need to do in the SVG DOM.

Here are the topics that we've already covered:

- *setAttributeNS()*

- *getAttributeNS()*

- *getElementById()*

- *createElementNS()*

- *appendChild()*

- *cloneNode()*

- *firstChild*

And here are the topics that we'll discuss in the final sections of the chapter:

- *previousSibling()* and *nextSibling()*

- *getElementsByTagNameNS()*

- *parentNode()*

- *removeChild()*

- *createTextNode()*

First, you will discover the utility of another method of a DOM object, called *getElementsBy TagNameNS()*. Those familiar with HTML DOM have probably noticed that some browsers (but not others) consider *white space* (which includes space characters, tabs, and carriage returns) that lie in between tags as separate nodes in the DOM. Trying to modify, for example, the third child of a node, might in one browser target a *#text* node and in another a *<stop>* node. Fortunately, for any given SVG element (in other words, a node in the DOM) you can ask for all its children of a given type using the *getElementsByTagNameNS()* method. Here's an example (visible at *http://granite.sru.edu/~ddailey/ svg/B/DOMplay3.svg*).

A key thing to note is that *getElementsByTagNameNS()* returns a node collection, but one that cannot be treated as a regular array. That is, its elements must be addressed using this special syntax: *getElementsByTagNameNS(namespace, name).item(n),* instead of the regular array notation *[n]*.

```
<svg xmlns="http://www.w3.org/2000/svg" width="100%"
  xmlns:xlink="http://www.w3.org/1999/xlink">
<script><![CDATA[
  xmlns = "http://www.w3.org/2000/svg";
  xlink = "http://www.w3.org/1999/xlink";
  var count = 0;
  var letters = ["A", "B", "C", "D", "E", "F", "G", "H", "I", "J"];
  var letco = 0;
  function add (evt) {
    var C = evt.currentTarget; // C.nodeName is g
    var N = C.cloneNode(true);
    var x = Math.random() * 700 + 5;
    var y = Math.random() * 400 + 5;
    N.setAttributeNS(null, "transform", "translate(" + x + "," + y + ")");
    var TspansN = N.getElementsByTagNameNS(xmlns, "tspan");
    var TspansC = C.getElementsByTagNameNS(xmlns, "tspan");
    if (TspansC.item(1).textContent == "Me") {
      N.setAttributeNS(null, "fill", Color());
      TspansN.item(1).textContent = letters[letco ++% letters.length];
    } else {
      N.setAttributeNS(null, "fill", C.getAttributeNS(null, "fill"));
      TspansN.item(1).textContent = TspansN.item(1).textContent;
    }
    TspansN.item(2).textContent = count++;
    document.documentElement.appendChild(N);
  }
  function Color () {
    return "rgb(" + parseInt(Math.random() * 255) + "," + parseInt(Math.random() * 255) + ","
      + parseInt(Math.random() * 255) + ")";
  }
]]></script>
<g onmousedown="add(evt)" fill="orange" transform="translate(300,200)">
  <rect height="30" width="80" fill="inherit" rx="10" stroke="black" stroke-width="2"
    fill-opacity=".7" />
  <text font-size="17" font-family="serif" transform="translate(6,20)" fill="black">
    <tspan>Click </tspan><tspan>Me</tspan><tspan></tspan>
  </text>
</g>
</svg>
```

Here are some notes about the preceding code:

- The event handler is added to the group so that the entire group (a *<text>*, a *<rect>*, and three *<tspan>* elements) can be cloned.

- We wished to give each new button its own identity, but while preserving a bit of family resemblance to the button that was used to create it.

- Each new button is given a new location (based on a translation involving random horizontal and vertical displacements). In all other respects, it inherits the other attributes of its ancestor.

- If the first button is clicked, the new button gets a new number and a new random color.

- If a subsequent button is clicked, the new button is given a part of the name and color of that newly clicked button.

- The text contains three *<tspan>* elements, each of which is retrieved as a part of the collection through *getElementsByTagNameNS()*. Two elements of this collection are modified to change the text within the button's group, based, in one case, on the text found inside the activating button.

Another example in which the use of *getElementsByTagNameNS()* is well motivated and perhaps slightly less artificial (although it uses SMIL animation) can be seen at *http://granite.sru.edu/~ddailey/svg/B/DOMplay2.svg*.

Removing Content

Here's a simpler example (visible at *http://granite.sru.edu/~ddailey/svg/B/makeAndTake0.svg*) that shows the use of *removeChild()* to delete content from an SVG document:

```
<svg xmlns="http://www.w3.org/2000/svg" width="100%"
xmlns:xlink="http://www.w3.org/1999/xlink" >
<script><![CDATA[
  xmlns = "http://www.w3.org/2000/svg";
  xlink = "http://www.w3.org/1999/xlink";
  var lastOne;
  Root=document.documentElement;

  function Color () {
    var R = parseInt(Math.random() * 255);
    var G = parseInt(Math.random() * 255);
    var B = parseInt(Math.random() * 255);
    return "rgb(" + R + "," + G + "," + B + ")";
  }
  function add (evt) {
    var C = document.getElementById("C");
    var NC = C.cloneNode(false);
    NC.setAttributeNS(null, "cx", evt.clientX);
    NC.setAttributeNS(null, "cy", evt.clientY);
    NC.setAttributeNS(null, "fill", Color());    NC.removeAttribute("id");
    Root.appendChild(NC);
  }
    function remove (evt) { Root.removeChild(evt.target); }
]]></script>
  <defs>
    <circle r="20" fill-opacity=".5" id="C" onclick="remove(evt)" stroke="black"
      stroke-width="2" stroke-dasharray="8,4" />
  </defs>
  <rect width="100%" height="100%" fill="white" onclick="add(evt)"/>
  <rect x="25" y="30" height="50" width="235" stroke="#800" stroke-width="2" fill="grey"
    opacity=".65">
  </rect>
  <text x="37" y="50" font-size="12" font-family="arial" fill="#800">
```

```
      Click on blank space to add something</text>
    <text x="59" y="70" font-size="12" font-family="arial" fill="#800">
      Click something to get rid of it</text>
  </svg>
```

This example requires only a few comments:

- Rather than typing *document.documentElement* whenever you wish to insert or remove things from the SVG DOM, it is common to use the variable *Root* (or *SVGRoot*) to refer to that entity.

- After finding the invisible circle (hidden inside the *<defs>* element), all its attributes, including the *onclick* attribute, are cloned. Its color and position are determined dynamically.

- Each circle, as cloned, has the built-in event handler to call the remove function.

- Each center's new center *(cx,cy)* is taken from the coordinate of the mouse click *(evt.clientX, evt.clientY)*.

- The *remove()* function uses the event to determine which object was clicked. That object—namely the target of the click event—is then removed from *Root* using *Root.removeChild()*.

- There is a problem with this script: all cloned circles share the same *id*. We address that by using the *removeAttributeNS()* method of the object. Alternatively, you could give each element a unique *id* (by, for example, counting mouse clicks and folding that number into the *id*), or you could simply not give the circle an *id* in the first place, and instead access it through other DOM techniques, such as *getElementsByTagNameNS()*.

The next example contains a button that recolors the most recent addition to a drawing. Rather than illustrating the entire document, we'll present the relevant code snippets. Look at the source of the example (visible at *http://granite.sru.edu/~ddailey/svg/B/makeAndTake1.svg*) if you need to examine it more closely. Changes from the previous example are illustrated in bold.

```
Root = document.documentElement;
var lastOne = Root;
function add (evt) {
var C = document.getElementById("C");
var NC = C.cloneNode(false);
NC.setAttributeNS(null"cx", evt.clientX);
NC.setAttributeNS(null "cy", evt.clientY);
NC.setAttributeNS(null "fill", Color());
Root.appendChild(NC);
lastOne = NC;

}
function colorit(){
if (lastOne.nodeName != "circle") return;
lastOne.setAttributeNS(null, "fill", Color());
}

function remove (evt) {
lastOne = evt.target.previousSibling;
```

```
Root.removeChild(evt.target);
}
]]></script>
<defs>
<!--here would be material that is identical to last example-->

<text x="50" y="100" font-size="12" font-family="arial" fill="black">
Click here to change color of last</text>
<rect x="40" y="80" height="30" width="200" onclick="colorit()"
stroke="blue" stroke-width="2" fill="red" opacity=".35" rx="10">
</rect>
```

Here, the primary addition is a function called *colorit()* that finds the last circle added and changes its color. However, this brings about the following issues:

- You need a button to activate the *colorit()* function.

- You need to keep track of which circle was added last. So, the code contains a variable named *lastOne* that gets set to point to the last circle created.

- Now suppose someone removes the last circle. In that case, the variable *lastOne* would point to a nonexistent object. So, when an object is removed, the variable gets pointed to the previously added circle. This is done by retrieving the *previousSibling* of the clicked item and assigning it to *lastOne*.

- Finally, suppose *all* the circles have been deleted. In that case, *lastOne* will point to *Root* or to the last element in the DOM—and that will not be a circle! Therefore, the test to check whether *lastOne* points to a circle allows the change in color to happen safely.

Next, we'll expand this example with one more feature: to allow text (in this case, a numeric digit) to be placed physically inside one of the circles after it has been created. This actually requires a bit more reworking of the conceptual model employed and a bit more code. We'll include only the parts that change (in bold). The example is visible at *http://granite.sru.edu/~ddailey/svg/B/makeAndTake2.svg*.

```
<svg xmlns="http://www.w3.org/2000/svg" width="100%"
  xmlns:xlink="http://www.w3.org/1999/xlink" >
<script><![CDATA[
  var xmlns = "http://www.w3.org/2000/svg";
  var xlink = "http://www.w3.org/1999/xlink";
  var Root = document.documentElement;
  var lastOne = Root;

  function Color () {
    var R = parseInt(Math.random() * 255);
    var G = parseInt(Math.random() * 255);
    var B = parseInt(Math.random() * 255);
    return "rgb(" + R + "," + G + "," + B + ")";
  }
```

```
      function add (evt) {
        var G = document.getElementById("C");
        var NG = G.cloneNode("true");
        var C = NG.firstChild;
        C.setAttributeNS(null, "cx", evt.clientX);
        C.setAttributeNS(null, "cy", evt.clientY);
        C.setAttributeNS(null, "fill", Color());
        Root.appendChild(NG);
        lastOne = C;
      }

      function content () {
        if (lastOne.nodeName != "circle") return;
        var x = lastOne.getAttributeNS(null, "cx");
        var y = lastOne.getAttributeNS(null, "cy");
        var T = document.createElementNS(xmlns, "text");
        Msg = document.createTextNode(Math.floor(Math.random() * 10));
        T.appendChild(Msg);
        T.setAttributeNS(null, "x", x - 10);
        T.setAttributeNS(null, "y", parseInt(y) + 10);
        T.setAttributeNS(null, "font-size", 36);
        T.setAttributeNS(null, "fill", "black");
        lastOne.parentNode.appendChild(T);
        lastOne = lastOne.parentNode.previousSibling.firstChild;
      }

      function colorit () {
        if (lastOne.nodeName != "circle") return;
        lastOne.setAttributeNS(null, "fill", Color());
      }

      function remove (evt) {
        lastOne = evt.currentTarget.previousSibling.firstChild;
        Root.removeChild(evt.currentTarget);
      }
]]></script>

  <defs>
    <g id="C" onclick="remove(evt)">
      <circle r="20" fill-opacity=".5" stroke="black" stroke-width="2" stroke-dasharray="8,4"/>
    </g>
  </defs>
  <rect width="100%" height="100%" fill="white" onclick="add(evt)"/>
  <rect x="15" y="20" height="50" width="235" stroke="#800" stroke-width="2" fill="grey"
    opacity=".65"/>
  <text x="27" y="40" font-size="12" font-family="arial" fill="#800">Click on blank space to add
    something</text>
  <text x="49" y="60" font-size="12" font-family="arial" fill="#800">Click something to get rid
    of it</text>
  <text x="40" y="100" font-size="12" font-family="arial" fill="black">Click here to add content
    to last</text>
  <rect x="30" y="80" height="30" width="200" onclick="content()" stroke="black"
    stroke-width="2" fill="blue" opacity=".35" rx="10"/>
  <text x="40" y="140" font-size="12" font-family="arial" fill="black">Click here to change
```

```
      color of last</text>
   <rect x="30" y="120" height="30" width="200" onclick="colorit()" stroke="blue"
      stroke-width="2" fill="red" opacity=".35" rx="10"/>
</svg>
```

Here's what happens in the preceding code:

- A new blue button is created that adds content (a random digit between 0 and 9) to the last node.

- To let that content be a part of the node, the node to be cloned, "C", is made into a group containing the circle. That way, when content is to be added, it can be added to the group. When it is time to remove content, the entire group may be deleted.

- The cloning operation now needs to remember that "C" is a group instead of a circle. This means that to change attributes of the circle within the group, you have to get the *firstChild* of the group.

- The cloning operation uses the parameter *true* because the group's child (the circle) is needed.

- The new group is appended to *Root* and the variable *lastOne* is left pointing at the circle so it may be easily accessed when the user decides to change colors (paralleling the earlier example).

- The *content()* function first checks to see if *lastOne* points to a circle. If not, the function exits.

- If *lastOne* is a circle, then the code finds out what its coordinates are, because those will be needed to position the text.

- A new SVG node of type *text* is created.

- Then a rather odd thing happens: to set the *textContent* of the new node, you have to create a *textNode* inside it. This is the actual text itself—the typewritten characters that appear inside the *<text>*—for example *<text>content of textNode</text>*. You do this in SVG by using the method *createTextNode(string)*, where the string contains the content of the text.

- The method *parseInt()* is once again applied to the y-coordinate before doing the addition so that the addition operation is not confused with a concatenation operation.

- At this point, the code can append the text node and its contents—not into the node referenced by *lastOne*, which you'll recall is a *<circle>*—but rather into the group to which *lastOne* belongs. That group is *lastOne.parentNode*.

- Finally, because one does not (typically) wish to overwrite the contents of this text node again, *lastOne* gets redirected to point to the circle inside the preceding group within the document. (This is not a foolproof technique, because the earlier nodes may have been given textual content already, but it's good enough for now. You could strengthen this example by checking to see whether the previous node has a text child or not, and then continuing from there.)

Measurements

This section addresses the topics *getBBox()*, *getTotalLength()*, *getPointAtLength()*, and *viewBox*, because all are helpful in scripting when you need to be precise about element positioning.

You can use the *getBBox()* method, which stands for *get bounding box*. It finds the coordinates of the smallest rectangle (parallel to the edges of the browser window) that contains the geometry of a given shape.

Given a shape such as a 7-pointed purple star, like so:

```
<path onclick="displayBB(evt)" fill = "#837fc0" id = "P9" stroke = "black" stroke-width = "1"
    d="M 96 110.5 Q 191 132 96 154 1 176 77.5 115 154 54 111.5 142 69 230 69 132.5 69 35 111.5
    123 154 211 77.5 150 1 89 96 110.5 z" />
```

you can use *getBBox()* as follows:

The JavaScript used here (see *http://granite.sru.edu/~ddailey/svg/BBoxOM.svg*) that finds the bounding box looks like this:

```
function displayBB (evt) {
  var P = evt.target;
  var BB = P.getBBox();
  var msg1 = "This " + P.nodeName + " has upperleft corner at (" + BB.x + "," + BB.y + ")";
  var msg2 = "and it has width and height of " + BB.width + " and " + BB.height;
  buildBox(BB);
  alert(msg1 + "\n" + msg2);
}
```

You can see a complete example that additionally creates a visible rectangle with the coordinates of the bounding box at *http://granite.sru.edu/~ddailey/svg/B/BBox0M.svg*.

> **Note** Through a click event, the path activates the function *displayBB()*. Then *evt.target* is used to identify the path itself. *BB.x*, *BB.y*, *BB.width*, and *BB.height* are the four crucial measurements of the bounding box. The example finally just calls a small function that builds a red rectangle at those coordinates.

Armed with that information, let's consider a classic packing problem: how to fit a bunch of starlike objects together in a box. Suppose that you have some SVG stars like these (from *http://granite.sru .edu/~ddailey/svg/B/BBox0.svg*):

Further, assume that while duplicating and scattering them, you don't want the objects to overlap, as shown in this output of a small script (see *http://granite.sru.edu/~ddailey/svg/B/BBox1.svg*) that produces these results by applying random transforms:

It would be better to have a bit of space left over than to have all of the objects on top of one another. The classic packing problem is to minimize the amount of space left over—in other words, to constrain the area needed for packing to the smallest area possible.

One simplifying assumption that packers often make is to wrap each item in a nicely sized rectangle (with padding to prevent breakage!) and then fit the rectangles together inside the larger rectangle—which is the screen in this case. (Alternatively, because these shapes are just irregular enough that packing them truly tightly, rotating and adjusting them so that the space between them is minimized might be a more economical packing solution than a rectangular one.) Furthermore, assume (because this is SVG after all) that you can resize the stars to fit the boxes. That's how *getBBox()* can come in handy.

The preceding image was generated by the following JavaScript program embedded in SVG (visible at *http://granite.sru.edu/~ddailey/svg/B/BBox2.svg*). At present, this example works in all browsers except Firefox (which has a known bug related to trying to measure something that has not actually been rendered).

This example involves a bit of algebra and some programming, so it may seem a little opaque—but we'll give a general description of the gist of the program. We set the following listing inside Table 4-1 to display the commentary side by side with the program listing. The hope is that you will be able to see the flow of the program and the descriptions simultaneously.

TABLE 4-1 Creating Boxes Sized for Their Contents

Code	Description
```<svg xmlns="http://www.w3.org/2000/svg" width="100%"` `xmlns:xlink="http://www.w3.org/1999/xlink"` `onload="startup()">` `<script><![CDATA[` `xmlns = "http://www.w3.org/2000/svg";` `xlink = "http://www.w3.org/1999/xlink";` `Root = document.documentElement;```	The standard beginning declares namespaces, and then the *startup()* function is called immediately. It begins the program and draws the graphics.
```var Nacross = 12; //this is how many boxes across we'd like` `var Ndown = 7; //this is how many we'd like vertically```	The code tiles 12 stars across and 7 down. These are global variables defined early in the program so that a programmer can find and change them easily.
```function Color () {` ` var R = parseInt(Math.random() * 255);` ` var G = parseInt(Math.random() * 255);` ` var B = parseInt(Math.random() * 255);` ` return "rgb(" + R + "," + G + "," + B + ")";` `}```	This is the same *Color()* function presented before.
```function startup () {` ` var Stars = document.getElementsByTagNameNS(xmlns, "path");` ` var R = document.getElementById("R");` ` var BB = R.getBBox();` ` var littleBoxw = BB.width / Nacross;` ` var littleBoxh = BB.height / Ndown;```	We measure the screen using *getBBox()* and determine the size of the boxes.
``` for (var i = 0; i < Nacross; i++) {` ` for (var j = 0; j < Ndown; j++) {```	In these two nested loops, the outer loop is controlled by the variable *i* and works across the screen, while the inner one works downward. You could reverse this order without difficulty.
``` var R = document.createElementNS(xmlns, "rect");` ` R.setAttributeNS(null, "width", littleBoxw);` ` R.setAttributeNS(null, "height", littleBoxh);` ` R.setAttributeNS(null, "x", littleBoxw*i);` ` R.setAttributeNS(null, "y", littleBoxh*j);` ` R.setAttributeNS(null, "fill", Color());` ` R.setAttributeNS(null, "stroke", "black");` ` R.setAttributeNS(null, "stroke-width", 1);` ` R.setAttributeNS(null, "fill-opacity", .80);` ` Root.appendChild(R);```	The code creates one small rectangle whose height and width are an appropriate fraction of the available screen size. The starting position is determined by multiples of the values of *i* and *j*.
``` var rS = Math.floor(Stars.length * Math.random());` ` var SC = Stars.item(rS);` ` SBB = SC.getBBox();```	This code chooses a random star from among the total number of paths in the document. Then it measures the selected star.
``` var StarClone = SC.cloneNode("false");` ` var scale = "scale(" + littleBoxw / SBB.width + "," +` `littleBoxh / SBB.height +")";` ` var trans = "translate(" + (littleBoxw * i -BB.x *` `(littleBoxw / SBB.width)) + "," + (littleBoxh * j - SBB.y *` `(littleBoxh / SBB.height)) + ")";`  `StarClone.setAttributeNS(null, "transform", trans + scale) ;```	Here, the code clones the randomly selected star and performs some nasty algebra to rescale and translate the star from its original bounding box and location into the cell reserved for it in the grid.
```StarClone.setAttributeNS(null, "fill-rule", "evenodd");` `StarClone.setAttributeNS(null, "fill", Color());` `Root.appendChild(StarClone);`  `}}}` `]]></script>```	This code changes the color and fill rule of the star to make it more interesting.

Code	Description

```<defs>```
 	
```<path fill="#63f721" d="M 114.5 290.5 Q 213 280 114.5 270 Q 16 260 110.5 290.5 Q 205 321 119 271.5 Q 33 222 106.5 288.5 Q 180 355 121.5 274.5 Q 63 194 103.5 285 Q 144 376 123.5 278.5 Q 103 181 103 280.5 Q 103 380 123.5 282.5 Q 144 185 104 276 Q 64 367 122 286.5 Q 180 206 106.5 272.5 Q 33 339 119 289.5 Q 205 240 110.5 270.5 Q 16 301 114.5 290.5 z" id="P18" stroke="black" stroke-width="1"/>```
 	
```<path fill="#837fc0" d="M 96 110.5 Q 191 132 96 154 Q 1 176 77.5 115 Q 154 54 111.5 142 Q 69 230 69 132.5 Q 69 35 111.5 123 Q 154 211 77.5 150 Q 1 89 96 110.5 z" id="P9" stroke="black" stroke-width="1"/>```
 	
```<path fill="#6fcf96" d="M 347 442 Q 408 393 347 344.5 Q 286 296 252 366.5 Q 218 437 294.5 454.5 Q 371 472 371 393.5 Q 371 315 294.5 332.5 Q 218 350 252 420.5 Q 286 491 347 442 z" id="P47" stroke="black" stroke-width="1"/>```
 	
```<path fill="#d17943" d="M 239 313.5 Q 329 284 239 255 Q 149 226 204.5 303 Q 260 380 260 284.5 Q 260 189 204.5 266 Q 149 343 239 313.5 z" id="P3" stroke="black" stroke-width="1"/>```
 	
```<path fill="#3b63db" d="M 193.5 112 Q 290 129 193.5 146.5 Q 97 164 182 114.5 Q 267 65 204 140.5 Q 141 216 174.5 123.5 Q 208 31 208 129.5 Q 208 228 174 135.5 Q 140 43 203.5 118.5 Q 267 194 182 144.5 Q 97 95 193.5 112 z" id="P1" stroke="black" stroke-width="1"/>```
 	
```<path fill="#c44c80" d="M 374 192.5 Q 459 157 374 122 Q 289 87 324.5 172 Q 360 257 395 172 Q 430 87 344.5 122.5 Q 259 158 344.5 193 Q 430 228 394.5 142.5 Q 359 57 324 142.5 Q 289 228 374 192.5 z" id="P6" stroke="black" stroke-width="1"/>```
 	
```</defs>```
	The actual Bézier paths are placed inside a *<defs>* element so that they're defined but not drawn. That way, they are available to script. The actual star paths were first drawn using the star tool in a drawing program at this author's website (*http://srufaculty.sru.edu/david.dailey/svg/Draw018.html*). Then the results were smoothed and resulting source code was copied.

```<rect id="R" x="0" y="0" width="100%" height="100%" fill="#ddd"/>``` ```</svg>```	The *<rect> R* is added so you can measure the screen.

Before moving on to *getTotalLength()* and *getPointAtLength()*, we'll show one more application of a bounding box to set the stage for what follows.

Following is a script that draws a bounding box around a simple Bézier curve. You can find this example at *http://granite.sru.edu/~ddailey/svg/B/bbox2.3.svg*.

```
<svg xmlns="http://www.w3.org/2000/svg" width="100%" xmlns:xlink="http://www.w3.org/1999/xlink"
  onload="initialize()">
<script><![CDATA[
  xmlns = "http://www.w3.org/2000/svg";
  xlink = "http://www.w3.org/1999/xlink";
  Root = document.documentElement;
  function initialize () { //some global variables
    B = document.getElementById("B");
    BB = B.getBBox();
    R = document.getElementById("R");
  }
```

```
  function measure () {
    var Rnew = R.cloneNode(false);
    Rnew.setAttributeNS(null, "x", BB.x);
    Rnew.setAttributeNS(null, "y", BB.y);
    Rnew.setAttributeNS(null, "width", BB.width);
    Rnew.setAttributeNS(null, "height", BB.height);
    Rnew.setAttributeNS(null, "fill", B.getAttributeNS(null, "stroke"));
    Rnew.setAttributeNS(null, "pointer-events", "none");
    Root.appendChild(Rnew);
  }
  function hilight (evt) {
    var P = evt.currentTarget;
    var Ps = P.childNodes.item(3);
    if (evt.type == "mouseover") Ps.setAttributeNS(null, "stroke", "red");
    else Ps.setAttributeNS(null, "stroke", "black");
  }
]]></script>
<path d="M 30 120 C -30 250 350 20 420 70" id="B" stroke="#008" fill="none" stroke-width="30"/>
<g id="H" onmouseover="hilight(evt)" onmouseout="hilight(evt)" onclick="measure()"
  transform="translate(170,-50)">
<rect id="R" x="100" y="160" height="37" width="115" fill="#888" stroke-width="2" stroke="black"
  fill-opacity=".3"/>
<text x="120" y="190" font-size="30" width="115" fill="#bbb" stroke-width="1"
  stroke="black">Click</text>
</g>
</svg>
```

The following remarks are relevant to this example:

- This example works properly in Internet Explorer 9, Firefox, Opera, and Internet Explorer with ASV. Chrome and Safari, as of this writing, both miscalculate the object's bounding box rather dramatically.

- Realizing that in the examples to follow you might have to click the Click button many times, we moved several global variables into an initialize function. Different programmers have different styles, and some would rather spend the day in a pool of sludge than use global variables. However, in this case, we didn't want to have to reenter the DOM each time the button is clicked and reassign values of things such as curve B. Another approach makes good sense: set a reference to a node (which is the best thing to do when a node is intended for manipulation). Regarding the question of global variables, it's also a good practice to protect a variable with a namespace instead. This can be used to avoid collisions when mixing modular works (external files, libraries, etc.).

- Additionally, you cannot create a reference to an object that does not yet exist. That's why *initialize()* is called from the *onload* event associated with the *<svg>* element itself.

- Before the button is clicked, the bounding box of curve B is retrieved. That information about the bounding box is used to construct a new rectangle.

- The new rectangle takes its fill color from the stroke color of the curve itself. This will prove useful in the next example, in which different curves will produce different-colored bounding rectangles.

- Note that the bounding *<rect>* constructed does not take into account the stroke width. This may seem counterintuitive, and the SVG Working Group is considering alternatives for future versions of the specification.

- The new rectangle has *pointer-events* set to *"none"* meaning that the button still is accessible to mouse events, even though the rectangle is on top of it. This allows you both to see the rollover effect on the button's text and to use the buttons to create more rectangles. An alternative approach would be to change the stacking order of elements in the DOM by deleting the button and then adding it back in, hence putting it on top again.

> **Note** It's useful to point out that *appendChild()* removes an element and appends it to the top of the document or of a layer.

The example at *http://granite.sru.edu/~ddailey/svg/B/bbox2.4.svg* indicates that a bounding box measures the initial state of a path's animation. This is true regardless of whether the animation is running before or after the measurement of the bounding box.

Points on a Curve

This section introduces two more allied methods: *getTotalLength()* and *getPointAtLength()*, which can be used to calculate positions along complex curves; such calculations might otherwise defy simple arithmetic. The example shown also provides a good lesson in DOM manipulation, because it involves repeatedly filling a group with objects and then deleting them all again. You'll also see a combination of SMIL animation and JavaScript in this example, with each type used for what it does best: SMIL for animating the oscillation of a Bézier curve (which is difficult to interpolate through script) and JavaScript for accessing the DOM. The example, visible at *http://granite.sru.edu/~ddailey/svg/B/bbox4 .svg*, is shown with interleaved discussion.

```
var animate = false
function startup (evt) {
  bunch = document.getElementById("bunch");
  E = document.getElementById("E");
}
Col = new Array("red", "magenta", "blue", "cyan", "green", "yellow", "orange");
```

The Boolean variable *animate* is used to start and stop the animation. When it is *false*, the animation will be stopped. One of the buttons will turn it on and off by changing the value of this variable. An array of colors, *Col*, is defined, in which *Col[0] becomes "red"*, *Col[1]* becomes "magenta", and so forth, so the code can assign colors deterministically rather than randomly.

```
function populate (n) {
  if ((n > maxn) || (n < minn)) {
    incr =- incr;
    maxn = 60;
  }
  var v = n + incr;
```

```
    var p = "M 10 150 C 200 "+(5*n)+" 350 "+(300-5*n)+" 450 100";
    var B = document.getElementById("B");
    B.setAttributeNS(null, "d", p);
    var l = B.getTotalLength();
    if (bunch.childNodes.length > 0) DOs(bunch);
      for (i = 0; i < n + 1; i ++) {
        P = B.getPointAtLength(l * i / n)
        px = Math.ceil(P.x)
        py = Math.ceil(P.y)
        Enew = E.cloneNode(false)
        Enew.setAttributeNS(null, "cx", px);
        Enew.setAttributeNS(null, "cy", py);
        Enew.setAttributeNS(null, "fill", Col[i%Col.length]);
        bunch.appendChild(Enew);
      }
      if (animate) window.setTimeout("populate(" + v + ")", 10)
}


    if (animate) window.setTimeout("populate("+v+")",10)


}
```

The function *populate()* calls itself recursively and updates the screen every 10 milliseconds. This is because JavaScript will not redraw the screen while functions are still processing. Using this recursive call mechanism in HTML is a fairly standard trick. Each time the animation runs, the code deletes all the existing ellipses and introduces n new ones (where n increases for a period of time and then decreases). Each new ellipse is positioned 1/nth of the way along the curve further than the preceding one. The position of the curve is updated too, just for fun.

```
function Dos (s) {
    num = s.childNodes.length;
    for (i = s.childNodes.length; i > 0; i--){
        s.removeChild(s.childNodes.item(i - 1));
    }
}
```

When deleting objects, make sure you don't try to delete nonexistent nodes.

```
//]]></script>
<defs>
  <ellipse id="E" rx="10" ry="6" opacity=".75" stroke="black" stroke-width="2">
    <animateMotion dur="2s" rotate="auto" repeatCount="indefinite" begin="H.click">
    <mpath xlink:href="#B"/></animateMotion>
  </ellipse>
</defs>
```

A version referenced at *http://granite.sru.edu/~ddailey/svg/B/bbox4.svg* does something similar, but does not employ SMIL.

```
<g>
  <path d="M 10 150 C 200 80 350 300 450 100" id="B" stroke="black" fill="none"
    stroke-width="4"/>
  <g id="bunch"></g>
```

```
    </g>
    <g id="G" onmouseover="hilight(evt)" onmouseout="hilight(evt)"
      onclick="animate=false;populate(n=n+incr)" transform="translate(60,-170)">
      <rect x="90" y="393" height="47" width="115" fill="#bbb" stroke-width="2" stroke="black" />
      <path fill = "#663e16" id = "P6" stroke = "black" stroke-width = "1"
        transform="translate(93,393) scale(.10,.09)"
        d =[..... very long path data consisting of handwritten letters....]/>
    <g id="H" onmouseover="hilight(evt)" onmouseout="hilight(evt)"
      onclick="animate=!animate;populate(7)">
      <rect x="150" y="283" height="47" width="115" fill="#bbb" stroke-width="2" stroke="black" />
      <text x="155" y="325" font-size="47" width="115" fill="#bbb" stroke-width="2"
        stroke="black">Click</text>
    </g>

    </svg>
```

One button adds nodes manually to the path, and the other starts and stops the animation.

Another version (at *http://granite.sru.edu/~ddailey/svg/B/BBox3.5.svg*) shows that—at least in some browsers—shows that positions of objects at a given time in the animation can be accessed, since artifacts are left at their initial positions.

viewBox

While on the topic of measuring things, it is appropriate to discuss the *viewBox*, which is actually an attribute of the *svg* element itself. The topic is not directly related to scripting, but allows you to determine exactly how large drawings will be.

> **Note** For a deeper treatment, read the W3C specification on the subject (*http://www.w3 .org/TR/SVG/coords.html#ViewBoxAttribute*).

To set the stage for this discussion, the following example (visible at *http://granite.sru.edu/~ddailey/ svg/viewBox0.svg*) provides a brief review about relative coordinates in SVG:

```
<svg  xmlns="http://www.w3.org/2000/svg" width="100%"
  xmlns:xlink="http://www.w3.org/1999/xlink" >
<rect width="100%" height="100%" fill="#acf"/>
<ellipse rx="14%" ry="10%" cx="50%" cy="50%" fill="#79f"/>
<text font-size="45" textLength="150" lengthAdjust="spacingAndGlyphs" font-family="arial"
  font-weight="bold" x="44%" y="53%" >TEXT</text>
<path stroke="#207" stroke-width="2" d="M 460 220 C 560 320 660 320 760 220 z" fill="none"/>
</svg>
```

This code succeeds nicely in centering the ellipse on the screen; however, note that the path and the text are centered only at certain screen sizes. In this code, we attempted to center the text by aiming it a bit to the left of the center of the screen, and we also tried to stretch the text so that its width in pixels remained constant (through the use of *textLength*="*150*" and *lengthAdjust*="*spacingAndGlyphs*"—code currently supported in all browsers except Firefox). However, the path is drawn in absolute coordinates, so the results vary considerably as a function of screen size.

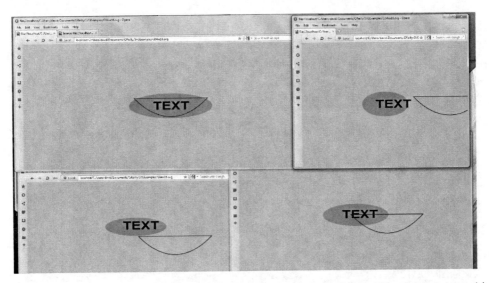

The following example (visible at *http://granite.sru.edu/~ddailey/svg/viewBox1.svg*) provides a way to make sure the text and graphics retain similar relations to one another regardless of the screen's size or aspect ratio:

```
<svg xmlns="http://www.w3.org/2000/svg" width="100%"
  xmlns:xlink="http://www.w3.org/1999/xlink"
  viewBox="0 0 100 100" preserveAspectRatio="none">
<rect width="100" height="100" fill="#acf"/>
<ellipse rx="10" ry="12" cx="50" cy="50" fill="#79f"/>
<text font-size="4" textLength="20" lengthAdjust="spacingAndGlyphs" font-family="arial"
  font-weight="bold" x="40" y="52" >TEXT</text>
<path stroke="#207" stroke-width=".5" d="M 35 46 C 45 60 55 60 65 46 z" fill="none" />
</svg>
```

The primary difference here, other than some of the coordinates having been reworked, is the use of the *viewBox* attribute in the *<svg>* element itself. It works by declaring that all geometric values, including font sizes and path coordinates, will be reworked as relative coordinates—in this case, relative to a rectangle that is 100 units wide and 100 units high. The *preserveAspectRatio* attribute is set to "none" because the horizontal and vertical units would otherwise be set to the same size, meaning that, for example, the *<rect>* would fill only the center of the screen on a typical browser screen that is wider than it is tall. As shown in the next illustration, this allows text, paths, ellipses, and rectangles to retain the same position and size relative to one another.

Clearly, this approach might not be optimal if you are interested in preserving the aspect ratios of things like circles, or preserving the legibility of text, which is often designed for legibility with a fixed aspect ratio. Nevertheless, the advantages of this method give the designer a powerful set of tools.

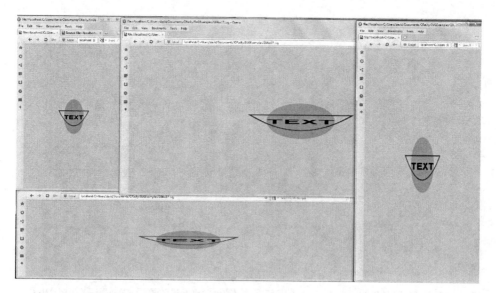

You can see another example of the use of *viewBox* and other scaling methods, which shows how an SVG document can take the place of a PowerPoint-based or HTML-based presentation, at *http://srufaculty.sru.edu/david.dailey/svg/devcon5.svg*. This particular example does not take advantage of the *textLength* attribute, because at the time the example was created, Firefox didn't support that feature.

Messages Between SMIL and Script

In this section we'll discuss two techniques (one a SMIL attribute and one a JavaScript method) that are useful in harnessing the power of both SMIL and JavaScript:

- **beginElement**   This is used for activating SMIL from JavaScript.

- **onend**   This is used for running a JavaScript function upon completion of a SMIL animation.

This section will be rather brief, consisting of two simple examples that illustrate the major principles, followed by a more complex illustration of the principles.

From SMIL to Script

The following code (from an example visible at *http://granite.sru.edu/~ddailey/svg/SMILscript1.svg*) illustrates the typical way of invoking JavaScript from SMIL:

```
<svg xmlns="http://www.w3.org/2000/svg" width="100%"
  xmlns:xlink="http://www.w3.org/1999/xlink" >
  <script><![CDATA[
    xmlns = "http://www.w3.org/2000/svg";
    xlink = "http://www.w3.org/1999/xlink";
  function stuff (evt) {
    O = evt.target.parentNode;
    O.setAttributeNS(null, "fill", "red");
  }
```

```
]]></script>
  <ellipse fill="lightgreen" cx="40" cy="100" rx="22" ry="14" stroke="#804" stroke-width="5">
    <animate attributeName="cx" dur="3s" onend="stuff(evt)" values="40;400;40"/>
  </ellipse>

</svg>
```

It includes an *<animate>* element that terminates after three seconds. When the animation finishes, the *end* event is fired, which activates the function *stuff()*, passing the event as a parameter. The target of the event received by the function is in fact the *<animate>* element itself. Having retrieved the *<animate>* element, you can now use script to enter the DOM and find its parent, the ellipse. That ellipse is then colored red.

You could achieve this functionality quite easily through SMIL alone, using a *<set>* with something like a *begin="idOfTheAnimate.end"* statement. However, this example demonstrates a role that is often very useful in building complex animations.

From Script to SMIL

This example (see *http://granite.sru.edu/~ddailey/svg/SMILscript2.svg*) uses a mouse click on an object to send a parameter to script that identifies which (of possibly many) animations to trigger.

```
<svg xmlns="http://www.w3.org/2000/svg" width="100%"
  xmlns:xlink="http://www.w3.org/1999/xlink" >
<script><![CDATA[
  xmlns = "http://www.w3.org/2000/svg";
  xlink = "http://www.w3.org/1999/xlink";
  function start (id) {
    document.getElementById(id).beginElement();
  }
]]></script>
<ellipse fill="blue" onclick="start('A')" cx="40" cy="140" rx="22" ry="14">
  <animate id="A" attributeName="cx" dur="3s" begin="indefinite" values="40;400;40"/>
</ellipse></svg>
```

The key statement involves *beginElement()*, a method applied to any identified *animate* or *set* object. It is used to trigger the animation itself, namely to instigate the change in attribute values specified by the *animate* or change.

As before, you could achieve the same results quite easily with *<set>* instead of relying upon script. But you might want to use the script technique to select an object at random and vary certain of its attributes before launching its animation.

Next, you'll see a combination of these two methods (SMIL-to-script and script-to-SMIL) that produces a moderately entertaining animation: one in which an object follows a curve and then morphs into a different shape when its flight path is complete. The following example is visible at *http://granite.sru.edu/~ddailey/svg/SMILscript5.svg*.

```
<svg xmlns="http://www.w3.org/2000/svg" width="100%"
  xmlns:xlink="http://www.w3.org/1999/xlink">
<script><![CDATA[
  xmlns = "http://www.w3.org/2000/svg";
  xlink = "http://www.w3.org/1999/xlink";

  function start (evt) {
    var T = evt.target;
    var TP = T.parentNode;
    var rn = Math.floor(Math.random() * 6) + 3;
    var d = "M 40 0 ";
    for (var I = 0; I < 2 * rn - 1; i++) {
      if (i % 2 == 0) d + = "Q ";
      var rx = Math.random() * 100 - 50;
      var ry = Math.random() * 100 - 50;
      d += rx + " " + ry + " ";
    }
    TP.setAttributeNS(null, "d", d + "80 40 z");
    TP.setAttributeNS(null, "fill", Color());
    T.beginElement();
  }
  function Color () {
  // same function used before to create a random color
  }
]]></script>
<path fill = "none" id = "P1" stroke = "black" stroke-width = "1" opacity = "0.5"
  d = "M 325 158 Q 293 107 260.5 166.5 Q 228 226 181.5 256 Q 135 286 227.5 255.5 Q 320 225
  350.5 263 Q 381 301 402 290 Q 423 279 412 234 Q 401 189 448.5 193.5 Q 496 198 523.5 251.5 Q
  551 305 538 192 Q 525 79 460 89 Q 395 99 376 154 Q 357 209 325 158 z"  />
<path id="PQ" fill="blue" stroke="black" stroke-width="2" d="M -50,-50 50,-50 50,50 -50,50 z"
  fill-rule="evenodd" >
  <animateMotion dur="2s" rotate="auto" onend="start(evt)" begin="0;indefinite" fill="freeze">
    <mpath xlink:href="#P1" />
  </animateMotion></path>
</svg>
```

Note the following about this example:

- *begin="0;indefinite"* in *<animateMotion>* allows the animation both to start as soon as the page loads (at time zero) and to be started by script, using the *T.beginElement()* statement.

- The traveling shape (initially a square) is instructed, through *<animateMotion>*, to travel around the path once every two seconds.

- *fill="freeze"* in *<animateMotion>* ensures that the traveling shape remains at the end of the path instead of reverting to its initial position at the end of one cycle. If it didn't, you would see the shape flicker momentarily in the upper-left corner of the screen.

- When a circuit of the path is complete, the *start()* function is invoked.

- A path is constructed at random. An initial start point at (40,0) and an endpoint at (80,40) are provided. The remainder of the points (between three and eight of them) are inserted into the path, with every other point being a quadratic control point. This allows for a relatively interesting set of shapes that combine curvilinear components and sharp edges. Varying the complexity of the shapes by changing the number of points allows for even more variety.

- With some considerable effort, this animation could be done without SMIL, but it could not be done without script. The SMIL handles the automatic rotation as well as the traversal of a fairly complex cubic spline that would be a bit tricky without some fancy footwork, math, and geometry.

Here are some other examples of animations you can explore that combine script with SMIL in various ways:

- *http://srufaculty.sru.edu/david.dailey/svg/newstuff/SMIL7g.svg*   Allows you to start and stop animations with SMIL and script.

- *http://srufaculty.sru.edu/david.dailey/svg/bezierovals.svg*   Displays ellipses on a Bézier curve that add new numbers when the script terminates.

- *http://srufaculty.sru.edu/david.dailey/svg/followPath.svg*   Builds a random path for an *<animateMotion>* element.

- *http://srufaculty.sru.edu/david.dailey/svg/followPath6.svg*   Also builds a random path to be followed through an *<animateMotion>* element, but a wilder version.

- *http://srufaculty.sru.edu/david.dailey/svg/followPath10.svg*   Grows a random path, but gradually. It answers the question of how to animate the drawing of a path.

- *http://srufaculty.sru.edu/david.dailey/svg/svgopen2008/makestars2.svg*   Displays Bézier starflakes calculated with a rather fun bit of modular arithmetic.

- *http://srufaculty.sru.edu/david.dailey/svg/stars3.svg*   Displays falling starflakes with a bit of wind applied. The wind is actually an invisible object that changes the horizontal velocity of things within a certain radius of it.

- *http://srufaculty.sru.edu/david.dailey/svg/swatch3.svg*   Entitled "Starflake expressway," this one moves stars, each clipped by a common clip path along Bézier curves.

Passing Messages Between HTML and SVG

This is not only a large, complex topic, but also a fun one. In this section, we'll provide just the basics to get you started, but if you need to, you can look at "An SVG Primer for Today's Browsers."

Ways of Putting SVG in HTML

There are five ways of putting SVG content in an HTML document: you can use *<embed>*, *<object>*, *<iframe>*, or *<img>*, or you can do it inline (in HTML5). All are acceptable according to the emerging standards for both HTML5 and SVG. The *<img>* method, for various reasons, will not allow script to run, but the others will. Inline support also has, at present, some rather major cross-browser inconsistencies. The *<iframe>* method has, according to our experiments, several cross-browser inconsistencies in accessing the SVG DOM. The *<embed>* method has problems with fallback content for browsers that don't support SVG, and *<object>* has some security problems associated with running script via the Adobe plug-in. Currently, the recommended technique is to use *<object>*, although we will also present an example of inline SVG support because direct interspersing of SVG code inline in HTML is the current trend.

The Other Way Around: Putting HTML in SVG

For HTML-centric people, it is natural to think of putting SVG in HTML. On the other hand, the concept of communication encompassed by HTML is perhaps neither as adaptable nor as broad as that of SVG, so in fairness, it is appropriate to mention that one can go the other way around, and use *<foreignObject>* from within SVG to embed HTML. This has the advantage that the powerful filters, masks, clipping paths, and animation of SVG can be brought to bear upon the stodgier and text-heavy HTML. Fortunately, most browsers have at least partial implementations of *<foreignObject>*, as the example at *http://srufaculty.sru.edu/david.dailey/svg/foreignObject.svg* (which runs in Opera, Firefox, Chrome, and Safari) demonstrates. This example loads an HTML document into SVG using *<foreignObject>* and then rotates it. The links on the page work, text remains selectable, and the HTML scroll bars still work. Some authors have gone so far as to use SVG filters (discussed in the next chapter) to restyle color themes of HTML documents in a way that may aid their legibility for people with certain kinds of color blindness.

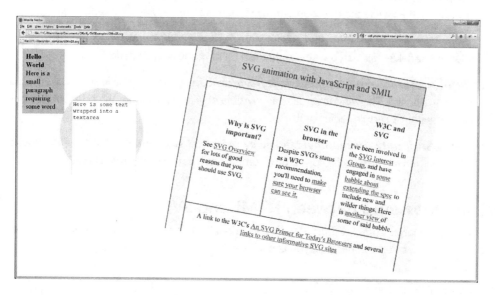

Using <object> to Embed SVG in HTML

Let's get started with something that works pretty much everywhere—a sort of simplest case (visible at *http://granite.sru.edu/~ddailey/svg/simplestSVG.html*):

```
<!doctype html>
<html>
<body>
   <object type="image/svg+xml" data="simplest.svg">
   <!-- fall-back HTML content goes here -->
      <p>Sorry! Your browser does not support SVG!
      Please use a modern browser.</p>
   </object>
</body>
</html>
```

It's important to note three things:

- As of this writing, the HTML5 doctype statement *<!doctype html>* is needed for Internet Explorer 9 to switch out of quirks mode so it can see the SVG in HTML.

- If you're using the Adobe plug-in with older versions of Internet Explorer, you should use *<embed>* instead of *<object>*—this works across all modern browsers, but does not have the advantage of supporting a statement to address browsers that don't support SVG. Alternatively, you could use the advice at *w* to use *<param>* inside *<object>* to address those idiosyncrasies.

- Inside the *<object>* tag, you can include a more extensive message that instructs the visitor about which version of their own software would support SVG, or suggest alternative workarounds (such as getting the Adobe plug-in for older versions of Internet Explorer).

getSVGDocument()

Here's a slightly more complex example (visible at *http://granite.sru.edu/~ddailey/svg/peruse.html*) that allows one, from HTML, to interrogate properties about an embedded SVG document. You do this by using the method *getSVGDocument()* in association with the *<object>*, *<embed>*, or *<iframe>* HTML object.

```
<!doctype html>
<html>

<script>
  function peruse () {
    var D = document.getElementById("O");
    var SVGDoc = D.getSVGDocument();
    var SVGRoot = SVGDoc.documentElement;
    var who = SVGRoot.firstChild.nextSibling;
    var whoName = "<" + who.nodeName;
    var whoHow = who.attributes.item(0);
    var whoNow = whoHow.nodeName;
    var whoWhat = whoHow.nodeValue + ">";
    alert(whoName + " " + whoNow + "=" + whoWhat);
  }
</script>
```

```
<body>
<button onclick="peruse()">open</button><br>
<object id="0" type="image/svg+xml" data="simplest.svg">
   <p>Sorry! Your browser does not support SVG!
   Please use a modern browser.</p>
</object></body>
</html>
```

The SVG itself is the simple example shown in Chapter 1, "SVG Basics":

```
<svg xmlns="http://www.w3.org/2000/svg">
   <circle r="50"/>
</svg>
```

Three key concepts are important here:

- The *<object>* tag has been given an *id*, which is used so that the tag and the SVG DOM within it can be retrieved from the HTML DOM using *getElementById()*.

- The method *getSVGDocument()* retrieves the SVG document itself. If you were to insert the statement *alert(SVGDoc.nodeName)* just after defining *SVGDoc*, you'd see that the *nodeName* would be *#document*.

- *SVGDoc.documentElement()* retrieves the SVG DOM itself. An inserted *alert(SVGRoot.node Name)* would reveal *svg*, and it is from there that you can traverse the node hierarchy of the SVG document.

You can see similar examples using *<iframe>* and *<embed>* instead of *<object>* at *http://srufaculty .sru.edu/david.dailey/W3CCourse/week4/SVGinHTML.html*.

Now let's extend the concepts here just a bit. In the example shown below (and visible at *http:// granite.sru.edu/~ddailey/svg/wordsput.html*), an HTML table contains a group of words. Any word, when clicked, creates a new SVG text node containing that word, positioned at some random location within the SVG document.

```
<!doctype HTML>
<HTML><head>
<style>
   div.u{float:top;  height:30%}
   div.d{float:bottom; height:70%}
   td{text-align:center;font-family:impact;width:15%;background:#eee}
</style>
<script>
function init () {
   var Ds = document.getElementsByTagName("td");
   for (var i in Ds) Ds[i].onclick = function () {add(this);};
   var D = document.getElementById("E");
   SVGDoc = D.getSVGDocument();
   SVGRoot = SVGDoc.documentElement;
   svgns = "http://www.w3.org/2000/svg";
}
```

```
function add (o) {
  var word = o.firstChild.nodeValue;
  var T = SVGDoc.createElementNS(svgns, "text");
  var MsgNode = SVGDoc.createTextNode(word);
  var fontratio = 0.05;
  var adj = (1 - fontratio);
  x = Math.random() * .9 - 2 * fontratio;
  y = Math.random() * .5;
  T.setAttributeNS(null, "x", x);
  T.setAttributeNS(null, "y", y);
  T.setAttributeNS(null, "font-size", fontratio);
  T.setAttributeNS(null, "font-family", "serif");
  T.appendChild(MsgNode);
  SVGRoot.appendChild(T);
}

</script></head>
<body>
<div align="center" class="u">
<table border=1>
  <tr><td>artichoke</td><td>balustrade</td>
    <td>cantaloupe</td><td>dandelion</td></tr>
  <tr><td>elephant</td><td>familiar</td>
    <td>groundhog</td><td>Hydrophlorone</td></tr>
</table>
Click on any word above
</div><hr>
<div class="d">
<object onload="init()" id="E" type="image/svg+xml" data="simplerect.svg" height="100%"
  width="100%">
<p>Message for browsers that don't support SVG</p>
</object>
</div>
</body></html>
```

The SVG itself is quite a simple document (to begin with):

```
<svg xmlns="http://www.w3.org/2000/svg" viewBox="0 0 1 1" preserveAspectRatio="none">
  <rect x="0" y="0" width="100%" height="100%" fill="#ddd"/>
</svg>
```

Note the following about this example:

- Each table cell, when clicked, sends itself (an object) as a parameter to the function *add()*.

- *add()* receives the table cell, determines what text is inside it, and then builds an SVG text node whose content is equal to the table cell's content.

- The new SVG node is inserted into the SVG DOM at a random location (taking into account the size of the screen and the size of the font employed).

One more example (visible at *http://granite.sru.edu/~ddailey/svg/wordsput2.html*) demonstrates a round trip from HTML to SVG and back. Here's some new material from the script in HTML:

```
function respond (evt) {
  var w = evt.target.firstChild.nodeValue;
  document.getElementById(w).style.background = "red";
}
```

The SVG document used is the following:

```
<svg xmlns="http://www.w3.org/2000/svg" viewBox="0 0 1 1" preserveAspectRatio="none"
  onload="init()">
<script><![CDATA[
  function init () {
    Root = document.documentElement;
    Root.addEventListener("click", top.respond, false);
}
]]></script>
<rect x="0" y="0" width="100%" height="100%" fill="#ddd"/>
</svg>
```

Note the following about this example:

- This example makes a minor change to the SVG from the previous example—it adds an *init()* function that runs when the document loads. This function makes each object responsive to the mouse click.

- The clicked object triggers a function in *top*—namely, the HTML container. If the SVG is not inside a container of some sort, then clicking the object will throw an exception. (Please realize that this code has been kept simple to illustrate the more important issues.)

- The *addEventListener()* method is used to assign the event to the objects in the SVG DOM. *Root.setAttribute("onclick", "top.respond")* would have done the same job.

- In the HTML, this time, instead of just adding an event handler to each *<td>* of the table, we also give each one an *id* equal to the text inside it. This allows the text in SVG to be able to find its parent.

- The click event inside the SVG document sends the event back to HTML, where the properties of the object that instigated the event are then examined and used to relate back to the object of that name in HTML. Specifically, the SVG text will correspond to an item in HTML. The button that originally led to the development of a node is thus identified.

- Experienced programmers will recognize that there are many other ways to accomplish the same thing. However, this example provides a crucial illustration of how to access scripts in HTML from events and scripts in SVG.

You can see an example (*http://granite.sru.edu/~ddailey/wordtable.html*) that starts with the above code but mixes it with some simple AJAX-like round-tripping to the server to retrieve definitions dynamically from a dictionary. The example then lets users click the retrieved words as well. This example is a little too complex to describe here, but the server-side script is the very simple PHP script shown below (in case you're interested in actually examining how the code for the example actually works):

```
<?
$num = 10;
$f = "/homes/ddailey/public_html/data/wordstudy/webster1913/ubest";
$o = file($f);
$c = count($o);
for ($i = 0; $i < $num; $i++) {
  $r = rand(0, $c-1);
  echo $o[$r];
  $l = $o[$r][0];
  echo "<br>";
}
?>
```

SVG Inline in HTML5

The still-evolving HTML5 standard has a requirement to maintain close integration between HTML and SVG. This means several things, but among the most important is that HTML allows the direct insertion of SVG code into HTML, interleaved, as it were, among HTML tags, inline. The inline model is not yet implemented consistently across browsers. There is ongoing discussion about ways that HTML and SVG might share animation, filters, and fonts, and possibly even coexist within the same namespace. However, it will be a few years before these decisions are finalized and broadly implemented by browsers. What follows are a couple of examples that seem to work fairly consistently even at present. In the following example (visible at *http://granite.sru.edu/~ddailey/svg/htmlsvg.htm*), clicking either a button in HTML or a circle in SVG changes an attribute of its counterpart in the other environment.

```
<!DOCTYPE HTML>
<html>
<script>
  function f () {
    document.getElementById("C").setAttributeNS(null, "fill", "orange");
  }
  function g () {
    document.getElementById("I").setAttribute("value","hello");
  }
</script>

<body>
```

```
Here is standard HTML, complete with the HTML5 doctype
<br>Following is some SVG:<br>
<svg width="300" height="250" xmlns="http://www.w3.org/2000/svg">
  <circle id="C" cx="100" cy="50" r="40" stroke="black" stroke-width="2"
    fill="lightgreen" onclick="g()"/>
  <text x="65" y="54" font-size="16" font-family="arial" pointer-events="none">
  click here</text>
</svg>


Later we revert to HTML and include a button:
<input id="I" type="button" onclick="f()" value="click here">
<br>The button and the circle can speak to one another.
</body>
</html>
```

In the next example (visible at *http://granite.sru.edu/~ddailey/svg/svginHTML.html*), an example previously used to demonstrate the simplest principles of scripting SVG is folded into a simple HTML container to show how the combined DOMs can actually work to your advantage.

```
<!DOCTYPE HTML>
<html>
<script>
function startup () {
  S = document.getElementById("SVG");
  for (i in S.childNodes) S.childNodes[i].onclick = removeIt;
}
xmlns = "http://www.w3.org/2000/svg";
xlink = "http://www.w3.org/1999/xlink";

function removeIt (e) {
  T = e.target;
  if (T.nodeName == "rect") add(e.clientX, e.clientY);
  else T.parentNode.removeChild(T);
}
function add (x,y) {
  var C = document.createElementNS(xmlns, "circle");
  C.setAttributeNS(null, "r", 50);
  C.setAttributeNS(null, "cx", x);
  C.setAttributeNS(null, "cy", y);
  C.onclick = removeIt;
  S.appendChild(C);
}
</script>
<p onclick="removeIt()">Hello there!</p>
<svg xmlns="http://www.w3.org/2000/svg" width="100%" xmlns:xlink=http://www.w3.org/1999/xlink
  id="SVG" onload="startup()">
  <rect width="100%" height="100%" fill="white" />
  <circle r="50" />
  <text font-size="12" x="50" y="20" onclick="removeIt()">Click something to remove it</text>
  <text font-size="12" x="50" y="80">Click nothing to add something</text>
</svg>
</html>
```

Summary

The opportunities for making SVG come alive with motion and interactivity are rich and multifaceted. In SMIL, the nonprogrammer has available a delightfully expressive vocabulary that allows almost any collection of attributes to be animated with minimal code and conceptual ease. And for the programmer, or even the novice, DOM methods allow you to use JavaScript to build sophisticated interfaces. The only limitations are, in the case of SMIL, the fact that implementations are still catching up with the standard, and in the case of script, the complexity of code. In Chapters 6 and 7, you will see ways of coming to terms with some of the issues related to code complexity.

CHAPTER 5

SVG Filters

The texture of experience is prior to everything else.

Willem De Kooning, 1948

The topic of filters is a complex one. There are many kinds of filters of varying complexity. You can chain filters together in rather complex ways, storing intermediate results in temporary locations, and then combine those temporary results together using a variety of methods of blending and composition. Rather than thinking of single filters, or even chains of filters, think of a flowchart of filters hooked together in a network.

As in Adobe Photoshop, where you can overlay different layers while applying different filters to each, and then extract color channels from those layers and calculate differences between the resulting layers, you can do such work in SVG. The difference is that in SVG you can do it programmatically and dynamically on a web page through script or animation.

Another important thing to realize is that as some of the wonderful things developed within SVG start to propagate outward, the proponents of HTML5 are beginning to recognize just how wonderful SVG is, and have begun to borrow, carte blanche, many of the good ideas, including gradients, clip paths, client-side graphics (e.g., using the *<canvas>* element), animation, fonts, and filters. In some cases, this works relatively painlessly, and in other cases (such as with web fonts and animation), it is not so clear whether the architectural crispness of SVG will be preserved, nor, indeed, whether its expressive power will be preserved. So, while HTML5 and CSS3 are still in flux, it is premature to say quite how this will all work out; but suffice it to say that learning about filters within SVG should

145

create neural pathways that will have some probability of enduring even after the conceptual framework has been altered. It is clear that the elusive boundaries between semantics and presentation, once so touted as crucial to all human intellect, have now been a bit fuzzified by this new zeal to bring the glitz of SVG (sans, perhaps, its elegance) into both sides of the text-and-graphics dialectic.

The Basic <filter> Element

A *<filter>* is applied to another object much as a clip path or gradient is applied—namely, through an attribute defined within the object to which the filter will be applied. The attribute looks something like this: *filter="url(#filtername)"*. The *<filter>* element itself must have one or more filter primitives inside it; those primitive operations will be conducted in the order they are defined, from top to bottom.

Here's an example of the syntax of the *<filter>* element:

```
<filter id="F">

  <anyParticularPrimitive1>
  <anyParticularPrimitive2>
  ...
  <anyParticularPrimitiveN>
</filter>
<anyParticularSVGObjectOrGroup filter="url(#F)"/>
```

The chapter begins with some examples using the simplest of the filter primitives, *<feColorMatrix>* and *<feGaussianBlur>*, to give an illustration of the sorts of things you can accomplish.

> **Note** As of this writing, cross-browser support for filters is not complete, but is improving dramatically. To properly view the most complex of these examples, you will need either Opera or the Adobe ASV plug-in for Internet Explorer. Internet Explorer 9, Microsoft's first release with native SVG support, did not yet support filters, but Internet Explorer 10 does.

The Basic Primitives

In the SVG specification, the discussion on filter primitives (at *http://www.w3.org/TR/SVG/filters.html*) lists 16 different filter primitives ordered alphabetically. Since the topic is a complex one, this book will attempt to bring a bit more organization to the subject, though clearly the specification provides considerably more detail (but fewer examples).

The treatment begins with those primitives that blur, distort, or change the colors of relatively simple content to which the filter is applied.

\<feGaussianBlur>

Perhaps the simplest of the SVG filter primitives is the *\<feGaussianBlur>*, which, stated simply, allows you to blur an image. This treatment is adapted from the W3C's primer, simply because I think it is the best way to open the topic of SVG filters.

The parameter associated with *\<feGaussianBlur>* is the standard deviation (*stdDeviation*). It controls the distance from which neighboring pixels will be allowed to influence a given pixel, and hence the amount of blurring. First, you set up a filter with an *\<feGaussianBlur>* inside:

```
<filter id="A">
  <feGaussianBlur stdDeviation="1" />
</filter>
```

Then you apply the filter to the element to be blurred:

```
<rect x="42%" y="10%" width="16%" height="25%" fill="white"
  filter="url(#A)"/>
```

The following shows the effect of increasing the value of *stdDeviation* on two different images on a black background:

```
<filter id="A"><feGaussianBlur stdDeviation=S/></filter>
<rect x="42%" y="10%" width="16%" height="25%" filter="url(#A)" fill="white"/>
```

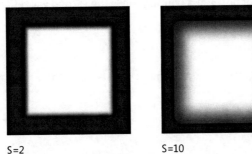 

S=2   S=10   S=25

```
<image x="42%" y="10%" width="16%" height="25%" filter="url(#A)" xlink:href="p0.jpg"/>
```

S=2   S=10   S=25

Notice that the blurred object expands beyond its original bounds and that values outside its boundary are considered to be transparent so that any background present (in this case, monochromatic black) will be visible inside the edges of the image itself. To restrict the image so that it does not bleed beyond its boundaries, you can either set the *x*, *y*, *height*, and *width* attributes of the filter itself (the easiest way), or use another filter primitive, *<feOffset>* (discussed later in this chapter).

The following is an example of restricting the extent of a filter to the size of the source image:

Restricted to Size of Source Image

Unrestricted to Size of Source Image

```
<filter id="B" x="0%" y="0%" width="100%"
    height="100%">
    <feGaussianBlur stdDeviation="25"/>
</filter>
```

```
<filter id="A">
    <feGaussianBlur stdDeviation="25"/>
</filter>
```

It is also worth noting that if *<feGaussianBlur>* takes two parameters, rather than one, for its *stdDeviation* attribute, then the first will represent horizontal blurring, while the second will represent vertical blurring. The statement

```
<feGaussianBlur id="fGB" stdDeviation="25, 0" />
```

will blur the object only horizontally in ways that, for a monochromatic rectangle, might resemble a linear gradient with three equidistant stops.

At *http://granite.sru.edu/~ddailey/svg/directionalBlur.svg*, you can see an example in which the blurring happens either horizontally or vertically, as illustrated here:

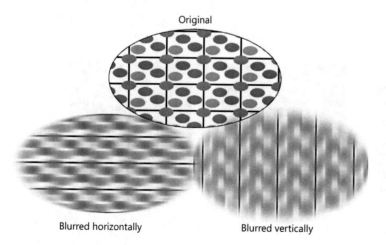

Original

Blurred horizontally

Blurred vertically

You can see a version that animates the blurring at *http://granite.sru.edu/~ddailey/svg/directionalBlurA.svg*.

<feColorMatrix>

The *<feColorMatrix>* filter primitive allows you to reconfigure the colors of an image. In the simplest case, you can use it to desaturate an image—that is, turn it from color to grayscale.

In the following example (also at *http://granite.sru.edu/~ddailey/svg/filter1.svg*), an unfiltered bit-mapped image is displayed next to a filtered version of the same image:

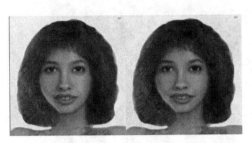

```
<filter id="F">
  <feColorMatrix type="saturate" values="0" />
</filter>

<image id="I" x="0" y="0" width="200" height="200"
  preserveAspectRatio="none" xlink:href="p17.jpg" />

<use xlink:href="#I" filter="url(#F)" transform="translate(200,0)" />
```

The filter consists of an *<feColorMatrix>* operation. Like a gradient, pattern, clip path, or mask, a filter is later applied to another SVG element—in this case a *<use>*—so that we can see what the object looks like before and after applying the filter. In this particular case, the image is desaturated so that it is, in effect, converted to a grayscale image. Note that animating the *values* attribute of this example is quite easy to do and is shown at *http://granite.sru.edu/~ddailey/svg/filter1a.svg*.

Currently in SVG1.1, the range of values is from 0 to 1, but it appears as though SVG will allow a broader range of values in the future (as in *http://granite.sru.edu/~ddailey/svg/filter1b.svg* and discussed at *http://lists.w3.org/Archives/Public/www-svg/2011Sep/0093.html*).

Observe that with just a tiny bit of play (reusing and reflecting the filtered and unfiltered image below the originals, within a pattern), you can achieve interesting effects using only one bitmapped image and a very small amount of code, as shown at *http://granite.sru.edu/~ddailey/svg/filter3.svg*:

```
<filter id="F">
  <feColorMatrix type="saturate"  values="0" />
</filter>
<pattern id="Pix" patternUnits="userSpaceOnUse" width="200" height="200" >
  <g id="g" transform="scale(.5)">
    <image x="0" y="0" width="200" height="200" preserveAspectRatio="none"
      xlink:href="p17.jpg" />
```

```
  <image x="200" y="0" width="200" height="200" preserveAspectRatio="none"
    xlink:href="p17.jpg" filter="url(#F)"/>
  </g>
  <use xlink:href="#g" transform=" translate(200,100) scale(-1,1)"/>
</pattern>
<rect x="0" y="0" width="100%" height="100%" fill="url(#Pix)" />
```

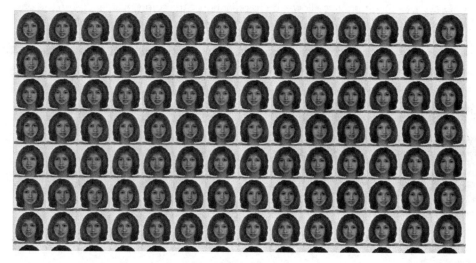

You can also use *<feColorMatrix>* to rotate the color values (through the circular scale that is the rainbow of hues) using *hueRotate*, as shown at *http://granite.sru.edu/~ddailey/svg/filter1f.svg*:

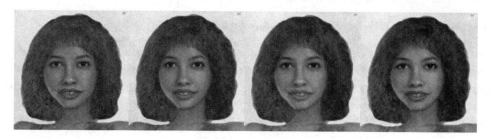

```
<filter id="F">
  <feColorMatrix type="hueRotate" values="90" />
</filter>
<filter id="G">
  <feColorMatrix type="hueRotate" values="180" />
</filter>
<filter id="H">
  <feColorMatrix type="hueRotate" values="270" />
</filter>
<image id="I" x="0" y="0" width="200" height="200" preserveAspectRatio="none"
  xlink:href="p17.jpg" />
<use xlink:href="#I" filter="url(#F)" transform="translate(200,0)" />
<use xlink:href="#I" filter="url(#G)" transform="translate(400,0)" />
<use xlink:href="#I" filter="url(#H)" transform="translate(600,0)" />
```

You can see a bit of further play with *hueRotate* at *http://granite.sru.edu/~ddailey/svg/filter1g.svg*, which, like the above example, uses *<pattern>*, but also uses animation to create an effect that plays a bit with the distribution of rods and cones in the retina to produce an interesting illusion. You can see another example that animates the rotation of the colors in a pattern at *http://cs.sru.edu/~ddailey/svg/feColorMatrixPattern.svg*.

In the illustration above, note how the color contrast between the lips and the skin does not seem to bear up so well under hue rotation; this is because the chromas are ultimately very similar. At the end of this section, we'll briefly discuss how to exaggerate color contrasts under rotation.

The *<feColorMatrix>* filter primitive is quite a bit more powerful, as the example shown below (and at *http://cs.sru.edu/~ddailey/svg/feColorMatrix.svg*) should indicate.

Without going into detail about the entire collection of effects, there are six bitmapped images (faces) atop three colored stripes. The first image, at left, is unfiltered. Each of the others has a filter somewhat like that of the third:

```
<filter id="inv">
  <feColorMatrix type="matrix"
    values="1  0  0 0 0
            0 -1  0 0 0
            0  0 -1 0 0
            1  1  1 0 0"
  >
  </feColorMatrix>
</filte
```

What this does is take each of the four color channels, treated as rows of the matrix—red, green, blue, and alpha (opacity)—and compose it out of color values of the other three channels. In this case, the red channel is kept unchanged:

Red = 1 * Red + 0 * G + 0 * B + 0 * A

The green and blue channels are, however, inverted, with their new color values being set equal to the inverse of their values. Finally, the alpha channel is contributed to positively by red, green, and blue values:

Alpha = 1 * Red + 1 * G + 1 * B

This has the effect that bright pixels (high on all three channels) are kept opaque, while dark pixels (low on all three channels) are converted to transparent. The last column of the matrix represents a constant used to adjust brightness on a channel, typically to scale the values so that the result is in the range from 0 to 1, though that is not strictly required.

In the above example, note that the final filter used is actually animated, demonstrating that two multivalued attributes, like matrices, can themselves be interpolated using *<animate>*.

Filter Chaining with <feColorMatrix>

We'll introduce one more topic before moving to the next filter primitive: the idea of chaining filter effects.

Above, one of our *<feColorMatrix>* filters succeeded in oversaturating an image. Note that in the example of *hueRotate*, the color values of the image were sufficiently similar such that when the hues of an image were rotated along the rainbow, the bluish image became uniformly bluish. You can adjust this by sending the results of one filter primitive to another. Consider this code:

```
<filter id="F">
  <feColorMatrix type="matrix"
    values=" 3 -1 -1 0 0
            -1  3 -1 0 0
            -1 -1  3 0 0
             0  0  0 1 0"
  />
  <feColorMatrix type="hueRotate" values="30" />
</filter>
```

In this filter, we have chained two different *<feColorMatrix>* effects. The result is that we first supersaturate the image and then rotate the color 30 degrees (toward yellow from red).

This is illustrated in the fourth illustration from the left in the following image (shown also at *http://cs.sru.edu/~ddailey/svg/filter1f3.svg*):

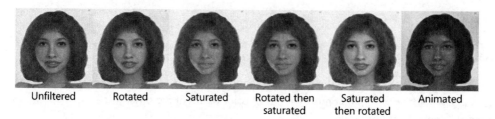

| Unfiltered | Rotated | Saturated | Rotated then saturated | Saturated then rotated | Animated |

It is noteworthy that the order of application of filters is significant. In this case, oversaturating before rotating the hue results in a ceiling effect on the red channel. Many pixels are shifted toward their highest possible red values. By rotating first and then saturating (see the fifth illustration from the left in the above image), you can better preserve the hue differential between lips and skin. This ability to chain filter effects together affords you a great deal of power in how you can combine the various effects.

You can see another comparison between the ordering of filter effects at *http://granite.sru .edu/~ddailey/svg/feColorMatrixBlur.svg*, at which we contrast the effects of first blurring and then applying *hueRotate* in the reverse order:

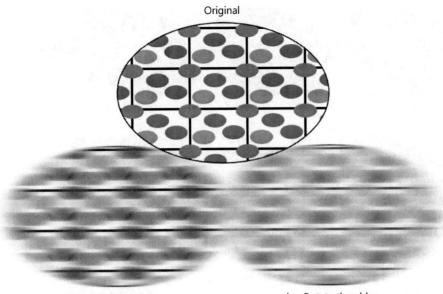

Original

Blur then hueRotate   hueRotate then blur

\<feComponentTransfer\>

While *\<feColorMatrix\>* allows remapping between color channels, you can achieve more precise control of remapping within an individual color channel by using *\<feComponentTransfer\>*. The *\<feComponentTransfer\>* primitive allows the independent redefinition of each of the four color channels R, G, B, and A. It allows the adjustment of brightness and contrast through the application of any of a variety of different functions to any or all channels of an image. The types of adjustment allowed include *identity*, *table*, *discrete*, *linear*, and *gamma*. *discrete* can be used to posterize an image (i.e., to reduce it to fewer color values). *linear* is used for simple brightening and darkening, contrast adjustment, or even inversion, while *table* can be used to remap a color's histogram—like *discrete*, only continuously. It is a powerful filter and can motivate a much deeper treatment than this chapter allows, but we'll consider some of its expressive range with some examples.

One of the most common uses of this filter primitive is likely to be posterization, or discretizing an otherwise smooth color-density function. The effect, also known as *color quantization*, results in the use of fewer overall colors in an image, generally with sharp boundaries between areas where one color is dominant.

Here's how it works. Shown in the next figure (and at *http://granite.sru.edu/~ddailey/svg/feComponentTransfer.svg*) is the effect of simply posterizing an image. The unfiltered image is at top left, and the posterized one is immediately to the right.

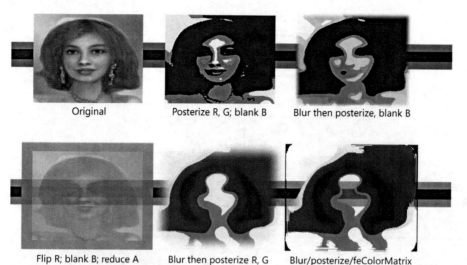

| Original | Posterize R, G; blank B | Blur then posterize, blank B |
| Flip R; blank B; reduce A | Blur then posterize R, G | Blur/posterize/feColorMatrix |

The filter applied to the second image looks like this:

```
<filter id="G">
  <feComponentTransfer>
    <feFuncR type="discrete" tableValues="0 .5 1"/>
    <feFuncG type="discrete" tableValues="0 1"/>
    <feFuncB type="discrete" tableValues="0"/>
  </feComponentTransfer>
</filter>
```

What it does is remap the red channel of the image so that the new image has only three values of red: 0, 127, and 255. All values that are closer to 127 get rounded to 127, with other values getting rounded either upward to 255 or downward to 0. The green channel is quantized to exactly two values, 255 and 0, and the blue channel is completely blackened (or blanked).

The third image is first blurred (reducing some of the discontinuities along the edge, effectively smoothing the effect of pixels that are different from their surroundings) prior to posterization. The green channel is given three values instead of two (to give it slightly more discriminant power), and the red is shifted higher a bit to increase subtleties in the lower range. This is done by dividing the range from 0 to 255 into four class intervals and rounding anything from 0 to 65 to 0, from 66 to 127 to 127, and from 127 to 255 to 255, resulting in a net reddening of the image. That is, using the following code, this option maps the red values in the interval [0,1] to one of the three values as follows:

(0 to .25) → 0; (.25 to .50) → .5; (.50 to .75 and .75 to 1.0) → 1

```
<filter id="H">
  <feGaussianBlur stdDeviation="3" />
  <feComponentTransfer>
    <feFuncR type="discrete" tableValues="0 .5 1 1"/>
    <feFuncG type="discrete" tableValues="0 .5 1"/>
    <feFuncB type="discrete" tableValues="0"/>
  </feComponentTransfer>
</filter>
```

That is, you can use *<feComponentTransfer>* to do a bit of manual equalization.

The bottom-left image uses a fairly simple set of transforms:

```
<filter id="F">
  <feComponentTransfer>
    <feFuncR type="table" tableValues="1 0 0"/>
    <feFuncB type="table" tableValues="0"/>
    <feFuncA type="table" tableValues=".75"/>
  </feComponentTransfer>
</filter>
```

It effectively inverts the red channel, mapping two-thirds of the red values to dark and the darkest one-third (on that channel) to bright. The green channel is left unaffected, and the blue channel (barely present in the original image to begin with) is completely suppressed (darkened). On the other hand, all alpha values (which are 1.0 to begin with, since this is an opaque image) are made slightly transparent by mapping alpha to 0.75.

The other two images, the source code of which you can examine at the web page, do a bit more play with the *discrete* attribute, with the last image additionally using *<feColorMatrix>* to recast just some of the pixels (the most yellow ones) to transparent. This ability to selectively turn certain pixels transparent is not something that *<feComponentTransfer>* has on its own, since it only works with one channel at a time. Used in conjunction with *<feColorMatrix>*, though, you can produce some quite interesting results.

Other attributes of *<feComponentTransfer>* include *identity*, *table*, *linear*, and *gamma*. *identity* appears to be the null filter, leaving its channel untouched; *gamma* adjusts the curvilinearity of a channel; *table* allows remapping of specific color values (as in an already discretized color distribution); *linear* is worth a bit of further mention.

Just as the *discrete* value establishes thresholds where the boundaries between a quantized channel's values map one direction or another, *linear* allows you to vary the slope of the function that transforms original pixels to new ones on a selected channel.

You can use this to actually invert an image (by turning each of its color channels upside down), as shown here (and at *http://granite.sru.edu/~ddailey/svg/feComponentTransfer3.svg*):

Using feComponentTransfer to form the photographic negative

The code to do this employs one new wrinkle: a slight change in color space from the default RGB color space used in SVG to sRGB (see *http://en.wikipedia.org/wiki/SRGB*). This alternative color space adjusts the gamma setting in a fairly fancy manner that maps more similarly across both printers and monitors. The code used looks like this:

```
<filter id="J" color-interpolation-filters="sRGB">
  <feComponentTransfer>
    <feFuncR type="linear" slope="-1" intercept="1" />
    <feFuncG type="linear" slope="-1" intercept="1" />
    <feFuncB type="linear" slope="-1" intercept="1" />
  </feComponentTransfer>
</filter>
```

As you can see, we merely plot a line from (0,1) to (1,0) instead of the usual (0,0) to (1,1), hence inverting the values on each channel.

While the resultant image may not be exactly equal to the photographic negative, I performed the following test: The two images were taken into Adobe Photoshop. The image on the left was pasted atop the one on the right, with a 50% opacity applied to the pasted layer. The result was an apparently monochromatic gray region (at least to the eye). Upon equalization of the area, subtleties of the difference appeared, but these were probably just artifacts of the browser's processing. In other words, the result is visually indistinguishable from a photographic negative!

When *type* equals *"table"*, it is similar to *discrete*, except that instead of clamping the values in the class interval to the specified value, it linearly interpolates the values in adjacent class intervals; so, instead of discretizing, *table* creates piecewise linear transformations such as sawtooth functions.

You can see the contrast between *type="discrete"* and *type="table"* in the following example (shown at *http://cs.sru.edu/~ddailey/svg/feComponentTable.svg*), in which a sawtooth function is applied either discretely or piecewise linearly on the blue channel.

Comparing fecomponentTransfer: Discrete and Table

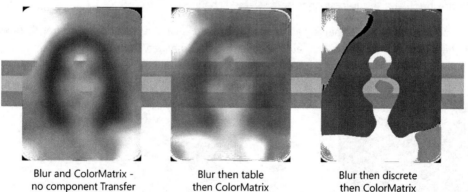

| Blur and ColorMatrix - | Blur then table | Blur then discrete |
| no component Transfer | then ColorMatrix | then ColorMatrix |

Here's a final example illustrating some of the richness of *<feComponentTransfer>* (here used with support from *<feGaussianBlur>* and *<feColorMatrix>*): *http://granite.sru.edu/~ddailey/svg/feComponentTransfer2.svg*.

It begins with an *<feGaussianBlur>* (animated on *stddeviation*) to vary the granularity of the edges. It uses a *discrete* function to quantize the dominant channel, red. Next, it uses a linear adjustment to animate both the blue and green channels. Finally, it uses an *<feColorMatrix>* to convert bright pixels to transparent ones. Since the slope of the functions on blue and green is oscillating (at different frequencies), it means that which pixels are transparent changes with time. Several screen shots are shown here:

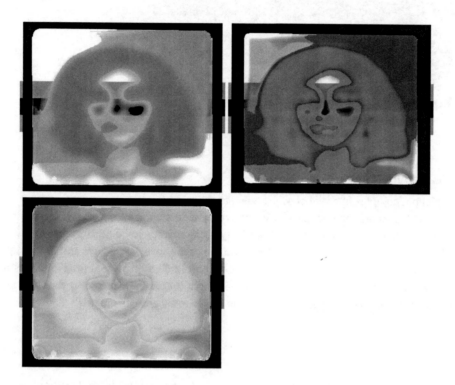

\<feMorphology\>

<feMorphology> is typically used as a part of the alpha channel of an image to thin or thicken an image. The W3C gives an example in which a boldface font is made thinner though the use of an *<feMorphology>* filter. See *http://en.wikipedia.org/wiki/Dilation_%28morphology%29* for a discussion of the mathematics of this filter effect.

In the example at *http://srufaculty.sru.edu/david.dailey/svg/feMorphologyDilate.svg*, you can see the effects of animating the two possible types of *<feMorphology>*: *dilate* and *erode*. When applied to an area having some transparency in it, it can either expand (dilate) or shrink (erode) the affected region.

The example at *http://cs.sru.edu/~ddailey/svg//feMorphology.svg* begins by using *<feComponentTransfer>* and *<feColorMatrix>* to convert a part of the image (the exaggerated green pixels) to transparent. The dilation morphology is then animated to slowly expand the transparent region, displacing other pixel values in its wake.

Animating feComponentTransfer with
Blur and ColorMatrix

<feConvolveMatrix>

This is a powerful but complex filter effect, well known to those in scientific image processing, since it is often used for sharpening images, or for boundary detection. It allows what is known as a *convolution filter*. To use it, you define a square matrix (typically $n×n$ for some odd number n) in which the center cell of the matrix refers to the pixel itself; and the cells above, left, below, and to the right of it within the matrix refer to the pixels above, left, below, and to the right of that pixel in the source image. The numeric coefficients in the matrix define the weight that each neighboring pixel will have in the calculation of the new color value of that pixel. In the simplest case, the matrix

```
0 0 0
0 1 0
0 0 0
```

leaves any image unaffected, since the new value of a pixel will be equal to 1 times its current value plus the sum of 0 times the values of its eight nearest neighbors (those immediately north, northeast, east, southeast, south, southwest, west, and northwest of it). That is, each pixel remains unaffected by its neighbors.

In a slightly different convolution, though, you can sharpen an image by letting each pixel be negatively influenced by its eight neighbors but still retain its own identity:

```
<feConvolveMatrix order="3"

    kernelMatrix=
    " -1 -1 -1
      -1  9 -1
      -1 -1 -1
    " />
```

Note that the sum of the coefficients is 1, meaning, generally, that the overall brightness values of the result (in each channel) will be roughly the same as the original. In general, you want to prevent the sum of the coefficients from being 0.

This effect is shown here and in the middle of the page at *http://cs.sru.edu/~ddailey/svg/feConvolveMatrix.svg*:

Some effects using feConvolveMatrix

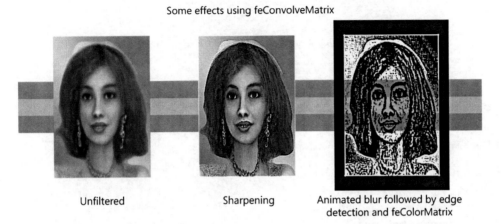

| Unfiltered | Sharpening | Animated blur followed by edge detection and feColorMatrix |

You can see a pleasant set of convolution filters at the Open GL website, at *http://www.opengl.org/resources/code/samples/advanced/advanced97/notes/node152.html*, should you wish to experiment further. In the meantime, here's another example that may help to explain how they work.

To accomplish an effect somewhat like vertical blurring, you can use a filter such as follows. In it, each pixel is enhanced if it is similar to the pixels in its same vertical "stripe," but also sharpens a bit if it differs from pixels further to its left or right.

```
<filter id="G">
<feConvolveMatrix order="7"
kernelMatrix="

  -1 0 0 2 0 0 -1
  -1 0 0 2 0 0 -1
  -1 0 0 2 0 0 -1
  -1 0 0 3 0 0 -1
  -1 0 0 2 0 0 -1
  -1 0 0 2 0 0 -1
  -1 0 0 2 0 0 -1

" />
</filter>
```

The result, as shown at *http://cs.sru.edu/~ddailey/svg/feConvolveMatrix2.svg*, is illustrated in the center image below and is contrasted with the effect of simply using a vertical *<feGaussianBlur>*. Note that the convoluted image, while vertically blurred, is done so much more clearly than with the use of the simpler blur filter, which smears pixel values. That is, the crispness of the shapes suggests a more discrete and less analog effect, which is to a large extent consistent with the nature of the underlying philosophy of the calculations.

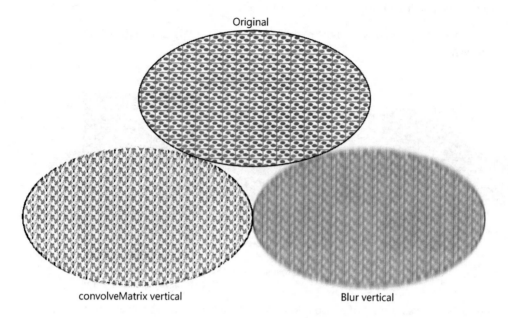

Original

convolveMatrix vertical

Blur vertical

Utility Filters

A number of filter primitives serve to merely provide some sort of necessary functionality, but would rarely be used alone. For example, some might introduce some sort of basic imagery into a filter chain. The most important of these are *<feTurbulence>*, *<feDiffuseLighting>*, and *<feSpecularLighting>*. Some others, *<feFlood>*, *<feImage>*, *<feTile>*, and *<feOffset>*, provide rudimentary operations that are useful within filter chains.

The presentation will begin gently, and build gradually toward more complexity.

Simple Utility Filters

The simpler utility filters allow ways to insert things into a filter chain. Each of the utility filters allows something to be entered into the filter chain through what we'll call *R*, which here refers to the rectangle subtended by the filter, either through its own *x*, *y*, *width*, and *height*, or through the geometry of the object to which it is applied.

- *<feFlood>* enters a single color into *R*.

- *<feOffset>* allows something in a filter chain to be translated horizontally and vertically.

- *<feImage>* enters an external file or local image (bitmapped or SVG) into *R*.

- *<feTile>* allows an input image in a filter chain to tile *R* like a pattern.

<feFlood> and <feOffset>

In the example at *http://cs.sru.edu/~ddailey/svg/feFlood.svg*, the two images in the top row show the effects of applying *<feFlood>*, in this case laid atop either an unfilled or a filled rectangle.

```
<filter id="f1">
  <feFlood x="10%" y="10%" width="80%" height="80%" flood-color="green" flood-opacity=".5"/>
</filter>
<rect x="15%" y="15%" width="20%" height="30%" fill="none" stroke-width="2" stroke="blue"/>
<rect x="15%" y="15%" width="20%" height="30%" filter="url(#f1)"/>
<rect x="60%" y="15%" width="20%" height="30%" fill="red" stroke-width="2" stroke="blue"/>
<rect x="60%" y="15%" width="20%" height="30%" filter="url(#f1)"/>
```

The advantage of this is that you can hence use a filter that applies a bit of green atop any other graphics that you might have, using the same filter wherever it is desired.

Note that the filter effect (like many others) bleeds outside of the rectangle of the graphic to which it is applied. As discussed earlier in this chapter, though, you can constrain this by setting the *x*, *y*, *height*, and *width* of the filter itself. Also note that applying *flood-opacity* leaves the underlying content visible through the filter effect, and, as you'll see later, adjusting the individual opacities of multiple *<feFlood>* filters in the same filter can prove quite useful.

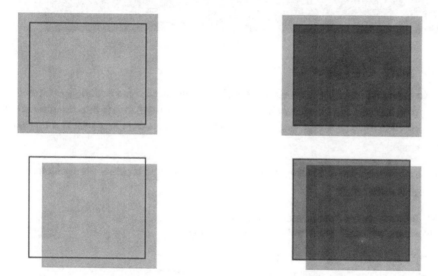

The bottom two examples in this illustration use *<feOffset>* in conjunction with *<feFlood>* to slide the effect over and down a few pixels.

```
<filter id="f2">
  <feFlood x="10%" y="10%" width="80%" height="80%" flood-color="green" flood-opacity=".5"/>
  <feOffset dx="40" dy="25"/>
</filter>
<rect x="15%" y="55%" width="20%" height="30%" fill="none" stroke-width="2" stroke="blue"/>
<rect x="15%" y="55%" width="20%" height="30%" filter="url(#f2)"/>
<rect x="60%" y="55%" width="20%" height="30%" fill="red" stroke-width="2" stroke="blue"/>
<rect x="60%" y="55%" width="20%" height="30%" filter="url(#f2)"/>
```

<feOffset> is frequently used to create drop shadows, such as shown below and at *http:// srufaculty.sru.edu/david.dailey/svg/text/offsetblur2.svg* (in this case using Gaussian blur for the shadow and something called *<feMergeNode>*, which will be discussed later, to recombine results of different primitives).

<feImage> and <feTile>

In each of the two examples at *http://cs.sru.edu/~ddailey/svg/feImage2.svg*, a rectangle is filtered using *<feImage>*, which allows the *interjection* of an external (or internal) image into the filter stream. The second instance of the image is then passed into a *<feTile>* filter, which acts a bit like *<pattern>*, but inside a filter chain.

In the first case (shown on the left in the graphic below), a rectangle is rather simply filtered while a bitmapped image is introduced:

```
<filter id="f1" primitiveUnits="objectBoundingBox">
  <feImage xlink:href="p84.jpg" preserveAspectRatio="none"/>
</filter>

<rect x="10%" y="10%" width="20%" height="30%" filter="url(#f1)" />
```

 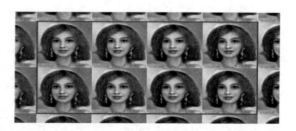

In the second case, we take the results of the *<feImage>* and direct it into an *<feTile>*, which rather simply allows content to be tiled as though in a *<pattern>* element:

```
<filter id="f2" primitiveUnits="objectBoundingBox">
  <feImage xlink:href="p84.jpg" x="0" y="0" width="25%" height="50%"
    preserveAspectRatio="none"/>
  <feTile/>
</filter>
```

In this case, *<feTile>* will make four copies of the image horizontally and two vertically because of the way the width and height attributes on *<feImage>* have been set. The outline of the blue rectangle shows the original size of the rectangle before filtering.

<feTile> is a rather simple primitive that just stretches the content to fill 100 percent of the area to be tiled. Its convenience is that it can easily be inserted into a filter chain and that the calculations of the size of the pattern space do not need to be manually calculated, as is often the case with *<pattern>*.

<feTurbulence>

<feTurbulence> is one of the most expressive and complex of the filter primitives. It is used, often in conjunction with others, to create textures and warps involving quasirandomness.

From the W3C's SVG 1.1 specification, we find that it "creates an image using the Perlin turbulence function (see *http://cs.nyu.edu/~perlin/*). It allows the synthesis of artificial textures like clouds or marble."

Like *<feFlood>*, *<feTurbulence>* fills a rectangle with new content. It has five specific attributes: *baseFrequency* (required), *numOctaves*, *seed*, *stitchTiles*, and *type*. In the simplest case, the primitive is used as follows:

```
<filter id="T1">
  <feTurbulence baseFrequency=".04"/>
</filter>
<rect x="30" y="10" height="100" width="100" filter="url(#T1)"/>
```

A more fully populated example of the syntax of the primitive is shown here:

```
<filter id="T2">
  <feTurbulence baseFrequency=".01" type="fractalNoise"
    numOctaves="3" seed="23" stitchTiles="stitch" />
</filter>
<rect x="30" y="10" height="100" width="100" filter="url(#T2)"/>
```

These two examples are shown next and at *http://cs.sru.edu/~ddailey/svg/feTurbulence1.svg*:

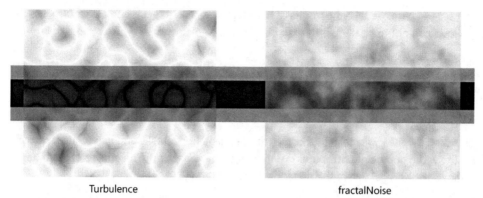

Turbulence   fractalNoise

The parameters governing *<feTurbulence>* are each worth of explanation, so we'll discuss them next.

baseFrequency

The most important of the parameters, *baseFrequency*, controls the scale or frequency of the noise. Larger numbers (approaching 1) result in a tighter grain, while smaller numbers (approaching 0) result in coarser, wider-grained textures. As with *<feGaussianBlur>*, you can control both the horizontal and vertical components of *<feTurbulence>*. Here are four examples in which, for *type="fractalNoise"*, the values of *baseFrequency* have been varied. You can see the example at *http://cs.sru.edu/~ddailey/svg/feTurbulence2.svg*.

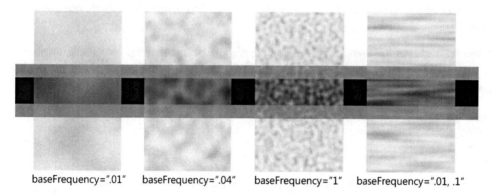

baseFrequency=".01"   baseFrequency=".04"   baseFrequency="1"   baseFrequency=".01, .1"

Note that in the last example, a lower value for *baseFrequency* has been provided in the horizontal direction, meaning that the frequency is higher in that direction, resulting in the appearance of horizontal streaking.

numOctaves

Variations in numOctaves essentially adjust the amount of detail present in the texture. Only integers are allowed, and in most cases, more than three octaves of turbulence (or grains of noise) does not increase the visual complexity of the filter. Generally, depending on the use, either one or two octaves of turbulence will suffice for most scenarios. In the example at *http://cs.sru.edu/~ddailey/*

svg/feTurbulence3.svg, you can see the effects of varying this parameter both for single values of *baseFrequency* and for a double-valued example.

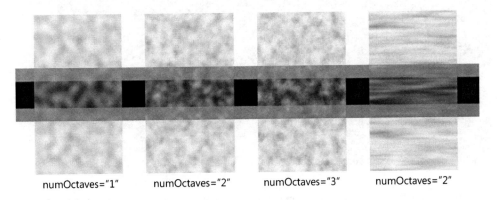

numOctaves="1"   numOctaves="2"   numOctaves="3"   numOctaves="2"

type

There are only two values for *type*: *turbulence* and *fractalNoise*. The default value is *turbulence*. The visual difference is primarily that *turbulence* appears stringier and *fractalNoise* looks cloudier. You can see the contrast below, and at *http://cs.sru.edu/~ddailey/svg/feTurbulence4.svg*.

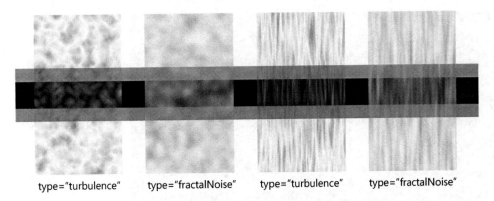

type="turbulence"   type="fractalNoise"   type="turbulence"   type="fractalNoise"

seed

<feTurbulence> accepts a *seed* value that allows different scenes of the same characteristics to be generated from instance to instance. In the example at *http://cs.sru.edu/~ddailey/svg/feTurbulence5. svg* (shown below), four adjacent rectangles in the top row are filled with turbulence having the same *seed* value. Note how all four adjoin with no seams. The bottom row, on the other hand, has four different *seed* values, and the seams between the four tiles are clearly visible (once the contrast has been enhanced and transparency eliminated to make the effect more obvious).

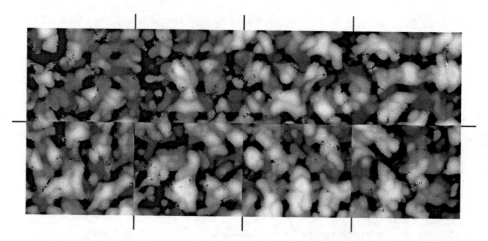

As shown in the above example, you can create new types of textures by further filtering the results of *<feTurbulence>*. We'll present some further examples of this, together with some ideas about how to create textures of given qualities.

Following is an example of simple turbulence from which the transparency channel has been effectively removed (by mapping alpha values everywhere to 1.0).

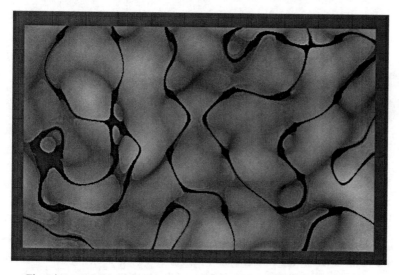

The above (visible at *http://cs.sru.edu/~ddailey/svg/feTurbulence11a.svg*) is created, quite simply, as follows:

```
<filter id="Q" x="0" y="0" height="100%" width="100%">
  <feTurbulence baseFrequency=".01" numOctaves="1" />
  <feComponentTransfer>
    <feFuncA type='linear' intercept="1" slope='0' />
  </feComponentTransfer>
</filter>
```

```
<rect x="15%" y="15%"  height="70%" width="70%" filter="url(#Q)"/>
```

Now, while it is easy to vary the specific pattern displayed in this rectangle by changing the value of *seed*, it is not so easy to simply move the pattern around. To make this point clearer, consider the following example:

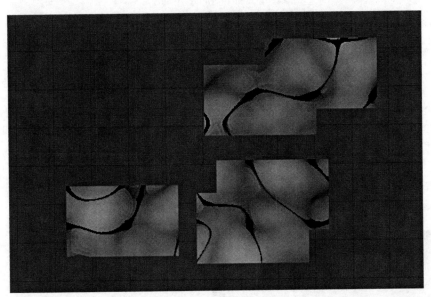

This example (at *http://cs.sru.edu/~ddailey/svg/feTurbulence11.svg*) shows five positions of a single filtered rectangle (filtered as in the previous example) as its location changes through an animation. Note how the rectangles that overlap share the same pattern. It is as though the rectangle is a window, moving through an infinite space populated with turbulence.

The rectangle is animated as follows:

```
<rect x="40%" y="40%"  height="20%" width="20%" filter="url(#T1)">
    <animate attributeName="x" values="10%;60%;70%;10%" dur="5s" repeatCount="indefinite" />
    <animate attributeName="y" values="70%;10%;30%;60%;70%" dur="7s" repeatCount="indefinite" />
</rect>
```

This example illustrates that *<feTurbulence>* is defined relative to absolute coordinates. The pattern does not move with the object that has been filtered with it!

This can create either obstacles or opportunities, depending on how you look at it and what you want to accomplish. But it should cause some rethinking of how you can use turbulence to animate certain types of things, such as clouds, fire, water, rain, bubbles, and smoke. In cases of fluid motion, you'll want the turbulence to "flow" continuously in a given direction.

An approach that has been around since the earliest days of SVG animation (used in the flickering candle from Adobe's SVG Zone; also visible at *http://svg.kvalitne.cz/adobe/candleinthewind.svg*) appears to solve this problem quite efficiently. You can also see another approach that we've used with the animated text examples at *http://srufaculty.sru.edu/david.dailey/svg/text/texteffects2.htm*. Since turbulence cannot easily be moved through a rectangle, the approach works as follows:

```
<g filter="url(#Q)">
  <animateTransform attributeName="transform" type="translate"
    from="0 0" to="0 -20000" dur="200" repeatCount="indefinite"/>
  <rect x="25%" y="25%"  height="50%" width="50%"/>
    <animateTransform attributeName="transform" type="translate"
      from="0 0" to="0 20000" dur="200" repeatCount="indefinite"/>
  </rect>
</g>
```

Essentially, this example (visible at *http://cs.sru.edu/~ddailey/svg/feTurbulence11b.svg*) drags the rectangle at the same speed in two opposite directions, with the net effect that it is left stationary. The reason that it works this way is that the *<g>* that is filtered, when dragged, brings both the filter region and the *<rect>* with it, but only the *<rect>* is retransformed, with the net appearance that only the filter region (and hence the pattern) appears to move.

This effect is used twice at *http://cs.sru.edu/~ddailey/svg/feTurbulence11g.svg* (shown below) to separately animate two different layers of clouds at differing speeds.

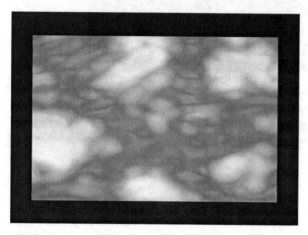

Likewise, using two layers of turbulence, together with lighting effects (discussed in the next section), allows the appearance of a flyover of a distant moon (see *http://cs.sru.edu/~ddailey/svg/feTurbulence11h.svg*):

This section concludes with a variety of effects using turbulence, and describes some of the ways that turbulence can be used in combination with other filter effects to create a variety of intriguing textures.

In the example at *http://cs.sru.edu/~ddailey/svg/feTurbulence16.svg*, you can see four different effects created by adjusting the chroma of turbulence using *<feColorMatrix>* and/or *<feComponentTransfer>*.

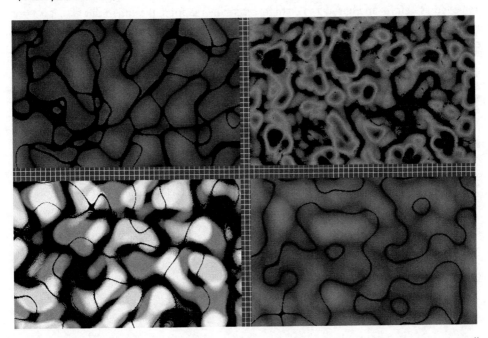

In the effect, in the example at the upper left, the transparency of the turbulence as well as the green and blue channels are simply eliminated, as follows:

```
<filter id="T1" x="0" y="0" height="100%" width="100%">
  <feTurbulence baseFrequency=".015" numOctaves="1" />
  <feComponentTransfer>
```

```
      <feFuncA type="linear" intercept="1" slope='0' />
      <feFuncG type="linear" intercept="0" slope='0' />
      <feFuncB type="linear" intercept="0" slope='0' />
   </feComponentTransfer>
</filter>
```

This is similar to the effect at the lower right, which eliminates the green, blue, and alpha channels through an *<feColorMatrix>*:

```
<feColorMatrix type="matrix"
   values="1 0 0 1 0
           0 0 0 0 0
           0 0 0 0 0
           0 0 0 0 1"
></feColorMatrix>
```

The effect at the lower left shows what happens if, again, the blue and alpha channels are eliminated, but if the red and green channels are discretized (mapping middle ranges of red or green to high values and eliminating low values through *<feComponentTransfer>*):

```
<feFuncR type="table" tableValues="0 0 1 1 1 1 1 1 1 1"/>
<feFuncG type="table" tableValues="0 0 1 1 1 1 1 1 1"/>
```

Finally, the most complex of the examples, at the upper right, has its blue, green, and alpha channels removed as before, and has its red channel discretely mapped; though in this case it is transformed nonmonotonically, so that very low, medium, and high values of red are eliminated, but low values are heightened.

```
      <feFuncR type="table" tableValues="0 0 .5 1 .5 0 0 0 0 0 0 "/>
```

The result is that the red "islands" have holes carved into them.

In the examples at *http://cs.sru.edu/~ddailey/svg/feTurbulence17.svg* (shown in the following figure), these concepts are explored a bit further.

The example at the upper left takes turbulence and, once more, adjusts the chroma:

```
<feTurbulence baseFrequency=".019,.06" numOctaves="1"/>
<feComponentTransfer>
  <feFuncA type="linear" intercept="1" slope='0' />
  <feFuncR type="linear" intercept="0" slope='.1' />
  <feFuncG type="linear" intercept="0" slope='.4' />
  <feFuncB type="linear" intercept="0" slope='.9' />
</feComponentTransfer>
```

Specifically, after eliminating transparency (by setting the alpha values to 1), instead of eliminating two of the channels, the red channel is severely dampened, and the green channel is partially dampened. The result is a texture vaguely reminiscent of water.

In the example at the top right, the blue channel is discretized, much as in the "islands" example discussed above, like so:

```
<feFuncB type="table" tableValues="0 0 0 1 1  0  0 0 0 0  0 0 "/>
```

Next, the boundaries of the pseudoglyphs (islands with holes) are smoothed, by first blurring and then sharpening:

```
<feGaussianBlur stdDeviation="3"/>
<feConvolveMatrix order="5"
  kernelMatrix="
  1  1   1  1  1
  1 -2  -2 -2  1
  1 -2 -.2 -2  1
  1 -2  -2 -2  1
  1  1   1  1  1
"/>
```

You might want to experiment with changing the number of octaves to one or three (from two) in this example to see how the complexity of the shapes can be increased or decreased accordingly. You can see an animated version of this at *http://cs.sru.edu/~ddailey/svg/feTurbulence19.svg*.

At the lower right, the example works much the same way as the blue pseudoglyphs. The differences are that the outer edges of the islands (the darker shades of blue) are turned blue and the inner parts are turned green. This is accomplished as follows:

```
<feComponentTransfer>
  <feFuncA type="linear" intercept="1" slope='0' />
  <feFuncB type="table" tableValues="0 0 .5 1 1  0  .5 .5 0 0  0 0 "/>

</feComponentTransfer>
<feGaussianBlur stdDeviation="2"/>
<feColorMatrix type="matrix"
  values=" 0  0  0 0  0
           0  0  1 0  0
           0  0  2 0 -1
           0  0  0 1  0"
/>
```

Specifically, *<feComponentTransfer>* is used to make the blue channel bimodal, with modes at 4/13 and 7/13 of the way across the 13 intervals established by the 12 table values. Then *<feColorMatrix>* is used to eliminate the red channel (it could also have been used to eliminate the alpha channel, hence sparing the earlier use of the *<feFuncA>*). The blue channel is preserved, but is forked into both blue and green. That is, in the result, pixels having both high and low values of blue will be turned green; those having only high values of blue will be made both blue and green, namely cyan.

The final of these four effects (at the bottom right) is accomplished as follows:

```
<feTurbulence baseFrequency=".08 .03" numOctaves="1" />
<feColorMatrix type="matrix" values="
  .5  .5  0  0  .1
  .4  .5  0  0 -.1
   0   0  0  0   0
   0   0  0  0   1"
>
</feColorMatrix>
<feGaussianBlur stdDeviation="1 2"/>
<feConvolveMatrix order="5"
  kernelMatrix="
  1  1   1  1  1
```

```
   1 -2  -2 -2  1
   1 -2 -.7 -2  1
   1 -2  -2 -2  1
   1  1   1  1  1"
/>
<feComponentTransfer>
  <feFuncG type="linear" intercept="-.5" slope='1' />
</feComponentTransfer>
```

In this code, several things happen:

1. *baseFrequency=".08 .03"* is used to make the frequency higher in the horizontal direction.

2. *<feColorMatrix>* succeeds first in eliminating blue and alpha, and then in yoking together (somewhat) the green and red channels, so that the result is predominantly orange, but with a bit of independence of green from red and a bit stronger redness than greenness.

3. We blur, slightly more vertically than horizontally, and then apply slight sharpening, to enhance the dark edges around the grains.

4. Finally, the green channel is further dampened to shift the image more toward red and away from yellow, using a component transfer effect. This last effect could perhaps have been accomplished within *<feColorMatrix>*, but a bit of fussing with the values didn't succeed, so I just slapped it in as an aftereffect.

Next, we'll explore a series of examples (visible at *http://cs.sru.edu/~ddailey/svg/feTurbulence18.svg*) involving the creation of a woodlike texture:

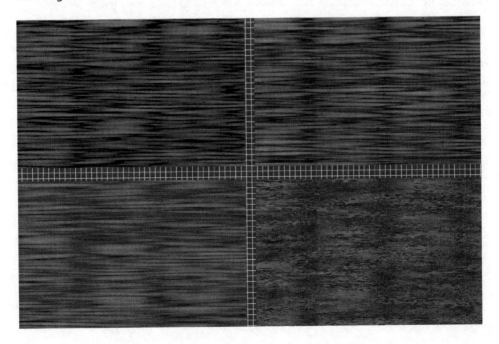

The first of these examples (top left) proceeds rather simply on the basis of previous examples:

```
<feTurbulence baseFrequency=".007,.15" numOctaves="2" />
<feComponentTransfer>
  <feFuncR type="linear" intercept="-.1" slope="1"/>
  <feFuncG type="linear" intercept="-.05" slope=".2"/>
  <feFuncB type="linear" intercept="0" slope="0"/>
  <feFuncA type="linear" intercept="1"/>
</feComponentTransfer>
```

That is, higher frequencies are used in the vertical direction, resulting in a horizontal grain. Blue and alpha channels are eliminated; while green is considerably dampened. This gives a plausible grain and range of coloration.

The second example (top right) shows that *<feColorMatrix>* can yield more precise control over the coloration:

```
<feTurbulence baseFrequency=".007,.15" numOctaves="2" />
<feColorMatrix type="matrix"
  values=" 1.2   0     0    0   -.1
   .05  .03    0    0    0
    0    0    .02   0    0
    0    0     0    0    1
"/>
```

In this example, red is again emphasized more than green, but instead of the two being independent, as in unprocessed turbulence, a bit of covariation is introduced, allowing the green channel to be influenced by both red and green. Blue is deemphasized and transparency is eliminated.

The third and fourth illustrations (bottom row) both use concepts developed in the next section: the introduction of new threads in a filter chain that are later recombined. We'll further articulate these concepts then, but for now, know that in both examples, an *<feFlood>* filter is used to introduce a particular color (in this case a reddish brown) into the filter, which is then used as the background of the texture. In the second, another filter, *<feDisplacementMap>*, is used to distort the grain using yet another source of turbulence to define the distortion.

Finally, the example at *http://cs.sru.edu/~ddailey/svg/feTurbulence14a.svg* shows the effect of concurrently varying the *<feBaseFrequency>* and the chroma of a texture applied to a pattern that itself has an animated pattern space:

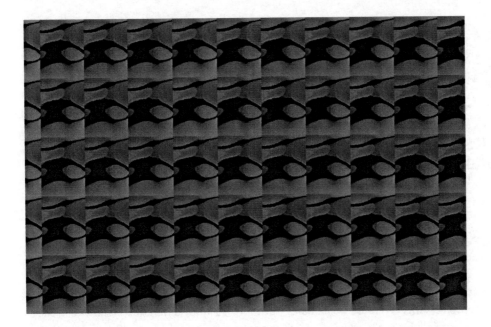

Lighting Effects

Two rather complex filters involve lighting effects: *<feDiffuseLighting>* and *<feSpecularLighting>*. Both are rather similar, in some ways, to *<feConvolveMatrix>* and *<feGaussianBlur>*, in that they allow for directional effects. That is, they allow for pixels to be influenced by their neighbors in certain directions. In the case of these lighting effects, we first convert an image to binary black and white, and then we pretend that these shades represent elevations and that a shadow is cast across the resulting contours. What is varied is the type and positioning of the light source. Lighting effects are often used in conjunction with other filters to create more complex effects. Basically, there are diffuse and specular effects filters into which you can place a collection of lights.

We'll present a few experiments with *<feDiffuseLighting>* first, with a link to an animated example that reveals the effects of simultaneously varying several of the parameters associated with the lighting effect.

In the example at *http://cs.sru.edu/~ddailey/svg/lighting.svg*, several different kinds of lights are placed into an *<feDiffuseLighting>* element (with one *<feSpecularLighting>* used last).

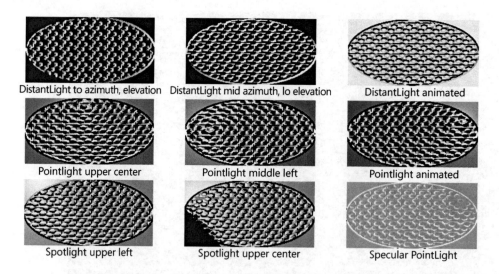

DistantLight to azimuth, elevation	DistantLight mid azimuth, lo elevation	DistantLight animated
Pointlight upper center	Pointlight middle left	Pointlight animated
Spotlight upper left	Spotlight upper center	Specular PointLight

In these examples, the same colored pattern that was used in the previous example (involving *<feConvolveMatrix>*) is reused nine times, each with a slightly different lighting effect. Each of the three basic lights is placed inside the filter primitive, using either *<feDiffuseLighting>* or *<feSpecularLighting>*. We'll show the middle effect ("Pointlight middle left") in some detail and leave inspection of the others to you if you wish to explore further.

Here are the filter and the effect object (an ellipse filled with a trichromatic pattern with a white background):

```
<filter id="pointLightB" filterUnits="objectBoundingBox" x="0" y="0" width="1" height="1">
  <feDiffuseLighting in="SourceGraphic" diffuseConstant="1" surfaceScale="10"
    lighting-color="white">
    <fePointLight x="40" y="50" z="10"/>
  </feDiffuseLighting>
</filter>

<ellipse fill="url(#OvalPattern)" stroke="black" stroke-width="2"
  filter="url(#pointLightB)" cx="50%" cy="50%" rx="10%" ry="10%"/>
```

In this case, you can imagine that a light source is located 10 pixels above the plane of the drawing and that each dark ellipse protrudes like a small half-sphere above the plane. The light emanates in all directions from a point located 10 units above the coordinate (40,50), as based on the affected rectangle of the filter (upper left being [0,0]). You can perhaps better understand the effect by animating the x, y, and z positions, as is done in the image immediately to the right (Pointlight animated).

You can also modify the color of the light, though if you want two different-colored lights, you would have to use different spot filters.

Ways of Combining Filters

There are several ways to combine or chain together two or more filter effects. You have already seen many simple examples of chaining: taking the output of one filter primitive and using it as an input to the next within a shared *<filter>* tag. You can even create veritable image-processing flow diagrams with the SVG filters module, allowing for enormous variation and sophistication in the effects that can be produced.

First, consider the default way in which filters handle multiple effects. Ordinarily, the first primitive within a *<filter>* receives as input the *SourceGraphic*—the element to which the filter has been applied. For example, if we define

```
<rect filter="url(#Fs)" ... />
```

then it is that rectangle that is considered to be the *SourceGraphic* of the filter *Fs*. Each primitive in succession (*FP1, FP2, . . . FPk*), takes the output, or *result*, from the previous filter as if it were its input. Here we'll demonstrate two equivalent approaches, the first of which just uses default values of the *in* and *result* attributes of successive filters, while the second makes all those default values explicit. There would be no reason to specify the values of *in* or *result* in the following example, but the example may help make it clear what is meant by the *in* and the *result* of a filter. In both cases, it is the final filter from which the output is rendered into the affected graphical objects.

```
<filter id="Fs">                  <filter id="Fs">
  <FP1/>                            <FP1 in="SourceGraphic" result="A"/>
  <FP2/>                            <FP2 in="A" result ="B" />
  <FP3/>                            <FP3 in="B" result ="C" />
  <FP4/>                            <FP4 in="C" result ="D" />
  <FP5/>                            <FP5 in="D" />
</filter>                         </filter>
```

In the above, *FPx* refers to any filter primitive (e.g., *<feGaussianBlur>*). Once you know where the *SourceGraphic* enters into the computations and how results are named and reused, then you are in a position to start varying the order and using those more complex filter primitives that combine results of two or more primitives, hence chaining filter primitives together in more complex and interesting ways.

SVG also gives access to the graphical content underneath a given image. That is, you can use the state of the rendered imagery in the layer below the filtered object itself as part of the filter. This allows combinations of an image with its background using techniques for combining two images: *<feMergeNode>*, *<feBlend>*, *<feComposite>*, and *<feDisplacementMap>*. We'll revisit the use of *BackgroundImage* to do this shortly.

<feMergeNode>

The *<feMerge>* filter allows the combination of filters concurrently rather than serially (as in the earlier examples). Rather than each filter being applied to the output of the preceding filter, *<feMerge>* gives us a way to temporarily store the output of each filter. Once several layers have been created and stored as the results of different primitives, you can place them on the canvas in order from bottom to top. The topmost layers should have some transparency (or incompleteness) in the fill area to allow those layers underneath to be visible (see *http://srufaculty.sru.edu/david.dailey/cs427/StateOfArt-Dailey.html#footnote20sym*).

In the following example (visible at *http://cs.sru.edu/~ddailey/svg/feMergeNode1.svg*), we are interested in converting an image from standard RGB to partial transparency, in this case using the darkest parts of the image so that an underlying color shines through. In this case, we're using yellow, created through *<feFlood>* as a part of the filter.

The code for the above illustration is shown next:

```
<filter id="twoF" x="0%" y="0%" width="100%" height="100%">
  <feFlood flood-color="yellow" result="A"/>
  <feColorMatrix type="matrix" in="SourceGraphic" result="B"
    values="
    1 0 0 0 0
    0 1 0 0 0
    0 0 1 0 0
    1 1 1 0 0
  "/>
  <feMerge>
    <feMergeNode in="A"/>
    <feMergeNode in="B"/>
  </feMerge>
</filter>
<image x="35%" y="20%" xlink:href="p84.jpg" filter="url(#twoF)" height="50%" width="30%"/>
```

<feFlood> has inserted a yellow rectangle into the filter stream, but it is temporarily held in memory as result *A*. As before, *<feColorMatrix>* is used to map dark parts of the image to transparent (keeping alpha high for bright values of red, green, and blue); the result is stored in *B*. Finally, the two effects are overlaid, as though stacked, and result *A* being under result *B*.

To bolster your understanding of these effects, it is worth pointing out that the following code (visible at *http://cs.sru.edu/~ddailey/svg/feMergeNode2.svg*) accomplishes essentially the same result.

```
<filter id="twoF" x="0%" y="0%" width="100%" height="100%">
  <feFlood flood-color="yellow" result="A"/>
  <feImage xlink:href="p84.jpg" preserveAspectRatio="none"/>
  <feColorMatrix type="matrix" result="B"
    values="
    1 0 0 0 0
    0 1 0 0 0
    0 0 1 0 0
    1 1 1 0 0
  "/>
  <feMerge>
    <feMergeNode in="A"/>
    <feMergeNode in="B"/>
  </feMerge>
</filter>

<rect x="35%" y="20%"  filter="url(#twoF)" height="50%" width="30%"/>
```

Here, instead of filtering an *<image>*, we filter a *<rect>*, inserting the image into the filter through *<feImage>*.

Two more examples that demonstrate alternative ways of accomplishing the same thing that *<feMergeNode>* does are shown at *http://cs.sru.edu/~ddailey/svg/feTurbulence8.svg* and *http://cs.sru.edu/~ddailey/svg/feTurbulence9.svg*. In the first, we introduce one kind of turbulence into another by laying one rectangle containing partly opaque turbulence atop another rectangle filled with higher-frequency turbulence. In the second, we accomplish this effect with a single filter by layering the effects with *<feMergeNode>*.

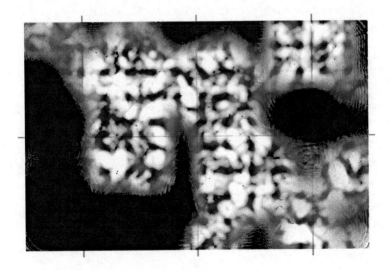

\<feBlend>

The *\<feBlend>* primitive enables the combination of two layers of an image using the methods *multiply*, *darken*, *screen*, or *lighten*—similar to those used in programs such as Adobe Photoshop—to logically combine color values of coincident pixels.

The example at *http://cs.sru.edu/~ddailey/svg/feBlend.svg* (shown below) demonstrates these four modes of composing an image with what lies underneath it.

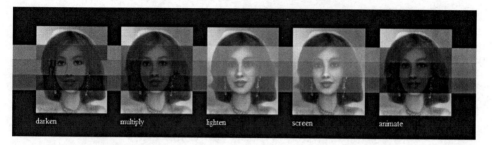

Except for the value of the *mode* attribute, all of these effects are the same, so we'll only illustrate the *multiply* example in detail.

The filter itself is relatively straightforward:

```
<filter id="multiply" x="0" y="0" height="100%" width="100%">
  <feBlend mode="multiply" in2="BackgroundImage" in="SourceGraphic"/>
</filter>
```

However, the code contains one significant exception—the use of two input images: *in* and *in2*. This allows what is underneath—namely, the three colored stripes—to be multiplied by the *SourceGraphic*. Inserting what is underneath and defined as *BackgroundImage* is done by enabling the background on a group element that contains both the three stripes and the filtered image:

```
<g enable-background="new">
  <rect x="0" y="10%" height="4%" width="100%" fill="red"/>
  <rect x="0" y="14%" height="4%" width="100%" fill="green"/>
  <rect x="0" y="18%" height="4%" width="100%" fill="blue"/>
  <image x="5%" y="5%" xlink:href="p84.jpg" filter="url(#multiply)" height="23%" width="15%"
    preserveAspectRatio="none"/>
</g>
```

Therefore, any content laid down before the filtered object in the group with *background* enabled will be used in the computation of the *\<feBlend>*.

Note that since the filter is applied to an image, the default value of *in* is in fact *SourceGraphic*, so stating *in="SourceGraphic"*, as above, is not strictly required.

The modes of *<feBlend>* work as follows:

- **normal**   Allows *BackgroundImage* (or another value for the *in2* attribute) to be visible only if *SourceGraphic* (or another value for the *in* attribute) contains transparency.

- **screen**   Allows each image's values to add brightness to the others. For example:

  ```
  white screen black = white
  and
  red (#FF0000) screen grey (#808080) = #ff8080 ("rose" or a rose-like color)
  ```

- **multiply**   Allows values of the images to subtract brightness from one. For example:

  ```
  white mult black = black
  and
  red (#FF0000) mult grey (#808080) = #800000 (a shade of red darker than "darkred")
  ```

- **lighten**   Takes the brighter value of the two images at each pixel. For example:

  ```
  white lighten black = white
  and
  red (#FF0000) lighten grey (#808080) = #ff8080 ("rose")
  ```

- **darken**   Takes the darker value of the two images at each pixel. For example:

  ```
  white darken black = black
  and
  red (#FF0000) darken grey (#808080) = #800000 ("darker red")
  ```

<feComposite>

Neither *<feMerge>* nor *<feBlend>* presents us with a way to either average or intersect two images. *<feComposite>* can be used for that work. It allows the superimposition of the footprints of images as well as the relative blending of their pixel values. Like *<feMerge>*, it takes two inputs, *in* and *in2*. By default, *in* is the *SourceGraphic*.

As of this writing, only two browsers, Opera and ASV, seem to handle *<feComposite>*, and though both appear to pass the SVG Working Group's two tests in the test suite at *http://www.w3.org/Graphics/SVG/Test/20110816/harness/htmlObjectApproved/index.html*, their treatment is different for the example at *http://cs.sru.edu/~ddailey/svg/feCompositeCompare.jpg*. The lower example, as rendered in ASV, is the correct rendition.

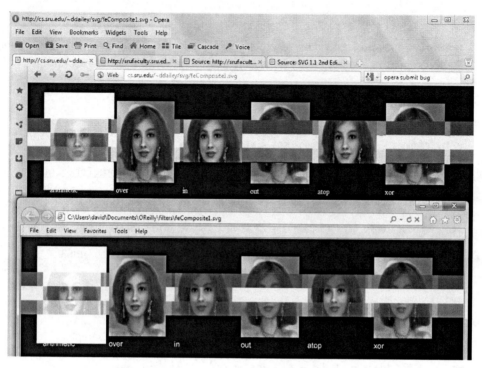

A representative example (with *operator="in"*) looks like this:

```
<filter id="in">
  <feComposite in2="BackgroundImage" in="SourceGraphic" operator="in" />
</filter>
```

The more complex operator, *arithmetic*, deserves a bit more explanation. When *arithmetic* is specified, four other parameters are invoked: *k1*, *k2*, *k3*, and *k4*. These assign weights, respectively, to a component representing the multiple of the two images, the linear effect of the first image, the linear effect of the second image, and an *intercept*, or brightness adjustment. In the following illustration, when the operator is *arithmetic*, then *k1* equals 0, *k2* equals 1, *k3* equals –1, and *k4* equals 1, meaning that the *SourceGraphic* (*in*) contributes positively, the *BackgroundImage* (*in2*) contributes negatively, and the brightness is boosted.

The example at *http://cs.sru.edu/~ddailey/svg/feComposite2.svg* (shown in the following figure) illustrates another set of uses for *<feComposite>*.

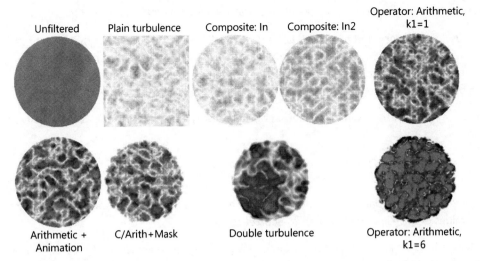

Unfiltered	Plain turbulence	Composite: In	Composite: In2	Operator: Arithmetic, k1=1

Arithmetic + Animation	C/Arith+Mask	Double turbulence	Operator: Arithmetic, k1=6

The first two illustrations (at the top left) show the basic forms to be combined: a simple ellipse and a turbulence map.

Third from the left in the top row shows the result of combining the two using *operator="in"*. Here's the corresponding code:

```
<filter id="compositeI" y="0" x="0" width="100%" height="100%">
   <feTurbulence baseFrequency=".05" numOctaves="3" result="A"/>
   <feComposite in="A" in2="SourceGraphic" operator="in" />
</filter>
<ellipse  cx="385" cy="87" rx="75" ry="87" fill="red" filter="url(#compositeI)"/>
```

Effectively, this constrains the turbulence to the ellipse itself. Immediately to the right of that image, the order of the composition is reversed:

```
<filter id="compositeJ" y="0" x="0" width="100%" height="100%">
   <feTurbulence baseFrequency=".05" numOctaves="3" result="A"/>
   <feComposite in2="A" in="SourceGraphic" operator="in" />
</filter>

<ellipse  cx="535" cy="87" rx="75" ry="87" fill="red" filter="url(#compositeJ)"/>
```

In short, by using *operator="in"*, you map the colors of one image to the shape of the other.

The rightmost image in the top row shows the same thing, but with *operator="arithmetic"* instead. Here's the code:

```
<filter id="compositeA" y="0" x="0" width="100%" height="100%">
   <feTurbulence baseFrequency=".05" numOctaves="3" result="A" />
   <feComposite in2="A" in="SourceGraphic" operator="arithmetic"
     k1="1" k2="1" k3="1"  k4="-1" />
</filter>
```

```
<ellipse filter="url(#compositeA)" cx="700" cy="87" rx="75" ry="87" fill="red" />
```

In its use of *operator="arithmetic"*, *k1*, *k2*, and *k3* are all equal to 1.0, meaning that both of the images, as well as their cross-product, contribute positively to the result. Since this results in a very bright image, *k4*, the adjustment (or brightness) coefficient, is adjusted downward to ensure that, among other things, the composition remains within the footprint of the ellipse.

Immediately below that image, another set of values for *operator="arithmetic"* is shown. Here's the code:

```
<feComposite in2="A" in="SourceGraphic" operator="arithmetic"
  k1="8" k2="1" k3="1"   k4="-1" />
```

This has the result of clamping the colors of the areas where the shapes overlap more closely to the red values of the ellipse represented by *SourceGraphic*.

Generally, it would appear that the most interesting sets of values associated with the parameters in this case arise from varying *k1*.

The remaining effects on the page experiment with animation as well as masking. By applying a mask that fades to transparency at the outer edge of the ellipse, the appearance of bumpiness at the edges is conveyed, which, when combined with animation, gives the illusion of a sphere being rotated.

<feDisplacementMap>

This effect is a bit different from others in the sense that it converts color values in one image into geometric distortions of pixels at the same location in another image.

<feDisplacementMap> takes *in* (*SourceGraphic* by default) and *in2*, and uses a specified channel (R, G, B, or A) of *in2* to serve as displacement value to determine the direction and distance each pixel of *in* will be moved in either the x or y direction (or both).

For example, if you wanted to use the red channel of *in2* to horizontally distort *in*, and if the underlying image represented by *in2* is, say, a red-and-black checkerboard (hence, high on red over the red squares and low on red over the black squares), then those pixels of *in* that lie above red squares would be moved to the right, while those above black squares would be moved to the left.

In the example at *http://cs.sru.edu/~ddailey/svg/feDisplacement1.svg*, a checkerboard pattern is used to fill the background. An *<image>* element is then filtered with a displacement that moves those pixels above the red squares and those above the black squares 150 pixels apart from one another in both the x and y directions.

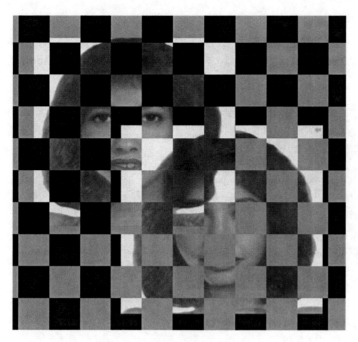

Here's the source code for this example:

```
<defs>
  <pattern id="Pattern" patternUnits="userSpaceOnUse" width="100" height="100">
    <rect x="0" y="0"  width="100" height="100"  fill="#f02"/>
    <rect x="0" y="0"  width="50" height="50"  fill="black"/>
    <rect x="50" y="50"  width="50" height="50"  fill="black"/>
  </pattern>
  <filter id="d" x="-20%" y="-20%" height="140%" width="140%">
    <feDisplacementMap scale="150" in2="BackgroundImage" yChannelSelector="R"
      xChannelSelector="R" />
  </filter>
</defs>
<g enable-background="new">
  <rect x="0%" y="0%" height="100%" width="100%" fill="url(#Pattern)"/>
  <image filter='url(#d)'  xlink:href="p17.jpg"  x="30%" y="25%"  width="40%" height="50%"
    preserveAspectRatio="none" />
</g>
```

This succeeds in separating every other square of the image and in moving each apart both vertically and horizontally, as shown.

<feDisplacementMap> is a remarkable tool when it comes to warping images and producing certain naturalistic effects, particularly when *<feTurbulence>* is used at the source of the displacement. Following are a collection of examples that use *<feTurbulence>*, together with brief explanations of how each is done.

Warping with a Simple Gradient

In the example at *http://cs.sru.edu/~ddailey/svg/feDisplacement4.svg*, a linear gradient is inserted into a filter through *<feImage>*. It is then used as the source of distortion for some other SVG content, as shown:

```
<defs>
  <linearGradient id="LG"  gradientTransform="rotate(12 .5 .5)">
    <stop offset="0" stop-color="black"/>
    <stop offset=".35" stop-color="#300"/>
    <stop offset=".45" stop-color="#8a8"/>
    <stop offset=".5" stop-color="blue"/>
    <stop offset=".57" stop-color="#8a8"/>
    <stop offset="1" stop-color="black"/>
  </linearGradient>
  <rect id="r" x="0" y="0" height="100%" width="100%" fill="url(#LG)"/>
</defs>

<filter id="D" height="165%" y="-30%" width="140%">
  <feImage xlink:href="#r" result="M" />
  <feDisplacementMap in="SourceGraphic" in2="M" scale="1" xChannelSelector="B"
    yChannelSelector="G">

    <animate attributeName="scale" dur="2s" values="0;85;0" repeatCount="indefinite"/>
  </feDisplacementMap>
</filter>
<use xlink:href="#r"/>
<g id="GEL" filter='url(#D)'>
  <ellipse cx="50%" cy="50%" fill="none"  stroke="#302" stroke-width="40"
    rx="20%" ry="15%" />
  <text x="40%" y="53%" font-size="55" fill="black" font-family="arial">Warping</text>
</g>
```

You can see similar examples at *http://cs.sru.edu/~ddailey/svg/feDisplacement4a.svg*, in which the gradient itself is rotated, and at *http://srufaculty.sru.edu/david.dailey/svg/newstuff/ filterDisplacementMap4.svg* (shown in the figure that follows), in which the gradient is a reflected radial gradient that is animated, instead of a simpler linear one.

Warping with Turbulence

The examples at *http://cs.sru.edu/~ddailey/svg/feDisplacement3.svg* and *http://cs.sru.edu/~ddailey/svg/feDisplacement2.svg* show how using *<feTurbulence>* as the source of distortion for an image can produce interesting results. The following illustration shows this effect manifest differently on four separate copies of the same image:

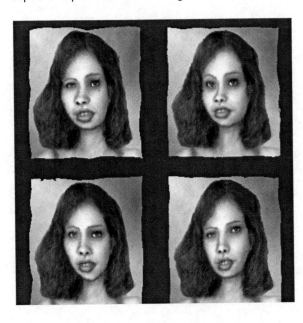

Spherical Warping

The illustration at *http://cs.sru.edu/~ddailey/svg/feComposite5.svg* (shown below) has two images that you can compare, one of which has had a lens effect applied (namely, a spherical gradient has been used as the source of displacement).

A close comparison of the two images will reveal that while the grain of the image on the right is similarly sized throughout the image, in the example on left, the grain tends to be larger toward the center. As the images rotate, the illusion of the image at left being spherical is more apparent.

The actual lens effect is imparted from a small PNG image found in the SVG test suite in the SVG Working Group's discussion, at *http://www.w3.org/Graphics/SVG/Test/20110816/harness/htmlObjectApproved/filters-displace-01-f.html*.

It is a pity, it might seem, that one has to resort to using a PNG file in order to introduce a lens effect into SVG, but we'll discuss alternatives to linear and radial gradients in a later chapter.

The following illustration shows how you can use the source raster image with *<feDisplacementMap>* to make a spherical transform, as in the example at *http://cs.sru.edu/~ddailey/svg/feComposite9b.svg*:

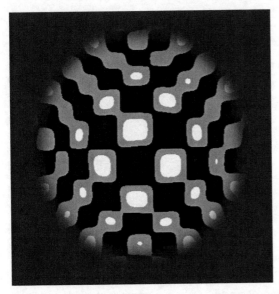

As in this other example, *sphere.png* is brought into the filter using *<feImage>*, where it is used to filter a simple rectangular grid:

```
<filter id="sphere" y="-60%" x="-60%" width="260%" height="220%" >
  <feImage  xlink:href="sphere.png" />
  <feOffset dx="-35" dy="15" result="Map" />
  <feDisplacementMap in="SourceGraphic" in2="Map" scale="250" xChannelSelector="R"
    yChannelSelector="G" result="C"/>
</filter>
```

<feOffset> is used to counterbalance the offset that *<feDisplacementMap>* imparts to the whole image, and then, owing to the nature of the map (*sphere.png*), the red channel is used to offset horizontally while the green is used for vertical offsets. The image is later blurred and posterized to induce the interesting visual pattern.

Other examples of the use of spherical distortion include *http://cs.sru.edu/~ddailey/svg/feComposite6.svg*, which demonstrates something resembling planetary motion, and *http://cs.sru.edu/~ddailey/svg/feComposite8.svg*, which demonstrates something vaguely reminiscent of a global weather system.

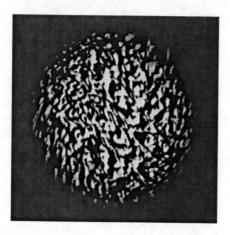

Summary

This concludes the study of SVG filters. We hope we have reached our goal of showing you how using them can be exciting and fun, without requiring extensive knowledge of mathematics.

CHAPTER 6

SVG Tools and Resources

An architect's most useful tools are an eraser at the drafting board, and a wrecking bar at the site.

Frank Lloyd Wright

Great discoveries and improvements invariably involve the cooperation of many minds.

Alexander Graham Bell

In this chapter:

The SVG language can be very expressive, but just like verbal language, it takes skill, tools, and mastery to empower its potential magic. The world of SVG is now a decade old, and during that time many tools specific to SVG have come about. Some preexisting authoring tools and vector graphics–editing software have adopted the technology, either as a native format or as an export option.

Whether your inclinations are more artistic, statistical, or programming oriented, you will find in this chapter a substantial set of tools that will be useful for enhancing your creativity and developing experience, and improving your workflow.

Just like in traditional drawing, SVG covers the two fundamental expressions of the discipline, free-hand drawing and technical drawing, thus constituting the ideal meeting point between artists and technicians. But this is not all; SVG has also been widely adopted by researchers in several domains like chemistry, physics, cartography, and so on, where in effect it is not uncommon to find individuals who shelter a bit of each under the same cap.

Libraries

Among the JavaScript libraries reviewed here, some are HTML legacy libraries that have had SVG plug-in modules added later, and others were written to use SVG natively. Thanks to the efforts led by the W3C to make SVG more interoperable, SVG can now coexist with HTML in a mixed namespace without any particular effort from the developer. The native SVG libraries are therefore probably best suited to produce modern applications. The solutions offered span the complete range of scenarios: HTML with embedded SVG, SVG and HTML in a mixed context, and SVG as stand-alone document. The legacy libraries, on the other hand, carry the overhead weight of backward HTML compatibility (one of their primary objectives). However, when using SVG, you will be necessarily targeting modern browsers, with their improved scripting engines and support for multicore and GPU processing, or the Adobe ASV plug-in, which is now well declining toward obsolescence.

If you've been using legacy libraries for a time, you may be tempted to continue using them in order to capitalize on your learning efforts; however, we encourage you to invest in the discovery of modern SVG-dedicated libraries, as this effort may prove worthwhile in the short run, in terms of efficiency and development costs.

Before reviewing the libraries, we'd like to mention debugging. Whether you will be using libraries or not, the developer tools built into modern browsers can be extremely useful when developing applications. The console can be used to quickly view and update object data and DOM elements. You can access any global object or property of an object by simply typing its name. You can assign a new value and see the result applied in real time. You can inspect the complete DOM tree and check, for instance, that the value of an attribute effectively corresponds to what was expected. A typical example is when a value yields *NaN*; if a value relates to a geometrical attribute, this does not throw a script error; the script continues execution and the elements are built and rendered, but a particular action (e.g., a transformation on an element) will simply not be applied. It is then just a reflex for you to jump directly to the offending portion of your code. The DOM inspector is the perfect debugging companion.

SVG Native JavaScript Libraries

There are several SVG libraries available that you can use when building SVG-based applications. These include D3, Pergola, Raphaël, Polymaps, and carto:net, each of which is described in the following sections.

D3: Data-Driven Documents

D3, distributed under an open source license, is ideal for building interactive SVG, HTML, and other DOM-based animations, visualizations, and applications. D3 emerged from the realm of visualization science, and borrows ideas from the open source Protovis (*http://mbostock.github.com/protovis/*) library. It has been well received by the SVG and web visualization communities. This section will get you up to speed with D3—and there is a lot to explore.

Primarily through the keen insights and focused efforts of Mike Bostock, D3 was designed specifically to facilitate the integration and visualization of data using W3C DOM-based languages. A quote from the D3 website concisely explains its purpose:

> *D3 is not a traditional visualization framework. Rather than provide a monolithic system with all the features anyone may ever need, D3 solves only the crux of the problem: efficient manipulation of documents based on data.*

Besides allowing for a low-level representation of dynamic data sources on top of the selection-based "kernel," D3 includes a collection of helper modules for creating advanced graphs and for mapping. D3 also provides convenient abstractions that support highly complex visualization tasks, including transitions and animation.

A few of the core concepts that you need to understand are the following:

- Element creation and selection

- Data and DOM manipulation

- Displaying quantitative ordinal data to scale

To start programing with D3, you will first need to download the D3 library, which you can find here: *https://github.com/mbostock/d3*.

After downloading the D3 library, you'll find that several of the examples will not run out of the box due to their use of external data files. This is due to the XMLHttpRequest 1 security restrictions of most browsers. However, as of this writing, Firefox implements XMLHttpRequest 2, where those restrictions do not apply. You will then be able to run the scripts on your local computer using Firefox. Alternatively, you can either set your browser's "Allow file access from files" security setting to *true* or run the examples in a local web server environment. If you do not have a local web server yet, you can use the Python web server included in the D3 package.

To keep things simple and demonstrate how D3 is DOM agnostic, this first example uses D3 to create an HTML table. This will show how you can create, select, and set element and attribute values to produce the graphic based on data.

First, set up your HTML document shell:

```
<html>
<head>
<title>D3 Example 1 ~ HTML Table</title>
<script type="text/javascript" src="http://mbostock.github.com/d3/d3.js">
</script>
<style type="text/css" media="screen">
    table {
        border: solid 1px #ccc;
    }
</style>
</head>
<body>
<h1>Generating HTML with D3</h1>
<div id="vis" style="width:100%;height:100%;"></div>

<script type="text/javascript">
// Code goes here, just before the end of the HTML body tag.
</script>
</body>
</html>
```

Next, here's the script to insert into the *<script>* tag:

```
// The data is stored in an associative array, as per D3's requirement.
var data = [[11, 22, 33, 44, 55, 66, 77, 88, 99, 'aa', 'bb', 'cc', 'dd', 'ee', 'ff']];
var t = d3.select("#vis")
    .append("table")
      .selectAll("tr")
      .data(data);
```

```
t.enter().append("tr")
 .selectAll("td")
    .data(function(d) { return d; })
 .enter().append("td")
    //    .attr("style", function(d) { return "background-color:#cc" + d + "33"; })
    // Values can be numeric
    .style("padding", 4 )
    // Values can be strings
    .style("background-color", function(d) { return "#cc" + d + "33"; })
    .text(function(d) { return d; });
```

Notice that the preceding code illustrates alternative ways of setting the style using the *style()* method or the *attr()* method.

Although creating SVG with D3 is useful, the primary benefit of D3 is that it can efficiently select SVG, HTML, or MathML DOM objects, which is useful for data manipulations and data-driven documents. You can use both custom input controls and the standard HTML input controls that have become familiar to developers over the past 15 years to implement interactivity.

The D3 library provides *scales* to help with mapping raw data points to the correct scale within the visualization. The basic concept is that you will have a domain or raw input data points and a corresponding range of possible output values that map to the visualization. Rather than having to write functions to perform the mathematical calculations for each data point, you can simply choose one of the D3 quantitative or ordinal scales, which greatly simplify the programming. Scales are one of the core features of D3.

Quantitative Scales

The quantitative scales currently support linear, power, logarithmic, quantize, and quantile scales. The simplest way to explain how D3 scales work in practice is with real numbers and the standard linear scale:

```
var x = d3.scale.linear()
      .domain([0, 10])
      .range([0, 200]);
```

In this case, when the raw data input value is 5, the range output value, *x(0)*, would equal 100. Likewise, *x(1)* equals 20 and *x(8)* equals 160. For example, when creating the HTML table in the preceding image, rather than using the raw data values in the associative array, we could have instead run the input data values, or the domain values, through the D3 linear scale to map these values to a range of output values. Linear scales work well for linear graphs such as bar charts and other common visualizations; however, the other scales make it just as easy to transform the same input data into graphs that use logarithmic, exponential, or other nonlinear scales.

Ordinal Scales

The ordinal scales map logical categories over a discrete domain. The next example uses the ordinal scale to map US state data along the y-axis using the height value, as in the following image.

```
y = d3.scale.ordinal().rangeRoundBands([0, h], .1);
yAxis = d3.svg.axis().scale(y).orient("left").tickSize(0);
```

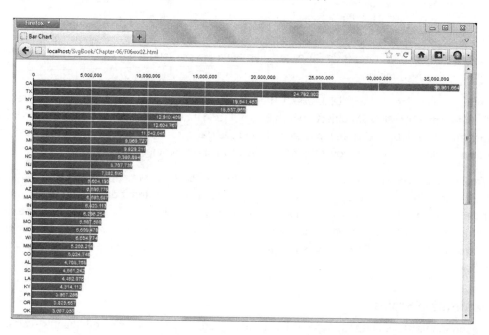

Colors

Ordinal scales also define categorical colors that are useful for quickly adding ranges of colors and mapping the colors to graph data. Because one of the primary goals of D3 is to empower visualizations, and because the SVG language is able to create vector graphics, the D3 library has several SVG-specific functions and classes, including shapes, events, axes, controls, and behaviors.

The following image (from *http://www.jasondavies.com/bloomfilter/*) shows the Bloom Filter using the *d3.svg.diagonal* shape.

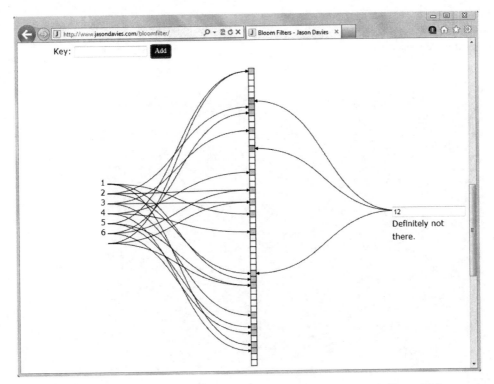

Similarly, this next example also uses the *d3.svg.diagonal* shape, but adds transitions to create an interactive pedigree visualization. You can expand or collapse the pedigree tree by clicking any of the light-blue nodes within the graphic. All the child nodes of the clicked node then transition toward the parent node as their opacity fades away throughout the transition.

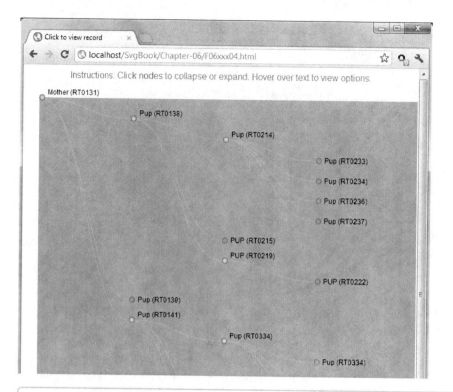

Note You can find a large number of appealing and instructive examples at *http://mbostock.github.com/d3/ex/*.

Pergola

The Pergola library is the creation of developer and early SVG inventor Domenico Strazzullo, a coauthor of this book. His goal was to design a library that provided developers with a powerful tool for building web apps, user interfaces, and mapping applications.

The Pergola library has a very cleanly designed JavaScript framework architecture that is dedicated to effectively generating SVG through class inheritance, constructors, prototype superclass and subclass extensions, and assemblies that comprise interface elements. JavaScript developers who are already familiar with SVG should be able to grasp the SVG-centric architecture of Pergola quickly. As the Pergola documentation states (see *http://www.dotuscomus.com/pergola/pergola_1.4.0/Documentation/documentation.html*):

> Pergola also implements a very powerful feature to some of its classes which allows the user to define, very simply in the call to the constructors, any SVG attributes as instance properties, using SVG grammar. This mechanism also has the advantage of producing SVG elements which are clear of all those attributes that have initial values, as per the specification, resulting in an optimized SVG file as it would be if written manually by a competent SVG developer.

This is also true for single elements built by the user through the DOM helper. For more details, see the article "JavaScript DOM Helper" in SVG Magazine, at *http://www.svgmagazine.com/jul2011/dom-helper.html*.

You can find a quick introduction to the capabilities of this library at *http://www.dotuscomus.com/pergola/overview.html*. Chapter 7, "Building a Web Application: Case Studies," goes into more depth on using both the Pergola and d3.js libraries to build modern web applications.

Raphaël

Raphaël was designed to make use of Microsoft's VML (Vector Markup Language) when the browser is unable to display SVG, and has been a significant factor in allowing a greater number of businesses to more seriously consider the use of SVG in their applications. For this reason, you can consider Raphaël to be a hybrid library. Nevertheless, Raphaël does use SVG as its primary display, and therefore it can be categorized as a native SVG library.

Raphaël has a number of useful graph and animation capabilities, and provides a few helpful methods for visualizing data. For example, you can pull data directly from an HTML table and use it within a graph, as shown in the following graphic.

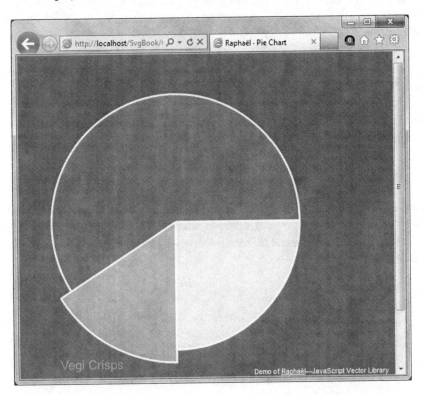

The library provides a means of quickly creating a basic set of graph layouts that will display in older Microsoft browsers. You can download the library on the home page of the Raphaël website, at *http://raphaeljs.com*, where you can also find a range of helpful starter examples.

Polymaps

Polymaps is a free JavaScript library for making dynamic, interactive maps in modern web browsers. It is a library specialized for mapping applications, and it uses SVG natively. It has a powerful layers module, a GeoJSON parser, and a collection of functions specific to mapping.

This library is used in the "Mapping Application" case study in Chapter 7. You can download it from the Polymaps home page, at *http://polymaps.org/*.

carto:net

In the domain of cartography, which greatly contributed to giving an early thrust to the popularity of SVG, carto:net was probably the first SVG library of dedicated JavaScript utilities. carto:net covers the domain exhaustively, and includes subjects such as server-side SVG generation, server-client communication, and XSLT-based generation. It also proposes a collection of GUI widgets, often accompanied by tutorials. The library is maintained by top-notch SVG developers Andreas Neumann and André Winter. It's available at *http://www.carto.net/svg/samples/*.

Legacy HTML Libraries

The rest of the JavaScript libraries discussed in this section were written primarily for HTML, but offer SVG support through plug-ins.

jQuery

The free, open source jQuery JavaScript library has become increasingly popular over the last several years. SVG support is provided by the *jQuery.svg.js* plug-in, which you can find at *http://keith-wood .name/svg.html*. Contrary to the current trend for modern libraries, jQuery defines a proprietary API and pseudolanguage.

Dojo

The developers of Dojo have regularly presented at SVG Open for several years, and make a good case for its utility. The library's support for SVG (*Dojox.drawing*) is rather consistent and reputed to be superior, in terms of features, to both the *jQuery.svg* module and Raphaël. You can find more information at *http://dojotoolkit.org/* (and more reference information at *http://dojotoolkit.org/ reference-guide/dojox/gfx/utils/toSvg.html*).

Sencha

Formerly known as *ext.js*, Sencha is a powerful and popular library oriented toward building interfaces and systemic applications. The latest release (4) includes a new module, named *Ext.draw*, which works with SVG and switches automatically to VML for compatibility with older versions of Internet Explorer. Its data visualization (charts) capabilities include transitions and animations. *Ext.draw* is backward compatible with previous versions of the software. Sencha is distributed under both a commercial license and the GPLv3 license.

Drawing Tools and Utilities

The following discussion of various drawing tools is by no means exhaustive of the programs that support SVG. In addition to the ones discussed here, CorelDRAW is also noteworthy (Corel was deeply involved in SVG development in the early 2000s), as is Xara X, both of which appear to have at least partial SVG support (see *http://www.unleash.com/davidt/svg/index.asp* and *http://site.xara.com/ products/xtreme/features/3.asp*).

Adobe Illustrator

Since 1988, Illustrator has been one of the premier professional graphics tools used by artists, designers, architects, and others. It is extremely powerful and serves as the de facto standard for vector-based drawing. Ever since Adobe's seminal involvement in the development of the SVG standard, Adobe Illustrator has exported content to SVG. Because of this heavy early involvement in SVG development, Adobe has recently recommenced its involvement in the SVG Working Group. The following image shows the four steps involved in creating a rectangle in Illustrator.

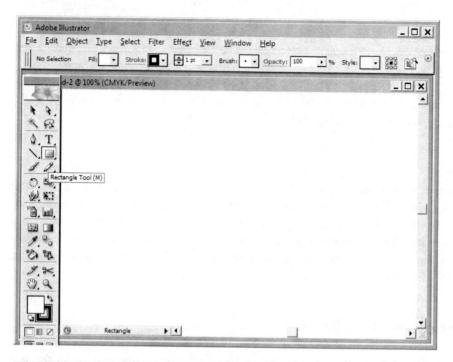

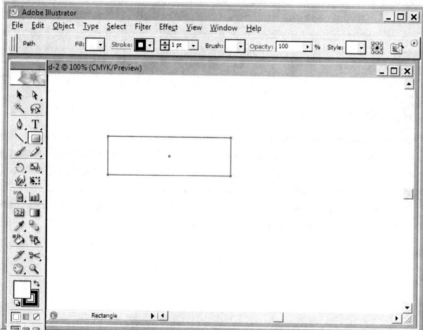

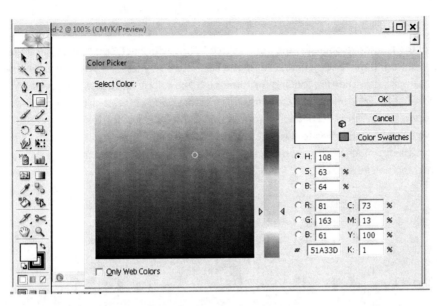

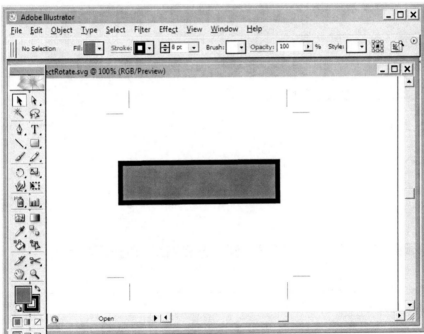

Inkscape

Jon Cruz, one of the lead developers for the open source Inkscape project, said that, in the beginning, the developers wanted to make something like Adobe Illustrator, only free. He went on to say that the objective has changed; now they are looking for something like Adobe Illustrator, only better. You can download this free software download from *http://inkscape.org/*, and you can install it on Windows, Mac, or Linux operating systems. Its native file format is SVG. Members of the Inkscape development team have begun contributing to the SVG Working Group within the past year. Inkscape is the software responsible for much of the open-license clip art available. The following image shows the creation of a rectangle in Inkscape.

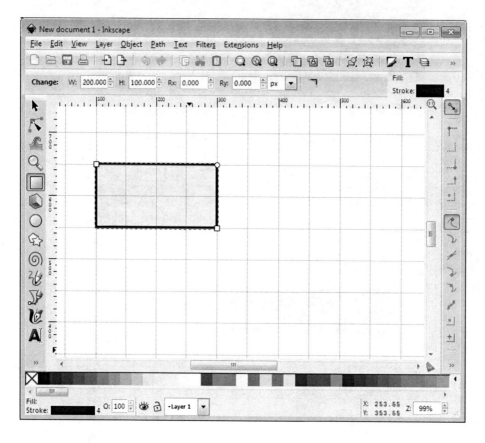

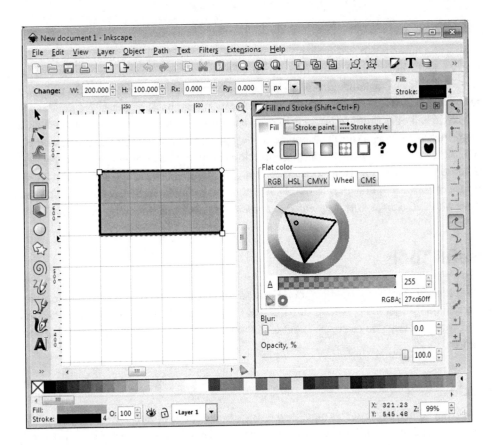

Scour

Much of the imagery available as public domain or open license on the web (particularly, that available from Wikimedia and OpenClipArt.org, as discussed in various places later in this chapter) has been created using either Adobe Illustrator or Inkscape. SVG developers may wish to take advantage of some of this imagery for creating animations or more complex scenes—but may find that it is hard to program with, or base derivations upon, because of the complexity of the output.

In such cases, a nearly indispensable tool that works in conjunction with drawing packages that produce SVG output is *Scour* (which is a part of Inkscape, actually), a small program created by Jeff Schiller for the purpose of cleaning up some of the bulky output that such programs sometimes create. Both Inkscape and Illustrator seem to have become sensitive to the occasional need of authors to be able to adjust SVG drawings programmatically, and Scour can dramatically simplify the markup to make it easier to do so.

Perhaps the easiest way to use Scour is simply to open a file in Inkscape and resave it as "optimized SVG." Scour allows users to specify the number of decimals of accuracy, as well as a number of other features.

SVG-Edit

We turn now to a new class of SVG drawing programs: web applications. The most important of these to date is SVG-Edit. The program is an open source, Google code project that enables web-based SVG drawing. SVG-Edit is well maintained, and it's still evolving, through the efforts of a sizable group of volunteers. Though SVG-Edit doesn't have the sophistication, user base, or expressive power of Illustrator or Inkscape, it does produce fairly clean code and provides an easy way to create SVG drawings without interrupting your workflow by opening a new application window. One enduring complaint with SVG-Edit is that its Bézier curve editor is bulky and counterintuitive. Many geometrically fluent SVG authors view this as a serious drawback. However, the simplicity of the web-based interface and the ease of converting drawings to usable SVG code make this limitation easier to bear. You can experiment with SVG-Edit at *http://svg-edit.googlecode.com/svn/trunk/editor/svg-editor.html*.

Other Useful Tools

Some other tools are worthy of brief mention because they either show promise for development or enable certain things that the programs described in the previous sections do not. They are also all web based, meaning that you can experiment with them easily, with very little investment of either time or effort.

Mugeda

From *https://www.mugeda.com/*, this quite new entry into the space of web-based drawing programs stems from a company headed by Lucas Wang. Mugeda has intuitive drawing tools, a crisp interface, and impressive animation capabilities. Its SVG support is still under development, but the sophistication of its user interface and overall functionality makes it worth keeping an eye on.

Pilat

In the cartographic domain, Michel Hirtzler, known for his pioneering work with the SVG DOM, created an interesting tool with two components. The first lets you choose from a list or load from a file system, and display a path itinerary in the GPX format, while the other lets you easily draw on a map and save or load an itinerary. You can then open the file with GPS software or transmit to a GPS. The tool uses IGN cartography (cartographic databases and infrastructures) and Open Layers (an open source mapping library); you can select maps, orthoimagery, cadastral parcels, or administrative display. Pilat provides some mapping widgets, and displays longitude and latitude with a selectable measurement system. Pilat is available at *http://pilatinfo.org/ign/index.html*.

SVG Editor

Web programmer Chris Peto developed this program (see *http://www.resource-solutions.de/svgeditor/*) several years ago, though it is still under development. It features a good interface and has many UI features to recommend it over SVG-Edit.

SVG Drawing Tool

This is another web-based program contemporary with SVG-Edit and SVG Editor (find it at *http:// srufaculty.sru.edu/david.dailey/svg/Draw018.html*). While it hasn't been actively maintained since 2005, it does produce cleaner output than many of the others, and supports path smoothing, path simplification, and a certain amount of intentional randomness. An allied program, available at *http:// srufaculty.sru.edu/david.dailey/svg/SVGOpen2010/Polygons/polygons8.html*, produces random polygons in polynomial time.

Grapher

A project begun at Carnegie Mellon in the mid-1980s, Grapher has been rebuilt in half a dozen platforms and languages since landing in SVG with JavaScript. This open source project, located at *http:// srufaculty.sru.edu/david.dailey/grapher/*, in its current incarnation, coded largely by Eric Elder, allows for the creation and editing of the mathematical objects known as graphs. The code base could be useful for people doing software project management, navigation research, website design, and other things network theoretic.

SCION

While not exactly a drawing tool, Statechart-to-ECMAScript Compiler (SCION) focuses on top-down construction of web programs and interfaces. It is one of several programs developed outside the web environment over the years involving a kind of visual programming. You can see more about it at *https://github.com/jbeard4/SCION* and *http://svgopen.org/2010/papers/45-Developing_a_ StatecharttoECMAScript_Compiler_Optimized_for_SVG_User_Interface_Development_for_the_World_ Wide_Web/index.html*.

Extension Tools

A variety of tasks, such as detecting whether or not an older browser supports SVG, are difficult or troublesome for web developers to perform. In addition, there are things that certain modern browsers don't do well (or at all)—for example, current versions of Internet Explorer lack SMIL support. Finally, there are operations that the SVG spec itself doesn't yet support. Fortunately, in the world around SVG, a number of programmers facing such issues have come up with some interesting tools that can help.

Batik

The Apache Batik project, available at *http://xmlgraphics.apache.org/batik/*, is a Java-based SVG engine that offers what may be the most comprehensive SVG implementation anywhere. As Cameron McCormack, one of the cofounders of the project, writes:

When you load a document in Squiggle (the stand-alone SVG viewer built with Batik) or in an SVG canvas embedded in your own Java application, it has access to all the regular Java classes that you can use. And you can access them directly from JavaScript embedded in the SVG document.

As such, it has numerous features that simplify the creation of data-driven SVG documents, as well as access to the powerful image manipulation libraries of Java and Linux. It also has facilities for exporting SVG to bitmapped formats such as JPEG and PNG so that older browsers that are not SVG enabled can display fallback content. From Java, you can invoke the Batik rasterizer and then inspect the pixel values of the results—a capability that is not currently implemented in stand-alone SVG. Cameron McCormack identifies Batik's most important features as the following:

- Squiggle, the stand-alone viewer

- The *JSVGCanvas* Java component, which can be embedded in any Java Swing application or in Java applets

- The *rasterizer* Java class and command-line program, which is capable of converting from SVG to PDF (even though PDF is not a raster format)

SmilScript and FakeSmile

In the somewhat complicated evolution of SVG from being a centerpiece of the W3C standards to becoming an unwelcome cousin of the *<canvas>* tag (Apple's darling), and then rebounding back to supplant Flash and Silverlight, SVG has been a complicated specification for browser developers to implement. Firefox, despite having an early native SVG implementation, lagged far behind Opera and ASV in implementing SMIL animation. Similarly, although Firefox now has very good support for SVG animation, some other browsers (notably WebKit and Internet Explorer) still lag behind. Between 2006 to 2008, the FakeSmile and SmilScript projects were developed to solve such problems by implementing in JavaScript what browsers were reluctant to support natively. For people who want animation content to play in recalcitrant browsers, FakeSmile and SmilScript may provide partial solutions.

SmilScript

This animation library was begun in 2006 by Doug Schepers, who, in his presentation at SVG Open in 2007, remarked that SmilScript was less of a serious attempt at implementing animation than an attempt to show the browser community that implementing animation was not as difficult a task as some had argued. SmilScript is still available at *http://schepers.cc/svg/smilscript/,* and is distributed under an open source artistic license. It interpolates between the values specified by *begin* and *end*— although it doesn't handle a *values* attribute—and overall, it manages to mimic a good number of the things that SMIL animation can do. Its list of supported and unsupported features lets SVG developers know exactly what it might help with.

FakeSmile

Development of FakeSmile was begun in 2008 by David Leunen, though the effort (licensed under the MIT and GNU licenses) seems to have attracted several other contributors. You can see the most recent version at *https://code.launchpad.net/smil*.

<replicate>

The *<replicate>* proposal for adding declarative drawing to SVG was first proposed to the SVG Working Group by David Dailey in 2008 (see *http://lists.w3.org/Archives/Public/ public-svg-ig/2008JulSep/0109.html*). A more formal proposal was presented at SVG Open 2010 (see *http://svgopen.org/2010/papers/46-A_proposal_for_adding_declarative_drawing_to_SVG/index .html*). Basically, *<replicate>* is an extension to the *<use>* tag that allows developers to create multiple instances of a drawing using *tweening* (the process of generating intermediate frames between two images), specified by syntax much like that used for *<animate>*, which interpolates over time. Hence, *<replicate>* is like *<animate>*, but for space instead of time. *<replicate>* is a Google code project with an open license. The proposal has recently gained some traction within the SVG Working Group, but it is unclear whether *<replicate>* will be adopted. In the meantime, the proposal is being extended to include animation support for browsers that don't yet support SMIL, and to include declarative randomness so that rich scenes may be generated relatively easily. You can see a large collection of examples of *<replicate>* that use the JavaScript code base at *http://srufaculty.sru.edu/david.dailey/ svg/SVGOpen2010/replicate.htm*. Interest in the proposal has come from outside the SVG group as well. For example, there are use cases for HTML form element replication (e.g., for repeating fields in data entry), InkML for multivariate time-series data, and 3D declarative applications. At present, *<replicate>* enables several things that SVG doesn't, including rich gradients, 3D drawing and animation, and perspective patterns. The following image shows an example.

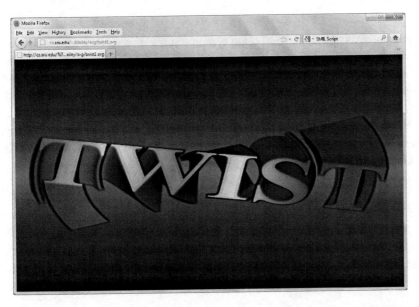

The code below shows the proposed *<replicate>* syntax:

```
<text id="T" fill="url(#g)" font-family="serif" stroke="black"
   stroke-width="1.5" stroke-opacity=".1"
   font-size="28" x="4" y="60" font-weight="bold">
   <replicate repeatCount="190">
     <replicateAttribute attributeName="transform"
       from="rotate(-20 50 50)" to="rotate(10 50 50)" />
   </replicate>
   TWIST
</text>
```

Integrated Development Environments

While a fair number of options exist that support HTML code development in the context of style sheets and web resources, SVG has not been quite so blessed, perhaps because of its complexity, or perhaps because of the longstanding uncertainty about whether Microsoft would support it. Here is a brief and current inventory of tools (which is likely to quickly become more substantial).

First, the perfect integrated development environment (IDE) for SVG does not yet seem to exist. The perfect IDE would have code hinting, would be aware of SVG syntax, would enable SVG previewing (which a few actually do), and most importantly, would provide the ability to edit a drawing in the preview window, thereby adjusting the code in a markup window. As the popularity of SVG continues to grow (which it has greatly over the past two years), such a development environment is likely to come into existence soon. Announcements by majors for this type of product were made at the SVG Open 2011 conference.

Oxygen

For several years, this powerful XML-based authoring system was the recommended environment for creating SVG documents and presentations for SVG Open. This Romanian-based product features code hinting and broad-based XML support, including support for XSLT and conversions between XML types. Oxygen is a powerful, professional-class IDE that connects programmers with the vast world of XML, of which SVG is just a part. Its SVG preview feature, as well as its ability to embed SVG in DocBook and XHTML documents, is quite thoroughly implemented, and has far better SVG support than some browsers. As of a year ago, Oxygen supported most of the SVG standard, with the exception of compound filters and SMIL animation.

Adobe Dreamweaver

Having both built and acquired a number of solid web development platforms, including those from Allaire, Aldus, and Macromedia, Adobe provides products that have long been choices for web developers. The next section mentions some of Adobe's other products, but the centerpiece of its web development lineup for the programmer/coder is Dreamweaver. Dreamweaver not only allows live previewing of SVG that has been embedded within an HTML document (through the *<object>* tag), but also supports code hinting and previewing for stand-alone SVG documents.

HTML-Kit

This freely downloadable software (with its companion professional edition) is available from *http://www.htmlkit.com/*. For those who have used Allaire's Homesite, the interface and IDE will be very familiar. To preview SVG, the free version requires that you download and configure a plug-in, but the professional version, HTML-Kit Tools, offers HTML5 awareness, including options for using a template to create SVG 1.1 documents and adding SVG 1.1 code blocks.

Other Useful Information

The SVG Interest Group (chartered by the W3C) organized some information in 2009 and 2010 at *http://www.w3.org/Graphics/SVG/IG/wiki/Authoring_tools_and_editors*. Based on an informal poll of the SVG community (through the svg-developers and SVG-IG lists), we found that SVG authors are also using the following tools:

- Chrome Developer Tools
- Opera Dragonfly
- Firefox Firebug
- Mozilla SeaMonkey
- Komodo Edit
- Notepad++
- TextPad
- Eclipse
- gEdit
- Safari Web Inspector
- WebDwarf

Other Tools That Support SVG

There are literally hundreds of applications, both conventional and web-based, that support SVG at some level. The software behemoths Microsoft and Adobe both have extensive SVG support in their product lines.

In addition to Illustrator, several other Adobe products support or use SVG, including the following:

- Edge
- InDesign
- Dreamweaver

Microsoft software (other than Internet Explorer 9) that supports SVG includes the following:

- Visio
- Expression
- Visual Studio
- Bing Maps
- PowerPoint Live (provides some support as an export format)

Miscellaneous

This section describes some other interesting things that you may want to know about SVG, including the extensive open source and public domain clip art libraries at Wikimedia Commons (*http://commons .wikimedia.org/*), the Open Clip Art Library (*http://openclipart.org*), and the fascinating OpenStreetMap project.

Wikimedia and Wikipedia

The SVG images used on Wikipedia (generally stored at Wikimedia) are browsable by category at *http://commons.wikimedia.org/wiki/Category:SVG*. These categories range from Astronomy, Biology, and Chemistry, to Flags, Ancient Egypt, and Vectorized Brick Wall Textures. Often, as discussed at some length in the article "Geometric Accessibility: Who Needs SVG?" (*http://cs.sru.edu/~ddailey/ svg/GeometricAccessibility.html*), such image files may come with considerably more bulk than strictly needed. Refer to the "Scour" section earlier in this chapter for ways of simplifying such files if you are interested in adapting them for your own use.

The Open Clip Art Library

At the Open Clip Art Library (*http://openclipart.org/*), you can find extensive (albeit a bit hard to browse) collections of quality vector graphics intended for use by the public. Wikipedia informs us:

The project started in early 2004 by Inkscape (http://en.wikipedia.org/wiki/Inkscape) developers Jon Phillips (http://en.wikipedia.org/wiki/Jon_Phillips) and Bryce Harrington to collect designs of flags from all around the world, having been inspired by the efforts to create a collection of flags created by users of vector graphics software Sodipodi (http://en.wikipedia.org/wiki/Sodipodi). It progressed very well and the project goals were extended to generic clipart, and as of October 2007 it incorporated over 10,000 images from over 500 artists, and offers the entire collection for free download. All images are dedicated to the public domain (http://en.wikipedia.org/wiki/Public_domain) by their contributors.

The project has grown considerably, attracting more than 5,000 unique visitors per day and containing more than 30,000 graphic files.

The OpenStreetMap Project

Finally, we'd like to mention the OpenStreetMap project (*http://www.openstreetmap.org/*). This project started in response to a need for better maps for bicyclists in England, but has expanded into a worldwide volunteer organization that consists of more than 100,000 volunteers. Volunteers from around the world upload GPS coordinates from their cell phones and other GPS devices, and then later annotate their coordinates, entering the data into an enormously successful map of the world.

One of the founders of OpenStreetMap, George James, tells many fascinating anecdotes about the power of crowdsourcing as practiced within the project (see *http://www.svgopen.org/2010/registration.php?section=keynotes*). One intriguing anecdote relates that when relief workers arrived in Haiti following the earthquake of 2010, much of the devastated area had not been mapped, complicating the relief effort. But volunteers using OpenStreetMap were able to map the affected area almost completely within three days. James points out that OpenStreetMap may produce as many as 10,000 SVG images per day.

Summary

This chapter described a number of tools that you can use to aid in SVG development. The past decade has seen a slow yet unstoppable snowball effect for SVG that has produced an avalanche of software and open source JavaScript toolkit libraries, and an associated rise in developer interest in the SVG language. This is an exciting time for web and SVG developers, because this coming decade will see even more improvements. The creators of the toolkits and applications described in this chapter are actively improving them at this very moment.

CHAPTER 7

Building a Web Application: Case Studies

All things were established in harmony

after the order of the numbers.

Boethius, circa 520 AD

This chapter will show you how to create web applications that can run equally well in a pure SVG context or in a mixed namespace HTML+SVG context, using available JavaScript tools and libraries. The chapter also covers the advantages of adopting an OOD model. The goal is to get an insight on how to build a rock solid, framed environment for your applications that can withstand browser or specification inconsistencies, migrations and other traps. You will see that once you integrate properly the concepts and definitions, you harness unlimited power in what you can make happen in a browser. Consider SVG a powerful and complete library that you can access through the DOM methods. Consider the DOM for what it is exactly, an Object Model, and although this may seem anodyne, in reality when you are writing code you are building an abstract representation of it; you are organizing its objects through representational objects. The keywords are: "architecture," you are designing a structure; "description," you are describing the procedural works; "conducting," you lead the execution of the works. Also consider learning to sight-read JavaScript code like you sight-read a newspaper. Off you go, you are in command, relaxed, ready to have lots of fun and satisfaction, while impressing your boss, your client, or your teacher.

The tools that you will be using for the two applications you are going to study are Pergola, d3.js (which we will refer to in this chapter as D3), and Polymaps. We will see how a well-written library is a library that is specialized, and can be plugged into another to create or extend a framework.

About Pergola

Pergola is composed of a native SVG framework and libraries that run equally well in HTML. It defines classes for creating widgets and system objects, libraries of SVG components, superclass prototype methods, classes' prototype extensions, and core utility functions. The core utility functions include a universal SVG DOM helper—an interfacing function allowing the creation of any SVG element with any attributes set, using SVG grammar and vocabulary, in one pass—and its sibling HTML DOM helper. By adopting the concept of considering the implementations as existing libraries, Pergola avoids the archaic approach of creating pseudo-classes of elements and primitives needing a proprietary pseudolanguage. The main purpose of Pergola is to allow the author to create web applications and user interfaces of systemic type thanks to its built-in low level system logic and extended User Events and Functions mechanisms.

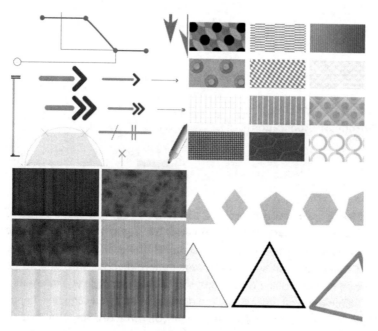

The preceding image shows objects from the Pergola plug-in libraries. Markers, patterns, and filters are functions, and the returned object is created and appended to the *<defs>* if it does not exist. It is not created and appended at runtime. A shape definition is an object defining *element* and *geometry* properties; the utility function *pergola.use(object)* allows you to use a shape definition, and because only the geometry is defined for shapes, this leaves total control over paint attributes and transformations, which are passed as object argument using SVG grammar and vocabulary. Thus, the *stroke-width* attribute can be controlled independently of any uniform scaling.

Pergola was created thanks to the experience acquired by the author during the development of GEMï, a web operating system prototype, itself inspired by the author's findings during an assignment he had in 2004: the superposition of an SVG-based interface layer onto a SoC (System on Chip), where the objective was to produce a visual debugger allowing engineers to trace the processes running simultaneously in a chip; a preexisting program would feed the interface in providing code dump and animated simulation for each process. The base requirement was a systemic interface showing at runtime one timeline window with tape transport and scrubbing features, one global animation window, and one global dump window. The user had the possibility of opening a dump window and an animation window for each individual process.

At the end of the line the constitutive elements of GEMï were organized into a framework with libraries. The entire rewriting of GEMï using Pergola served as a road test to see that the latter successfully met the requirements that the author had set for it, and that it responded to the needs of the developer in a real, complex situation.

All Pergola widgets and interface elements, some of which are shown in the following image, are highly customizable by overriding prototype properties, including the interactive behavior of some system objects, and their appearance can be configured globally through the skin engine, for accessibility purposes, for example.

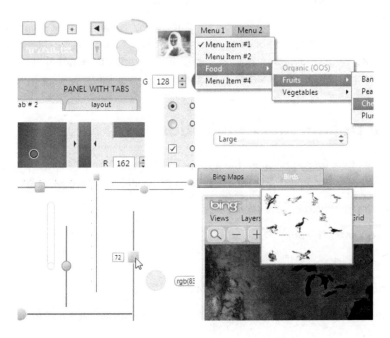

D3 Review

D3 stands for *Data-Driven Documents*. In a broad sense, D3 is a library specialized for producing charts, but it's also suitable for building an entire document from imported data, going beyond the simple definition of a chart by extending the definition. If it is true that a developer with substantial math skills can take full advantage of the library, the lambda developer will nevertheless find it useful and accessible. It uses SVG as its primary rendering mechanism.

D3 can be used with Pergola "as is"; the official distribution is 1.27.1 at the time of this writing. The example scripts require only very minor changes to avoid namespace collisions (because of the examples' original design as stand-alone demonstrations, not because of Pergola or D3) when they run together in the same application. The application demonstrates interactivity between the documents.

Polymaps

The version of Polymaps used here with Pergola to build a mapping application is 2.4.0. This version was modified precisely to eliminate crossing of domains of competency (what the libraries are specialized for), as well as to make it compliant in a stand-alone SVG context.

Polymaps is very compact and agile, yet it provides an API that is likely to fulfill all your mapping needs. In this respect it seems to outclass some of its competitors. Although it does not define cartographic utilities, this can in fact be considered an asset in respect to the symbiotic nature that should be, as we have seen, one of the essential characteristics of a library.

Interactive Multiple Documents Application

The first case study presented here is an application that groups multiple documents created with D3 into one single SVG or HTML+SVG document. The D3 example scripts used for this are:

- *force.js* (*http://mbostock.github.com/d3/ex/force.html*)

- *worm.js* (*http://bl.ocks.org/1216850*)

- *clock.js* (in the library's package)

- *stream.js* (*http://mbostock.github.com/d3/ex/stream.html*)

Each example will be integrated into a fully featured window with transformation tools, using Pergola.

The objective is to establish a level of interactivity among the different documents in the application. If you take a look at the D3 example *Force-Directed Graph*, you can easily imagine an application where you would be a click away from accessing the character diagrams of all of Victor Hugo's works, not just *Les Misérables*—provided they were all available from a database. You could have more than one diagram open for comparing. You could select the works from a pop-up list or from a menu, or perhaps content updates or other events in one window could update the current content of Victor Hugo's window using JSON. You will see that you do have the necessary tools at your disposal for doing all that.

To begin, an SVG document loads the libraries and the scripts (you will see the HTML version later):

```
<?xml version="1.0" encoding="UTF-8" standalone="no"?>
<?xml-stylesheet href="style.css" type="text/css"?>
<!DOCTYPE svg PUBLIC "-//W3C//DTD SVG 1.1//EN" "http://www.w3.org/Graphics/SVG/1.1/DTD/svg11.dtd">
<svg xmlns="http://www.w3.org/2000/svg" xmlns:xlink="http://www.w3.org/1999/xlink"
xmlns:ev="http://www.w3.org/2001/xml-events" version="1.1" baseProfile="full" width="100%"
height="100%" xml:space="preserve" zoomAndPan="disable" onresize="pergola.resize()">
  <title>Pergola windows- D3 multiple documents</title>

// Pergola
  <script xlink:href="../../pergola/pergola_min.es" type="text/javascript"/>
  <script xlink:href="config.js" type="text/javascript"/>
  <script xlink:href="../../pergola/lib/filters/filters.es" type="text/javascript"/>
  <script xlink:href="../../pergola/lib/markers/markers.es" type="text/javascript"/>
  <script xlink:href="../../pergola/lib/patterns/patterns.es" type="text/javascript"/>
  <script xlink:href="../../pergola/lib/shapes/shapes.es" type="text/javascript"/>
  <script xlink:href="../../pergola/lib/symbols/symbols.es" type="text/javascript"/>
  <script xlink:href="../../pergola/lib/cursors/cursors.es" type="text/javascript"/>
  <script xlink:href="../../pergola/lib/qtips.es" type="text/javascript"/>
  <script xlink:href="../../pergola/lib/msg.es" type="text/javascript"/>
  <script xlink:href="../../pergola/lib/skins/skins.es" type="text/javascript"/>
  <script xlink:href="../../pergola/c.es" type="text/javascript"/>

// D3
  <script xlink:href="../../pergola/extlib/d3-28b0e22/d3.js" type="text/javascript"/>
  <script xlink:href="../../pergola/extlib/d3-28b0e22/d3.geom.js" type="text/javascript"/>
  <script xlink:href="../../pergola/extlib/d3-28b0e22/d3.layout.js" type="text/javascript"/>
  <script xlink:href="../../pergola/extlib/d3-28b0e22/d3.time.js" type="text/javascript"/>

// D3 Examples
  <script xlink:href="stream_layers.js" type="text/javascript"/>
  <script xlink:href="stream.js" type="text/javascript"/>
  <script xlink:href=" clock.js" type="text/javascript"/>
  <script xlink:href=" force.js" type="text/javascript"/>
  <script xlink:href="worm.js" type="text/javascript"/>

</svg>
```

The order of the example scripts is irrelevant. We are going to start with *stream.js*.

Encapsulating the Stream Example

The first step is to define a Pergola window, the container for the stream document:

```
var streamWin = new pergola.Window("D3 Stream");
```

The preceding code line creates an instance of the *Window* class; it does not create the physical window. In this phase, the instance goes through the prototype inheritance process and gets a *name* property and a unique *id* (in the absence of the string parameter these will be generated XML names). This technique of splitting the instantiation and the actual building of an object into two separate calls offers multiple advantages: the second phase, the call to the *build()* method, can be executed remotely or dynamically; instance properties and methods can be defined in between the two phases; during the second phase, inherited properties can be overridden and the object can reference itself. Experience proves that this technique helps avoid downstream interactivity chokepoints and enhances code readability and maintenance.

The following image shows a Pergola window with its default settings, before it gets populated.

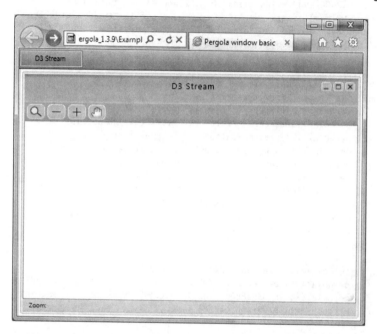

We can now define a simple interactive project where events from another window will change the base color of the stream diagram and will update the transition. You can explore more interesting ideas that use these techniques, but the goal here is to show how to apply the principle and methods concretely, without the overhead of more complex processing. We will also implement some private interactivity for this window: the user must be able to select a different type of diagram through a menu, and update the transition through a tool button in the toolbar.

Taking a look at the original *stream.js* example, you will notice that the container element *"#chart"* for the graph is assigned to the global variable *vis*:

```
var vis = d3.select("#chart")
```

A quick look at the other examples shows that the same variable name is used in some of them with the same purpose, and the same goes for other variables. We would normally reflexively rename each of those global variables with a unique name. But, come to think, we did say "Object Oriented Development model"; we will turn those variables into properties of the *streamWin* window, and therefore they will be protected. We will apply this change only to the D3 examples that we plan to make interactive.

The second step is to append the diagram to the window, no longer directly to the element with the ID *chart*, (which by the way does not exist in this environment). The goal here is not to learn the structure and the API of the *Window* class. All you need to know is that each window instance assigns a new *pergola.ChildDoc* instance to its *childDoc* property. This object, designed to host the window's contents, defines an *<svg>* element referenced by the property *port*, and a *<group>* element referenced by the property *transformable*. We have the options of appending static contents to *port* and transformable contents to *transformable*. In fact, Pergola keeps a shadow copy of the DOM for most critical objects: objects that are intended or likely to be manipulated.

> **Note** While some have argued that shadowing the DOM may hurt performance, this is not consistent with the experience of these authors and likely dates to a time when RAM was less carefully managed by the browsers.

The new container for the diagram example is now *streamWin.childDoc.transformable*. We will of course apply this change to all the D3 examples.

To append the contents, we have several methods at our disposal. The easiest and cleanest way is by setting the property *contains* of the window object. This property can get a node or a function. We then define a helper function as instance method and assign it to the property *contains*, which we will define in the call to the *build()* method. The D3 example script is the body of the function.

The resulting coding sequence is:

1. Instantiation of the window object *forceWin*

2. Definition of the instance method contents as wrapper for the D3 example script

3. Construction of the window (call to the *build()* method)

Put into practice, this results in:

```
var streamWin = new pergola.Window("D3 Stream");
streamWin.contents = function () {
// D3 example script goes here.
};
streamWin.build({
  properties
  ...
  contains : function () {return this.contents();}
});
```

This will produce a Pergola window with its default settings. Here we could override a variety of prototype properties that define the window's geometry, aspect, and options, as well as define new instance properties that we plan to use. For example, if we wanted our window without the default set of transformation tools, with a particular background color, and to start maximized, we would specify

```
hasZoomAndPan : false,
fill : value,
isFull : true
```

For *streamWin*, the default settings are just fine. We will simply override its default position and size.

Adding Interactivity to the D3 Stream Window

We will now prepare the interactivity for the *stream.js* script, which goes in the *forceWin.contents* function. One of the interactivity objectives that we have set is to be able to change the stream type of the chart. In the original example, stream layers are used. We add stream waves data:

```
this.data0 = d3.layout.stack().offset("wiggle")(stream_layers(n, m));
this.data1 = d3.layout.stack().offset("wiggle")(stream_layers(n, m));
this.data2 = d3.layout.stack().offset("wiggle")(stream_waves(n, m));
```

Note that the variables *data0* and *data1* (and the new *data3*) would be local variables once the script becomes the body of the *contents* function, and there would not be any risk of collision with variables with the same name declared in other scripts; but then they would no longer be available globally, and activity driven from external objects would not be possible. By declaring them instead as properties of the *streamWin* object, they can always be accessed. This will allow the interactivity to be triggered by events taking place in another window or any other object in the interface.

Now we have more than two transition data sets. We set two properties to store initial origin and destination of the transition:

```
this.transitFrom = this.data0;
this.transitTo = this.data1;
```

We will see later the construction of the menu for selecting the type of transition.

A note about property naming: All good programming books stress the importance of setting explicit names for variables. This is even more important when working with complex objects like windows, which may have a relatively large number of properties, many of which, being of a systemic nature, are hidden to the user. A window object may very well have instance properties named *from* and *to* (although it actually does not). Thus, not only *transitFrom* and *transitTo* are more explicit, but the risk of name collisions is also minimized. Equally, it would be sensible to rename *data0*, for example, to *streamTransitionData0*, or better, define a *streamTransitionData* array.

The other interactivity objective is to change the base color of the stream diagram and update the transition. We are going to make sure that the activity in *streamWin* can be driven by any object in the environment, and not just by the window designated for interaction in this example.

Extending the *transition* function, which now expects two parameters:

```
this.transition = function (destination, fill) {
/*
 * string.darken([f]) is a Pergola extension method of the String prototype.
 * string is any  rgb format. f is any number between 0 and 1.
 * If f is omitted, it defaults to 0.5.
 */
  color = fill ? d3.interpolateRgb(fill, fill.darken()) : color;
// If the Pergola debugger is loaded and enabled we can check the
// state of our variables without stopping the script with alerts.
  $D({"fill" : fill, "shade" : fill.darken()});
  this.chart.
  data(function() {
      o.transitTo = o.transitFrom;
      return o.transitFrom = destination;
    })
  .transition()
  .duration(2500)
  .attr("fill", function() { return o.color(Math.random()); })
  .attr("d", area);
}
```

Notice how in the callback function passed as parameter to the *data* method, the keyword *this* is not used. In the new execution context created by the function, the *this* value is not a reference to the *streamWin* object. In our script, the *this* value (the *streamWin* object) will be assigned to the local variable *o* (technically a property of the *Activation* object).

The Transitions Menu

We are now going to define the menu through which users can select the transition type, either Layers or Waves.

Simply setting the property *menu* in the call to the *build()* method will cause the window to create a menu bar. The property *menu* gets an object whose properties define *menu* objects. For each *menu* object, we define its *title* and *items:*

```
menu : {
  transitions : {
    title : "Transitions",
    items : {
      streamLayers : {
        string : "Stream Layers",
        active : true,
        check : true,
        exclusive : true,
        fn : function () {
          streamWin.transitTo = (streamWin.transitFrom == streamWin.data0) ?
            streamWin.data1 : streamWin.data0;
        }
      },
      streamWaves : {
        string : "Stream Waves",
        active : true,
        check : false,
```

```
        exclusive : true,
        fn : function () {streamWin.transitTo = streamWin.data2;}
      }
    }
  }
},
```

For each menu item, we can define: its initial state through the active property (redundant here because it defaults to true); determine whether it has a check mark by setting the check property, and control the initial display state (true or false); and whether its check mark acts like a radio button with sibling items by setting the exclusive property; a User Function.

The following figure shows the "Transitions" menu, the tool button for updating transitions (detailed in the next section) and the Pergola debugger active.

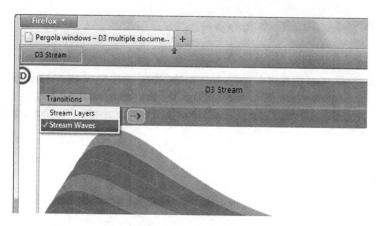

The Transition Tool Button

Now that users can select different transition types, we are going to add a tool button in the toolbar to update the transitions. In the original D3 example, this was done by an HTML button, but in this object-oriented environment, the type of interactivity we need could not be implemented through a hard-coded anonymous button:

<button class="first last" onclick="transition()">

or would at least represent a complication. A tool button in Pergola is a subclass of *Button*. The *Window* class allows a tool button or a group of tool buttons to be defined on the fly by setting the *tools* property in the call to the *build()* method. Alternatively, you can add these at a later stage, manually or dynamically, using the *Window* prototype method *addTools()*. This example uses the first technique:

```
tools : {
  streamGroup : {
    separator : true,
    transition : {
      symbol : {
        symbol : pergola.symbols.transition,
```

```
        x : 6,
        y : 11
      },
      quickTip : {tip : "Apply transition"},
      ev : "mouseup",
      fn : function () {this.owner.transition(this.owner.transitTo);}
    }
  }
},
```

Pergola objects can be completely customized during instantiation by overriding geometric and paint properties, or globally, for each individual class, in the skin file. Effects can be disabled or overridden to implement accessibility extensions by developers with the right know how. Here too it would be out of scope to customize a button; the default appearance and behavior are just fine. We only add a symbol from the symbols library, a quick tip, an event, and the associated handler. In this respect, it is interesting to note that the property *ev* can get an array of event types, and that the property *fn* can get several formats including a string expressing the function name. The function format is parsed and the function is then invoked through the prototype's *handleEvent()* method.

Note that the symbol used is not an SVG *<symbol>* element. It is a definition in the *pergola .symbols* library, which in this particular case uses a marker reference from the *pergola.markers* library. This symbol was defined ad hoc and added to the symbols library by the author, as a user.

The advantages in terms of flexibility, visualization, and maintenance offered by a pragmatic OOD model are now beginning to become apparent.

Here is the complete D3 Stream code:

```
var streamWin = new pergola.Window("D3 Stream");

streamWin.contents = function () {
  var n = 20,
      m = 200,
      w = 960,
      h = 500,
      o = this,
      color = d3.interpolateRgb("#aad", "#556");

  this.data0 = d3.layout.stack().offset("wiggle")(stream_layers(n, m));
  this.data1 = d3.layout.stack().offset("wiggle")(stream_layers(n, m));
  this.data2 = d3.layout.stack().offset("wiggle")(stream_waves(n, m));
  this.transitFrom = this.data0;
  this.transitTo = this.data1;

  var mx = m - 1,
      my = d3.max(this.data0.concat(this.data1), function(d) {
        return d3.max(d, function(d) {
          return d.y0 + d.y;
        });
      });
```

```
        var area = d3.svg.area()
          .x(function(d) { return d.x * w / mx; })
          .y0(function(d) { return h - d.y0 * h / my; })
          .y1(function(d) { return h - (d.y + d.y0) * h / my; });


      var vis = d3.select($C({element : "g", transform : "translate(" + 10 + "," + 40 + ")"}));
      this.chart = vis.selectAll()
        .data(this.data0)
        .enter().append("svg:path")
        .attr("fill", function() { return streamWin.color(Math.random()); })
        .attr("d", this.area);
      this.childDoc.transformable.appendChild(vis.node());

    this.transition = function (destination, fill) {
      color = fill ? d3.interpolateRgb(fill, fill.darken()) : color;
      this.chart.data(function() {
        o.transitTo = o.transitFrom;
        return o.transitFrom = destination;
      })
        .transition()
        .duration(2500)
        .attr("fill", function() { return o.color(Math.random()); })
        .attr("d", this.area);
    }
};

streamWin.build({
  x : 100,
  y : 100,
  width : 600,
  height : 420,
  menu : {
    transitions : {
      title : "Transitions",
      items : {
        streamLayers : {
          string : "Stream Layers",
          active : true,
          check : true,
          exclusive : true,
          fn : function () {
            streamWin.transitTo = (streamWin.transitFrom == streamWin.data0) ?
              streamWin.data1 : streamWin.data0;
          }
        },
        streamWaves : {
          string : "Stream Waves",
          active : true,
          check : false,
          exclusive : true,
          fn : function () {streamWin.transitTo = streamWin.data2;}
        }
      }
    }
  },
  tools : {
```

```
    streamGroup : {
      separator : true,
      transition : {
        symbol : {
          symbol : pergola.symbols.transition,
          x : 6,
          y : 11
        },
        quickTip : {tip : "Apply transition"},
        ev : "mouseup",
        fn : function () {this.owner.transition(this.owner.transitTo);}
      }
    }
  },
  contains : function () {return this.contents();}
});
```

If you run the code at this stage (*http://www.dotuscomus.com/pergola/pergola_1.4.0/Examples/D3/ D3_step1_stream.svg*), you will see a window with the stream example, where you can select transition types from the menu and apply transitions by clicking the tool button, which is next to the transformation tools group.

A few considerations on design:

1. Some of the local variables (*color, area*, and *vis*) have not been declared as properties of the *streamWin* object. This implies that the example works as long as the *transition()* function is executed in the same scope—only if it remains nested within the *contents()* function. If you needed to make the *transition()* function portable, for example by declaring it as a prototype method (or global function) rather than as an instance method, then the variables listed above would have the value *undefined* in the function's body, and the example would not work. Therefore they would need to be declared as instance properties. As such, they could be accessed from anywhere in the script, or dynamically from remote scripts.

2. In the original code you can see these two statements: *vis.selectAll("path")* and *d3.selectAll("path")*, meant to refer to the same group of paths (the *<visualization>* elements). This raises two problems, one minor and one critical. The first is that each time a transition is launched the selection process is reexecuted, because the value returned by the *selectAll()* method (the selected group of paths) in the first statement was not stored; the second is that, by using *d3.selectAll("path")* instead of *vis.selectAll("path")* in the *transition()* function, any path element that may have been added to the document, which is obviously the case in this application, will be affected by the transition, resulting in a free "artistic" reinterpretation of the works and of some interface elements. In the modified code we have then assigned the reference to the property *chart*. In this respect, note that a reference to a DOM node (shadowing the DOM) is simply a pointer to a memory address.

3. To ensure dynamic interactivity and content updates, the *pergola.Window* constructor registers the *DOMNodeInserted* and *DOMNodeRemoved* events on the group referenced by the *childDoc.transformable* property. Upon updates, the geometry of the relevant components of

the window is refreshed. The technique used in the original code (as well as in several other examples) for appending the path elements throws a cascade of errors in IE9, because the attempt to query the *BBox* of an element with no geometry, (for example, before setting the *d* attribute), fails. Although this behavior can be seen as particularly zealous, the *d* attribute is nevertheless "required" by the SVG specification. The code was then modified by deferring the appending of the paths' parent node (the *<g>* element), referenced by the *vis* object.

Encapsulating the Force Example

The same remarks made for the *stream.js* example apply. In particular, we need to declare the global variables as properties of the window object *forceWin*, and to replace the container.

Before proceeding, the time has come to see the benefits of adopting an OOD model, as mentioned in the introduction of this chapter, and how a different model, particularly one that extensively leverages functional programming, could possibly constitute a bottleneck in terms of interactivity design.

Designing software is a complex activity that involves, among other things, the anticipation of positive and negative effects that any constituent element or process of an entity can have on any other element or process of that same entity, as well as on its environment. Functional programming can provide terrific benefits: it is less bureaucratic, and hence smarter, and definitely a good performer. But to use it at the front end of the developer's interface is not the best method for opening communication channels, in that only experienced programmers can easily find their way through the jungle of functions returning functions, which in turn return other functions, and so forth. Doing so requires particular attention and certainly does not help with sight-reading (horizontal, vertical, and diagonal).

Going back to this precise case, we can see that the simple operation of declaring the variables as properties of the *forceWin* object through the *this* keyword is not possible for the *force.js* example because the function populating the diagram is called from a different execution context, and the caller does not provide a *this* value that then references the global object. Unfortunately the notion that this behavior is "wrong" seems to be widespread, but by the JavaScript specification, sections 10.4.3 and 11.1.1 (*http://www.ecma-international.org/publications/files/ECMA-ST/Ecma-262.pdf*), this behavior is correct. For the same design considerations evoked in the previous section, we will replace all local variables with properties of the *forceWin* object, and will use the same solution—that of declaring a local variable that remains a valid reference in the scope chain as a property of the *Activation* object: *var o = this;*.

We can then reassign the variables *force*, *link*, and *node* in the callback function like this: *o.force = d3.layout.force();*.

Those objects will then be accessible from a different scope. Why not simply hard-code the object's name in the callback function? Because that is not good design; at some point we might want the *contents* function to be multipurpose, a prototype method rather than an instance method. That way we could have several concurrent instances of the force diagram with different data, or a contextual instance that we could update dynamically with other data, which could be passed as parameter, or better, assigned upstream to a property of the containing object, although this would mean a complete redesign of the example. You can easily guess how this would give us the necessary freedom and ability to explore all the many opportunities.

Put into practice, this gives:

```
var forceWin = new pergola.Window("D3 Force-Directed Graph");

forceWin.contents = function () {
  var w = 960,
      h = 500,
      fill = d3.scale.category20(),
      o = this;

// replace <svg> with <g> (BBox needed). Replace container.
  this.vis = d3.select(forceWin.childDoc.transformable)
    .append("svg:g");

// sets a stable BBox
  $C({element : "rect", width : w, height : h, fill : "none", appendTo : this.vis.node()});

  d3.json("miserables.json", function(json) {
    o.force = d3.layout.force()
        .charge(-120)
        .linkDistance(30)
        .nodes(json.nodes)
        .links(json.links)
        .size([w, h])
        .start();

    o.link = this.vis.selectAll("line.link")
        .data(json.links)
      .enter().append("svg:line")
        .attr("class", "link")
        .attr("stroke-width", function(d) { return Math.sqrt(d.value); })
        .attr("x1", function(d) { return d.source.x; })
        .attr("y1", function(d) { return d.source.y; })
        .attr("x2", function(d) { return d.target.x; })
        .attr("y2", function(d) { return d.target.y; });

    o.node = this.vis.selectAll("circle.node")
        .data(json.nodes)
      .enter().append("svg:circle")
        .attr("class", "node")
        .attr("cx", function(d) { return d.x; })
        .attr("cy", function(d) { return d.y; })
        .attr("r", 5)
        .attr("fill", function(d) { return fill(d.group); })
        .call(o.force.drag);

    o.node.append("svg:title")
        .text(function(d) { return d.name; });

    o.vis.transition()
        .duration(1000)
```

```
    // register event on circle nodes
        for (var a in o.node[0]) o.node[0][a].addEventListener(
            "mousedown", xWindowinteractivity, false);

        o.force.on("tick", function() {
            o.link.attr("x1", function(d) { return d.source.x; })
                .attr("y1", function(d) { return d.source.y; })
                .attr("x2", function(d) { return d.target.x; })
                .attr("y2", function(d) { return d.target.y; });

            o.node.attr("cx", function(d) { return d.x; })
                .attr("cy", function(d) { return d.y; });
        });
    });
};

// handler for the "mousedown" event on circle nodes
function xWindowinteractivity(evt) {
    evt.stopPropagation;
    streamWin.transition(streamWin.transitTo, evt.target.getAttributeNS(null, "fill"));
}

forceWin.build({
    width : 600,
    height : 440,
    contains : function () {return this.contents();}
});
```

The *mousedown* event registered on the circle nodes (note that this can be done by registering
the event on the *<container>* element of the circles, as shown in Chapter 4) and the corresponding
handler, *xWindowinteractivity()*, interact with the D3 Stream window. The *fill* value of the circle that
was clicked is passed to the *streamWin.transition()* method, which obtains the darker shade of the new
transition color using the *darken* extension method of the *String* class—*fill.darken(f)*—which is specifically designed for *rgb* color strings in any format. This author never tried to darken other strings. The
base color and the shade are then passed to the *d3.interpolateRgb()* method, which expects upper
and lower color thresholds. When the user clicks any of the circles representing the characters in *Les
Misérables*, a new transition in the *stream* window is launched. It is interesting to see that the transition also applies from the current color to the color of the new group. A good exercise would be to
define individual transitions for each character, based on the traits and the role that he or she has in
the plot. Perhaps another type of chart could be more appropriate for this. D3 allows a theoretically
infinite variety of chart types. The work would then become academically interesting. It could also be
easily adapted for other scenarios.

To finish off the application, we add the two remaining D3 examples. Since we are not adding
any interactivity to them, we can just wrap the scripts in their respective *contents* functions with only
minor changes, basically skipping the outermost *<svg>* container, not needed in this scenario, and
small positioning tweaks. The *worm.js* example shows an animation controlled by the *mousemove*
event, and to ensure that the mouse coordinates and the resulting animation are consistent with the
window's position, this adaptation uses the pergola dragarea, which in this particular case is resized
and positioned to the window's geometry through the *pergola.dragarea.resize()* method.

The *worm.js* example:

```
var wormWin = new pergola.Window("D3 Worm");

wormWin.contents = function () {
  var repCountTunnel = 200,
      repCountSpace = 100,
      mouse = [400, 400],
      zoom = 1,
      color = d3.scale.linear()
        .domain([0, repCountSpace])
        .interpolate(d3.interpolateHsl)
        .range(["hsl(250,100%,50%)", "hsl(180,100%,50%)"]),
      vis = d3.select(this.childDoc.transformable),
      node = vis.node();

var gradient = $C({
    element : "linearGradient",
    id : "worm-gradient",
    x1 : "0%",
    y1 : "20%",
    x2 : "20%",
    y2 : "100%",
    appendTo : vis.node()
  });
  $C({element : "stop", offset : "20%", "stop-color" : "green", appendTo : gradient});
  $C({element : "stop", offset : "50%", "stop-color" : "blue", appendTo : gradient});
  $C({element : "stop", offset : "100%", "stop-color" : "orange", appendTo : gradient});

  $C({element: "rect", width: w, height: h, fill: "none", appendTo: vis.node()});

// Code for static centroid created using principles of the SVG-Replicate project.
  var tunnel = d3.select($C({element : "g", transform : "translate(150 54)", fill : "none",
"stroke-width" : 4, "stroke-opacity" : .1, appendTo : vis.node()}))
      .selectAll()
        .data(d3.range(0, repCountTunnel, 1))
      .enter().append("svg:circle")
        .attr("r", function(d) { return d * .62 + 4})
        .attr("stroke", function(d) { return color(d); })
        .attr("transform", function(d) {
          return "rotate(" + d / 4 + ")"
          + "translate(" + (d * 1.45).trim(3) + "," + (d * -.4).trim(3) + ")";
        });

    var g = d3.select($C({
      element : "g",
      "stroke-width" : 5,
      "stroke-opacity" : .25,
      fill : "url(#worm-gradient)",
      appendTo : node
    }));

    var e = g.selectAll()
        .data(d3.range(repCountSpace))
      .enter().append("svg:ellipse")
        .attr("rx", function(d) { return (repCountSpace - d) * .8; })
```

```
            .attr("ry", function(d) { return (repCountSpace - d) * .5; })
            .attr("stroke", function(d) { return color(d); })
            .map(function(d) { return {center: [250, 250], angle: 30}; });

    g.timer = pergola.Timer()
      .initialize({
        handle : this,
        callback : function (timer) {
          timer.count ++;
          timer.target.attr("transform", function(d, i) {
            d.center[0] += ((mouse[0] / zoom - d.center[0]) / (i + 10));
            d.center[1] += ((mouse[1] / zoom - d.center[1]) / (i + 10));
            d.angle += Math.sin((timer.count + i) / 10) * 3;
            return "translate(" + d.center + ") rotate(" + d.angle + ")";
          });
        },
        frequence : 25,
        target : e,
        count : 0
      });


    this.registerEvents(this.background.rect, "mouseover", function (evt) {
      var c = wormWin.childDoc,
          offsetX = c.absoluteX(c.port),
          offsetY = c.absoluteY(c.port);

      zoom = c.scaleFactor;
      pergola.dragarea.resize(offsetX, offsetY, c.width(), c.height());

      pergola.dragarea.activate({
        handle : wormWin,
        fn : function (evt) {
          var m = pergola.mousePoint(evt);
          mouse[0] = m.x - this.offsetX;
          mouse[1] = m.y - this.offsetY;
        },
        offsetX : offsetX,
        offsetY : offsetY,
        updateCoordinates : false
      });
    });
  };


wormWin.build({
  x : 120,
  y : 120,
  width : 600,
  height : 420,
  fill : "black",
  minimized: true,
  contains : function () {return this.contents();}
});
```

This window starts minimized at runtime. Window objects create window tab instances. Pergola automatically creates a taskbar, which is the container for window tabs. This behavior can be overridden.

Likewise, the *clock.js* example only receives minor tweaks, so we won't discuss it here.

Improving the Application Design

What we have done so far seems quite good. But we have made a mistake that would be unthinkable for an architect designing an apartment building: we forgot to build corridors.

Suppose that we have our four D3 examples and we plan to add other modular works. If you recall the advantages of the split method for instantiation of classes, we can go further in the organization of the work and separate the construction processes by first defining right off (or in a new file) the different works that we plan to use:

```
var clockWin = new pergola.Window("D3 Clock"),
    forceWin = new pergola.Window("D3 Force-Directed Graph"),
    streamWin = new pergola.Window("D3 Stream"),
    areaWin = new pergola.Window("D3 Worm"),
```

but also, for example:

```
    techDrawings = new pergola.Window("Technical Drawings"),
    svgEditor = new pergola.Window("SVG Editor");
```

This is what swings the communication portals wide open. Each of those components has now access to the other objects, their prototype and their properties, and an object and its properties (including methods) can be now referenced in expressions during the construction of another object, independently from its ordinal position in the definitions. Remember this recommendation: organize and define as soon as possible whatever can be organized and defined. That will help with your own mental organization in keeping a copy of the code in a dedicated portion of your memory, which is a key factor for maintenance. To not do that is like negligence, and there cannot be good design with negligence.

But what if we were really planning to override properties of any of those objects? For example, say that we need to override some properties of *streamWin* and perhaps define its data beforehand. We can then set those properties before proceeding:

```
streamWin.color = d3.interpolateRgb("#aad", "#556");
streamWin.x = value;
streamWin.myProp = value;
streamWin.myMethod = function () {...};
```

and to organize this in a more elegant way, we have a utility function at our disposal for extending classes, prototypes, or objects:

```
pergola.extend(streamWin, {
  color     :  d3.interpolateRgb("#aad", "#556"),
  x         :  value,
  myProp    :  value,
  myMethod  :  function () {...}
});
```

The target object (the first parameter) inherits those properties. Those that already exist are over-ridden. The gain in clarity is flagrant, and that can be invaluable in terms of maintenance or analysis.

Running in an HTML and SVG Context

You will see now how easy it is to port your work to HTML. The document has the same structure of the SVG document: you only need to define a *<div>* element as the container for the SVG work, *before* the script tags:

```
<div id="svg" style="width: 840px; height: 620px;"></div>
```

Pergola organizes the canvas into layers stacked according to their systemic rank. In a stand-alone SVG context, *pergola.doc* is a reference to *document.documentElement*. In an HTML context, we need to override *pergola.doc* to point to an outermost SVG element. This is done in the configuration file (*config.js*) that is bound to each project, by uncommenting these two statements:

```
pergola.container = document.getElementById("svg");
pergola.doc = $C({
  element : "svg",
  width : "100%",
  height : "100%",
  appendTo : pergola.container
});
```

The first statement assigns the new container. The second creates and appends the outermost SVG element—here you can specify any attribute of the *<svg>* element (*$C* is a shortcut reference to the universal DOM helper function *pergola.createSVGElement()*, which returns the requested element).

If the *<div>* container does not exist you can create one on the fly:

```
pergola.container = $html({
  element : "div",
  style : "margin : 40px; width : 840px; height : 620px;",
  appendTo : document.body
});
```

where *$html* is a shortcut reference to *pergola.createHTMLElement()*, the sibling function of *create-SVGElement*. In this case, you do not need to set its ID, the element is already referenced by *pergola .container*, and you will not need to use any selection method, either. There are several possibilities to play with for the dimensions of the *<svg>* and *<div>* elements.

This concludes the first study. The referenced work (see the following image) is visible at *http:// www.dotuscomus.com/pergola/download/pergola_1.4.0/Examples/D3/multiD3.svg*.

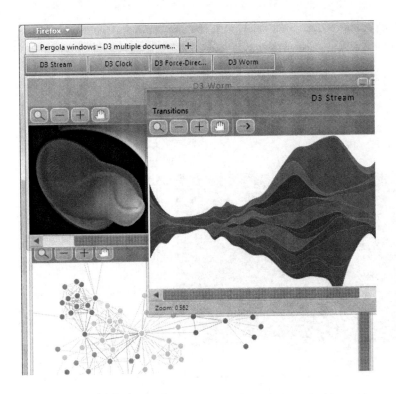

Mapping Application

For this second case study, you will be using the same mechanisms. The principle is the same: to have maps displayed in a window running as an independent application within an interactive environment. The focus here is specifically on mapping features and tools. The tools used for the mapping application are Pergola, Polymaps, and Bing tiles. You will learn how to use GeoJSON objects, projections, and custom feature layers as well.

Here's the code to initialize the mapping window:

```
var bingWin = new pergola.Window("Bing Maps");
bingWin.build({
  isFull : true,
  type : "map",
  mapWidth : 2048,
  mapHeight : 1536,
  fill : "#010413",
  ...,
  contains : function () {return this.mapMaker()}
});
```

The property *type: "map"* will produce a window with different behavior from a regular window. The class's prototype is extended with specific mapping properties and methods, and the behavior of the transformation tools, including scrollbars, overrides the regular behavior by sending requests rather than acting on the contained document's viewport. The *mapWidth* and *mapHeight* values should be equal to or greater than the screen dimensions, and in any case, should be multiples of 256.

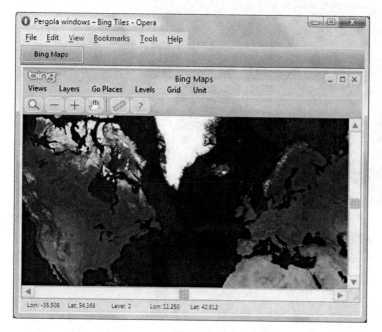

To populate the map, the *Window* class defines the *mapmaker()* method, which we have assigned to the property *contains*. For hardcore readers who may want more control, here is the code for appending the map manually, as per the Polymaps documentation:

```
pergola.Window.current = bingWin;
var doc = bingWin.childDoc;
polymaps.origin = {x: bingWin.x + doc.x, y: bingWin.y + doc.y};
bingWin.map = polymaps.map(doc).
container(doc.transformable.appendChild($C({
  element : "svg",
  id : bingWin.id + "_tiles",
  width : bingWin.mapWidth,
  height : bingWin.mapHeight
})))
.add(polymaps.interact())
.add(polymaps.hash());
```

Note that since version 1.3.9, Pergola windows have a status bar that, in a window of type *map*, displays center longitude and latitude by default, as well as some other information such as zoom level and location longitude/latitude following a mouse click (zoom level only for a regular window). This avoids the annoying side effect of precluding the use of the browser's back button when displaying the longitude/latitude and zoom level in the browser's address bar. Therefore, the Polymaps *hash* feature is not used. Other user-defined information can be added to the status bar.

The Menus

Through menus, the user will be able to do the following:

- Switch between different views

- Toggle layers on and off

- Go to different preset cities and places

- Select a zoom level

- Display a true longitude/latitude grid

- Select preferred units (kilometers, miles, or nautical miles)

The Views menu lets the user select three different views: *Aerial*, *Aerial With Labels*, and *Road*. Here's the code for the Views menu:

```
menu : {
  views : {
    title : "Views",
    items : {
      aerial : {
        string : "Aerial",
        check : false,
        exclusive : true,
        view : "aerial",
        fn : tileSource
      },
      aerialLabels : {
        string : "Aerial With Labels",
        check : true,
        exclusive : true,
        view : "aerialWithLabels",
        fn : tileSource
      },
      road : {
        string : "Road",
        check : false,
        exclusive : true,
        view : "road",
        fn : tileSource
      }
    }
  }
}
```

The initial display is "Aerial With Labels" because its *check* property is set to *true*.

The user function *tileSource* is in charge of switching scripts in order to request the appropriate tiles for each view. It is a function closely associated with the request callback function.

The Polymaps development model does not adopt a typical JavaScript OOD model. In order to facilitate communication with Polymaps, we define for the window the property *views*, an object designed to store information about Polymaps' tile layers. Its properties are referenced by the *view* properties of the corresponding menu items:

```
menu : {
  ...
},
views : {
  aerial : {},
  aerialWithLabels : {},
  road : {}
},
...
```

Remember that these are just definitions, and the order in which the properties of the window are defined in the object literal passed as parameter to the window's *build()* method is irrelevant. It is just convenient to analyze them thematically.

The Layers menu lets the user toggle layers on and off. You will learn how to build feature layers in the "Adding Map Features" section of this chapter (you can skip ahead and read that first if you wish).

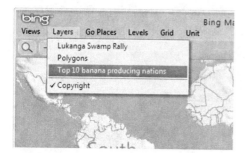

Of the four layers listed in this menu, the most interesting under different aspects is "Top 10 banana producing nations":

```
menu : {
  ...,
  layers : {
    title : "Layers",
    items : {
      ...,
      bananas : {
        string : "Top 10 banana producing nations",
        check : false,
        target : function () {
          return {
            layer : bingWin.layers.bananas,
```

```
            center : {lat : 10, lon : 100},
            zoom : 4,
            view : "aerial"
          }
        },
        fn : 'toggleLayer',
        separator : new pergola.Separator()
      },
      ...
    }
  },
  ...
}
```

Apart from the menu item (a *pergola.MenuItem* instance) prototype properties that we have already met, we have assigned the property *target*. This is a user property, technically an instance property. What does this mean exactly? It is a new property that we mean to process somewhere, in our case in the user function *fn*. Its value is arbitrary, and we have assigned a function returning an object containing data. Its properties define a world location, a zoom level and a view type, but the property *layer* references an object that we haven't defined. Here's the code for the *bingWin.layers* object:

```
layers : {
  ...,
  bananas : {
    feature : true,
    display : "none"
  },
  ...
},
```

Just like in the menu item *views* we were referencing the *bingWin.views* object, in the menu item *layers* we reference the *bingWin.layers* object.

The Go Places menu defines random world locations:

```
menu : {
  ...,
  go_places : {
    title : "Go Places",
    items : {
      venice : {
        string : "Venice",
        fn : function () {
          var c = pergola.Window.currentMap;
          c.centerMap({lat : 45.4351, lon : 12.3375});
          c.mapZoom(14);
        }
      },
      ...
    }
  },
  ...
}
```

The property *pergola.Window.currentMap* designates the active mapping window in a hypothetical application containing more than one concurrent map instance.

Basically, all this does is use the Polymaps functions for centering and zooming. However, Polymaps' zoom function is invoked through the prototype method of the *Window* class *mapZoom()*, which also carries out other interface updating tasks. Likewise, the Polymaps' *center* function is invoked through the method *centerMap()* for the same purpose.

The Levels menu allows the user to set the zoom level:

```
menu : {
  ...,
  zoomLevel : {
    title : "Levels",
    hasZoomLevels : true,
    items : {
      z1 : {
        string : "1",
        check : false,
        exclusive : true,
        fn : function () {pergola.Window.currentMap.mapZoom(1);}
      },
      ...
    }
  },
  ...
}
```

The Grid menu allows the user to toggle the grid on and off (the original Polymaps grid is jagged and buggy, and is replaced by a true longitude/latitude grid).

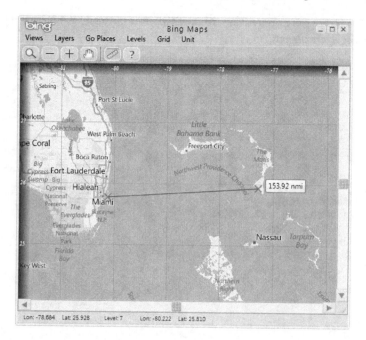

```
menu : {
  ...,
  grid : {
    title : "Grid",
    items : {
      grid : {
        string : "Grid",
        check : false,
        fn : function () {
          var map = bingWin.map,
              l = bingWin.layers.grid;
          l.display = l.display == "block" ? "none" : "block";
          if (!map.grid) {
            map.add(polymaps.grid());
            map.center(map.center());
          }
          map.grid.setAttributeNS(null, "display", l.display);
        }
      }
    }
  },
  ...
}
```

The user function *fn* creates the grid (and its layer) if it does not exist, and toggles the layer on and off. This technique proves very useful for reducing the load on the DOM when building large applications. A user may never use the grid layer during a session; therefore, it is not necessary to create it at runtime. The same technique is used for all the feature layers except the copyright static layer, which needs to be shown up front. The cost of the test of existence is irrelevant.

The Unit menu is used to set the units for the measure tool:

```
menu : {
  ...,
  unit : {
    title : "Unit",
    items : {
      km : {
        string : "Kilometres",
        check : true,
        exclusive : true,
        fn : function () {bingWin.map.unit = "Km";}
      },
      ...
    }
  }
}
```

The conversions between units are made in the measure tool functions.

Adding Map Features

Before implementing features, a little theory. Implementing a custom feature on a map involves a custom graphic, either scaled according to the map zoom level or not scaled. Paths showing itineraries or polygons for delimiting areas, for example, are meant to be scaled, while objects used to pinpoint a particular place or to show information about a particular region are just projected. Either way, you can implement these features using GeoJSON objects.

A custom feature is commonly placed in its own layer, overlaid on top of the map. Recall how in the previous section the property *layers* was defined in the call to the *build()* method of *bingWin*. That object defines the feature layers used in the application, or more precisely in this mapping window. They are c*opyright, bananas, polygons, lukangaRally, svgOpen2011*, and *grid*. In these objects we have stored information for the layers' management. The property *feature* indicates whether the layer is static (*false*) or a projection (*true*). The property *display* designates the initial state of the layer, and it is updated dynamically. Note that the control of a layer is not necessarily in the Layers menu; "SVG Open 2011" is in the Go Places menu, or could perhaps be in an external panel with check boxes.

GeoJSON

To give a quick overview, GeoJSON specifies an encoding format for geographical data. The second part of the acronym stands for JavaScript Object Notation, an OOP writing technique. A GeoJSON object may define a *geometry*, a *feature*, or a collection of *features*. A GeoJSON object can have any number of properties. The *geometry* object must have the properties "*type*" and "*coordinates*", both expressed as strings.

The property "*type*" can take any of the following values: "*Point*", "*MultiPoint*", "*LineString*", "*MultiLineString*", "*Polygon*", "*MultiPolygon*", or "*GeometryCollection*".

The property "*coordinates*" takes an array, the structure of which is determined by the type of *geometry*. The values are geographic coordinates (longitude and latitude units of decimal degrees).

Polymaps provides a GeoJSON parser where data is processed. The geographic coordinates are converted into projected SVG Path data (in most cases), but for "Point" and "MultiPoint," SVG Circle is used. All path-based geometries are projected and scaled according to the zoom level of the map. The scaling is not the result of an SVG transformation, hence strokes are not scaled. "Point" and "MultiPoint" are just projected and keep their original size at different zoom levels.

Often you will want to use your own custom objects to pinpoint places on a map, and if you take a look at some code examples, you will see that it can be quite a mission (nodes substitution, lengthy code, etc.). To facilitate this task, the GeoJSON parser was extended with some Pergola facilities that allow you to use any SVG object (artwork, shape, symbol, or clip art) either from a library or defined on the fly, as well as SVG images containing PNG or JPG images, for the "point" property. The parser is also enabled to process the "style" property for inline style, or more precisely, it just adds the style attribute to the object passed to the Pergola DOM helper. It also determines the appropriate parent node; therefore it is important to remember that the definitions of SVG elements are not calls to the DOM helper, which expects the *appendTo* property. Thus, when, for example, you define elements inline, you will use the same format of the libraries' definitions: the object carries the SVG element's name and its legal attributes only.

To use this functionality, you define in the "geometry" object the property "elements" and, if needed, a "scale" value. For example, the layer "Top 10 banana producing nations" uses the *pergola.symbols.banana*. If set, scaling is applied to a *<g>* element created dynamically by the parser. This transformation adds to transformations that you may define for a particular element by setting the *transform* attribute.

The value of "elements" is an array of one or more objects, and each object defines an SVG primitive element. Here's the banana definition from the *pergola.symbols* library:

```
banana : [
  { element : "path", fill : "#FADC74", d : "..." },
  { element : "path", fill : "#E8B84D", d : "..." },
  { element : "path", fill : "#C89943", d : "..." },
  { element : "path", fill : "#B2BC4B", d : "..." },
  { element : "path", fill : "#537F37", d : "..." },
  { element : "path", fill : "#4C4822", d : "..." },
]
```

A symbol is constituted of as many elements as you need, and can reference patterns, gradients, and filters. Here is an example of how you can use a Pergola symbol with the *pergola.symbol()* utility function:

```
var myIcon = pergola.symbol.call({}, {
  symbol : pergola.symbols.banana,
  x : 100,
  y : 100,
  scale : 3,
  parent : Node
});
```

The preceding image shows a banana symbol with a scale factor of 3.

The procedure for using a symbol with a GeoJSON "geometry" object is simplified; you just need to assign its reference to the "elements" property:

```
"geometry" : {
  "type" : "Point",
  "coordinates" : [ coordinates ],
  "elements" : pergola.symbols.banana,
  "scale" : "(...)",
}
```

This would show a banana at *coordinates*.

In the mapping application, the bananas are scaled according to the production classification and text labels are also added (see the following image).

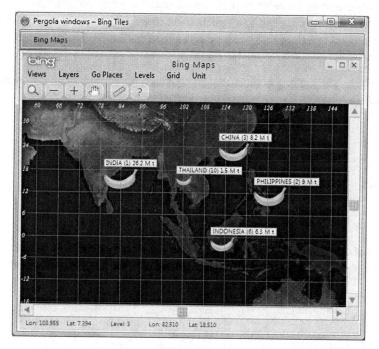

Here's the method that builds the "Top 10 banana producing nations" layer:

```
m.bananas.toggleLayer = function (evt) {
  var target = this.target(),
      o = target.layer,
      currentMap = pergola.Window.currentMap;
// Force selection in menu Views
  currentMap.mapViewsToggle(target.view);

// Build the layer if it doesn't exist
  if (!o.container) {
    var banana = pergola.symbols.banana,
        node,
        features = [],
        prod = [
          {coordinates : [79, 18], tag : "INDIA (1) 26.2 M t"},
          {coordinates : [122, 13.62], tag : "PHILIPPINES (2) 9 M t", scale : "(.94)"},
          ...
        ];
/*
 * Using Pergola's String prototype extension method width() to compute the text
 * width and assign the result to the property "width" for each object in "prod".
 */
    for (var a in prod) prod[a].width = prod[a].tag.width("10px");
```

```
    function tag(i) {
      return [
        {element : "rect", x : .5, y : -15, width : prod[i].width, height : 12, fill :
"url(#quickTipGrad)", stroke : "#808080"},
        {element : "text", x : 4, y : -5.5, "font-size" : "7pt", "pointer-events" : "none",
textNode : prod[i].tag}
      ];
    };
    function geometry(i, obj) {
      var scale = (obj == banana) ? prod[i].scale : 0;
      return {
        "geometry" : {
          "type" : "Point",
          "coordinates" : prod[i].coordinates,
          "elements" : obj,
          "scale" : scale,
        }
      };
    };

    for (var i in prod) {
      features.push(geometry(i, banana));
      features.push(geometry(i, tag(i)));
    }
    currentMap.map.add(polymaps.geoJson(o).features(features));
  }
  currentMap.centerMap(target.center);
  currentMap.mapZoom(target.zoom);
  currentMap.showMapFeatureLayer(o);
}
```

Note that although this function is an instance method of the menu item "Top 10 banana producing nations," this does not mean that the menu builds the layer. It is simply a convenient place to put
the layer code instead of defining an extra helper function that would be executed exactly zero or
one time. If you were to define such a function, the best place would be in the *bingWin.layers*
.bananas object:

```
bananas : {
  feature : true,
  display : "none",
  build : function () { layer's code }
}
```

The access would then be *bingWin.layers.bananas.build()*. However, this would be to the detriment
of readability of the window's definitions.

Note that most of the code of the *toggleLayer* function is for serializing the banana objects and
text labels. In terms of GeoJSON, you will simply retain the "geometry" objects returned by the
geometry function.

Adding Tools

Besides the transformation tools that are set by default (if not overridden) for every window instance, the *Window* class adds a measure tool and a navigation help tool for window instances of *type* "map," as shown in the following image.

In the previous application, you saw how to add a tool in the call to the *build()* method by setting the *tools* property. You also learned that tools can be added at a later stage through the *addTools()* prototype method. Here is an example of how to add a custom tool with this technique:

```
bingWin.addTools({
  group1 : {
    separator : Boolean,
    myTool : {
      symbol : {
        symbol : symbol,
        x : 4,
        y : 4
      },
      exclusive : true,
      quickTip : "...",
      ev : "mouseup",
      fn : function () {...}
    }
  }
});
```

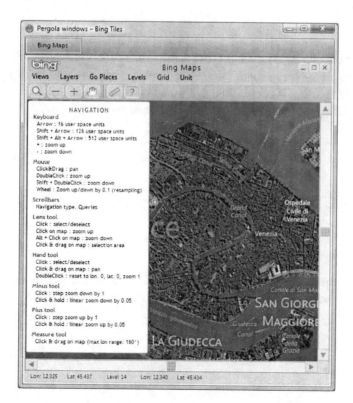

Window tools can have radio button behavior. You should always set the *exclusive* property to *true* for tools of this type—tools that cannot function simultaneously—or you will get strange results. Selection of an exclusive tool causes exclusive siblings (tools of the same window) to be deselected. It also temporarily disables mouse events on the map, while keyboard navigation remains active. To deselect, the tool must send a notification to the window object by calling the prototype method *toolInit()*:

```
bingWin.toolInit(evt, this)
```

If your tool is exclusive, the above must be the first line in your user function; if the tool is added dynamically and the window object's name is not known, you can use *this.owner* in its stead.

The Complete Code

```
var bingWin = new pergola.Window("Bing Maps");
bingWin.build({
  isFull : true,
  type : "map",
  mapWidth : 2048,
  mapHeight : 1536,
  fill : "#010413",
  menu : {
    views : {
      title : "Views",
      items : {
        aerial : {
          string : "Aerial",
          check : false,
          exclusive : true,
          view : "aerial",
          fn : tileSource
        },
        aerialLabels : {
          string : "Aerial With Labels",
          check : true,
          exclusive : true,
          view : "aerialWithLabels",
          fn : tileSource
        },
        road : {
          string : "Road",
          check : false,
          exclusive : true,
          view : "road",
          fn : tileSource
        }
      }
    },
    layers : {
      title : "Layers",
      items : {
        lukanga : {
          string : "Lukanga Swamp Rally",
```

```
            check : false,
            target : function () {
              return {
                layer : bingWin.layers.lukangaRally,
                center : {lat : -14.46, lon : 27.3125},
                zoom : 11
              }
            },
            fn : 'toggleLayer'
          },
          polygons : {
            string : "Polygons",
            check : false,
            target : function () {
              return {
                layer : bingWin.layers.polygons,
                center : {lat : 37.7590, lon : -122.4191},
                zoom : 14
              }
            },
            fn : 'toggleLayer'
          },
          bananas : {
            string : "Top 10 banana producing nations",
            check : false,
            target : function () {
              return {
                layer : bingWin.layers.bananas,
                center : {lat : 10, lon : 100},
                zoom : 4,
                view : "aerial"
              }
            },
            fn : 'toggleLayer', formats)
            separator : new pergola.Separator()
          },
          copyright : {
            string : "Copyright",
            check : true,
            target : function () {return bingWin.childDoc.copyright;},
            fn : function () { formats)
              if (!this.target()) return;
              var l = bingWin.layers.copyright;
              l.display = l.display == "block" ? "none" : "block";
              this.target().setAttributeNS(null, "display", l.display);
            }
          }
        }
      },
      go_places : {
        title : "Go Places",
        items : {
          paris : {
            string : "Paris",
            fn : function () {
              var c = pergola.Window.currentMap;
              c.centerMap({lat : 48.8553, lon : 2.3456});
```

```
        c.mapZoom(16);
      }
    },
    rome : {
      string : "Rome",
      fn : function () {
        var c = pergola.Window.currentMap;
        c.centerMap({lat : 41.9030, lon : 12.4664});
        c.mapZoom(14);
      }
    }
,
    tokyo : {
      string : "Tokyo",
      fn : function () {
        var c = pergola.Window.currentMap;
        c.centerMap({lat : 35.6429, lon : 139.8098});
        c.mapZoom(11);
      }
    },
    newyork : {
      string : "New York",
      fn : function () {
        var c = pergola.Window.currentMap;
        c.centerMap({lat : 40.7050, lon : -74.0093});
        c.mapZoom(11);
      }
    },
    sydney : {
      string : "Sydney",
      fn : function () {
        var c = pergola.Window.currentMap;
        c.centerMap({lat : -33.8654, lon : 151.2102});
        c.mapZoom(12);
      }
    },
    venice : {
      string : "Venice",
      fn : function () {
        var c = pergola.Window.currentMap;
        c.centerMap({lat : 45.4351, lon : 12.3375});
        c.mapZoom(14);
      }
    },
    riodejaneiro : {
      string : "Rio De Janeiro",
      fn : function () {
        var c = pergola.Window.currentMap;
        c.centerMap({lat : -22.9389, lon : 316.7979});
        c.mapZoom(12);
      }
    },
    buenosaires : {
      string : "Buenos Aires",
      fn : function () {
        var c = pergola.Window.currentMap;
        c.centerMap({lat : -34.6570, lon : 301.6016});
```

```
              c.mapZoom(11);
          },
          separator : new pergola.Separator()
      },
      northAmerica : {
          string : "North America",
          fn : function () {
              var c = pergola.Window.currentMap;
              c.centerMap({lat : 42.37, lon : 268.07});
              c.mapZoom(3);
          }
      },
      india : {
          string : "India",
          fn : function () {
              var c = pergola.Window.currentMap;
              c.centerMap({lat : 18.832, lon : 78.734});
              c.mapZoom(5);
          }
      },
      wEurope : {
          string : "Western Europe",
          fn : function () {
              var c = pergola.Window.currentMap;
              c.centerMap({lat : 46.588, lon : 5.938});
              c.mapZoom(5);
          }
      },
      patagonia : {
          string : "Patagonia",
          fn : function () {
              var c = pergola.Window.currentMap;
              c.centerMap({lat : -50.570, lon : -70.977});
              c.mapZoom(7);
          }
      },
      antartica : {
          string : "Antartica",
          fn : function () {
              var c = pergola.Window.currentMap;
              c.centerMap({lat : -79.1, lon : -10.5});
              c.mapZoom(2);
          },
          separator : new pergola.Separator()
      },
      svgOpen2011 : {
          string : "SVG Open 2011",
          target : function () {
              return {
                  layer : bingWin.layers.svgOpen2011,
                  center : {lat : 42.36131, lon : -71.08124},
                  zoom : 17,
                  view : "road"
              };
          },
          fn : 'toggleLayer'
      }
```

```
        }
    },
    zoomLevel : {
        title : "Levels",
        hasZoomLevels : true,
        items : {
            z1 : {
                string : "1",
                check : false,
                exclusive : true,
                fn : function () {pergola.Window.currentMap.mapZoom(1);}
            },
            z2 : {
                string : "2",
                check : false,
                exclusive : true,
                fn : function () {pergola.Window.currentMap.mapZoom(2);}
            },
            z3 : {
                string : "3",
                check : false,
                exclusive : true,
                fn : function () {pergola.Window.currentMap.mapZoom(3);}
            },
            z4 : {
                string : "4",
                check : false,
                exclusive : true,
                fn : function () {pergola.Window.currentMap.mapZoom(4);}
            },
            z5 : {
                string : "5",
                check : false,
                exclusive : true,
                fn : function () {pergola.Window.currentMap.mapZoom(5);}
            },
            z6 : {
                string : "6",
                check : false,
                exclusive : true,
                fn : function () {pergola.Window.currentMap.mapZoom(6);}
            },
            z7 : {
                string : "7",
                check : false,
                exclusive : true,
                fn : function () {pergola.Window.currentMap.mapZoom(7);}
            },
            z8 : {
                string : "8",
                check : false,
                exclusive : true,
                fn : function () {pergola.Window.currentMap.mapZoom(8);}
            },
            z9 : {
                string : "9",
                check : false,
```

```
        exclusive : true,
        fn : function () {pergola.Window.currentMap.mapZoom(9);}
      },
      z10 : {
        string : "10",
        check : false,
        exclusive : true,
        fn : function () {pergola.Window.currentMap.mapZoom(10);}
      },
      z11 : {
        string : "11",
        check : false,
        exclusive : true,
        fn : function () {pergola.Window.currentMap.mapZoom(11);}
      },
      z12 : {
        string : "12",
        check : false,
        exclusive : true,
        fn : function () {pergola.Window.currentMap.mapZoom(12);}
      },
      z13 : {
        string : "13",
        check : false,
        exclusive : true,
        fn : function () {pergola.Window.currentMap.mapZoom(13);}
      },
      z14 : {
        string : "14",
        check : false,
        exclusive : true,
        fn : function () {pergola.Window.currentMap.mapZoom(14);}
      },
      z15 : {
        string : "15",
        check : false,
        exclusive : true,
        fn : function () {pergola.Window.currentMap.mapZoom(15);}
      },
      z16 : {
        string : "16",
        check : false,
        exclusive : true,
        fn : function () {pergola.Window.currentMap.mapZoom(16);}
      },
      z17 : {
        string : "17",
        check : false,
        exclusive : true,
        fn : function () {pergola.Window.currentMap.mapZoom(17);}
      },
      z18 : {
        string : "18",
        check : false,
        exclusive : true,
        fn : function () {pergola.Window.currentMap.mapZoom(18);}
      },
```

```
        z19 : {
          string : "19",
          check : false,
          exclusive : true,
          fn : function () {pergola.Window.currentMap.mapZoom(19);}
        },
        z20 : {
          string : "20",
          check : false,
          exclusive : true,
          fn : function () {pergola.Window.currentMap.mapZoom(20);}
        },
        z21 : {
          string : "21",
          check : false,
          exclusive : true,
          fn : function () {pergola.Window.currentMap.mapZoom(21);}
        }
      }
    },
    grid : {
      title : "Grid",
      items : {
        grid : {
          string : "Grid",
          check : false,
          fn : function () { formats)
            var map = bingWin.map,
                l = bingWin.layers.grid;
            l.display = l.display == "block" ? "none" : "block";
            if (!map.grid) {
              map.add(polymaps.grid());
              map.center(map.center());
            }
            map.grid.setAttributeNS(null, "display", l.display);
          }
        }
      }
    },
    unit : {
      title : "Unit",
      items : {
        km : {
          string : "Kilometres",
          check : true,
          exclusive : true,
          fn : function () {bingWin.map.unit = "Km";}
        },
        mi : {
          string : "Miles",
          check : false,
          exclusive : true,
          fn : function () {bingWin.map.unit = "mi";}
        },
        nmi : {
          string : "Nautical Miles",
          check : false,
```

```
                exclusive : true,
                fn : function () {bingWin.map.unit = "nmi";}
            }
        }
    }
},
views : {
    aerial : {},
    aerialWithLabels : {},
    road : {}
},
layers : {
    copyright : {
        feature : false,
        display : "block"
    },
    bananas : {
        feature : true,
        display : "none"
    },
    polygons : {
        feature : true,
        display : "none"
    },
    lukangaRally : {
        feature : true,
        display : "none"
    },
    svgOpen2011 : {
        feature : true,
        display : "none"
    },
    grid : {
        feature : false,
        display : "none"
    }
},
contains : function () {return this.mapMaker()}
});
```

Summary

This concludes the second case study. The referenced work is visible at *http://www.dotuscomus.com/ pergola/pergola_1.4.0/Examples/BingMaps/BingWindow.svg.*

The authors hope that these studies will have achieved their purpose: demonstrating how well-designed libraries that define a consistent OOD model and that provide a clear and well-organized structure allow works of this type to be defined efficiently, while also producing compact files, which helps with ease of maintenance, readability, and debugging. This is possible thanks to the judicious use of the DOM and SVG DOM interfaces, which you are encouraged to study in depth. Integration of these concepts will help you gain a command of such coding practices.

Index

Symbols

3D drawing and animation, 17, 209

A

absolute path coordinates, 49
absolute value, 24
accessibility, 3, 27, 83–84
a command, 48
A command, 48
addEventListener() method, 140
add() function, 111, 114, 139
Adobe Dreamweaver IDE, 210
Adobe Illustrator application, 4
    creating rectangle, 201–203
    SVG support, 201
Adobe SVG Viewer (ASV) plugin, 4, 146, 192, 208
    downloading, 5
    history of, xv–xvi
<animateColor> element, 94
<animate> element, 107, 133, 152
    begin="G.click" attribute, 98
    controlling width and height, 91
    text following path, 13
    with color names, 94
animate() function, 107
<animateMotion> element, 96
    begin="0;indefinite" attribute, 134
    fill="freeze" attribute, 134
<animateTransform> element, 93, 94, 112, 114
animation. *See also* declarative animation; scripting;
SMIL (Synchronized Multimedia Integration Language)
    clip paths, 11
    clock, 14–15
    concentric circles, 16
    reflected gradients with transparency, 13–14
    simple example, 9–10
    text along Bézier curve, 13
Apache Batik project, 207–208
appendChild() method, 128
arcs, elliptical, 47–48, 48
arithmetic operator, 182, 184
ASV plugin. *See* Adobe SVG Viewer (ASV) plugin
attributeName attribute, 91
attributes
    categories, 22
    changing via scripting, 103–108
    defining style of shapes, 33
    setting, 146
averaging images, 181–184

B

Backus-Naur Form (BNF), 49
baseFrequency parameter, 164, 174
Batik project, 207–208
begin attribute, 134
beginElement() method, 132–134
bevel value, 34
Bézier curves, 64
    creating shapes using, 42–46
    cubic, 45, 46, 49
    defining paths, 126
    equidistant positioning points along, 8–9
    example graphic, 32
    oscillation, 128
    quadratic, 42–46, 49
    smooth, 46–47, 49
    SVG-Edit tool, 206
    text along, 13, 64–65
Bézier (Q) command, 42, 49
bingWin object, 239, 242, 245

M

N

O

About the Authors

 DAVID DAILEY was born and raised in Albuquerque, NM, receiving his bachelor's degree from the University of New Mexico and his doctorate from the University of Colorado. Having taught mathematics, psychology, and computer science at the Universities of Wyoming, Tulsa, and Alaska, he later moved east with appointments at Vassar, Williams, and Bay Path College, before settling in at Slippery Rock University in Pennsylvania where he is Professor of Computer Science teaching mainly in areas of web programming. He is married, has four children, and enjoys creating art, food, music, and games.

 JON FROST is a seasoned developer who has worked with SVG for more than a decade. The SVG applications he has developed include interactive web applications and dynamic reports. He dreamt up and collaborated on the books *Learn SVG: The Web Graphics Standard* and *Building Web Applications with SVG*.

 DOMENICO STRAZZULLO, founder and editor-in-chief of *SVG magazine*, is the author of both the Pergola JavaScript library for SVG and the open-source GEMï web operating system.

What do you think of this book?

We want to hear from you!

To participate in a brief online survey, please visit:

microsoft.com/learning/booksurvey

Tell us how well this book meets your needs—what works effectively, and what we can do better. Your feedback will help us continually improve our books and learning resources for you.

Thank you in advance for your input!

Lightning Source UK Ltd.
Milton Keynes UK
UKOW020816211112

202490UK00002B/10/P